Rev. Dr. Bayley

New Church Worthies

Rev. Dr. Bayley

New Church Worthies

ISBN/EAN: 9783741140891

Manufactured in Europe, USA, Canada, Australia, Japa

Cover: Foto ©Lupo / pixelio.de

Manufactured and distributed by brebook publishing software (www.brebook.com)

Rev. Dr. Bayley

New Church Worthies

NEW CHURCH WORTHIES

OR

EARLY BUT LITTLE-KNOWN DISCIPLES OF THE LORD IN DIFFUSING THE TRUTHS OF THE NEW CHURCH.

BY THE
REV. DR. BAYLEY
NEW JERUSALEM CHURCH, KENSINGTON
LONDON

"The Lamb shall overcome them: for He is Lord of lords and King of kings: and they that are with Him are CALLED AND CHOSEN AND FAITHFUL" (Rev. xvii., 14).

LONDON:
JAMES SPEIRS, 36, BLOOMSBURY STREET, W.
And all Booksellers.
1884.

PREFACE.

The object of the following biographical sketches is to endeavour to preserve the remembrance of those worthy men who, though they have not stood in the first rank as APOSTLES OF THE NEW DISPENSATION, have yet been distinguished for such faithful, steady assistance in the diffusion of New Church Truth, that we would willingly keep their memories fresh and green.

They are of the class of which it is written, "They that feared the Lord spake often one to another: and the Lord hearkened and heard, and a Book of Remembrance was written before Him, for them that feared the Lord, and that thought upon His Name. And they shall be mine, saith the Lord of hosts, in that day when I make up my jewels."

We have not confined our regard for these worthy fellow-labourers to England, nor indeed to Great Britain, for our desire was to give some information of the manner in which stream after stream was opened for the flow into other lands of those truths that, commencing with the One Saviour, the Father in the Son, God in Christ, in whom dwells "all the fulness of the Godhead bodily," will bring into loving unity all the nations of the earth: "I in them," as the Lord Jesus said, "and Thou in me, that they may be made perfect in One" (John xvii., 23).

We could not aim at being exhaustive in a small work like this. We could only hope to afford specimens and recollections we would not willingly let die, which may stimulate us all to diffuse truths which will brighten the intellect, animate the hope, and direct the steps of those who strive to prepare for heaven by becoming heavenly.

APPENDIX.

From a letter in the *New Church Messenger*, Jan. 21, 1885, signed by C. T. Odhner, it appears that in the article " CARL DELEEN, AND THE NEW CHURCH IN SWEDEN," several particulars are not quite as accurate as the more exact detailed knowledge of our friend, whom I presume is a Swede, would make them. My information has been obtained during my different visits to Sweden, but (in referring to details of time and place so distant may not always avoid inaccuracy, but are as accurate as I can make them) I accept our friend's corrections with thanks, and place them at the command of my readers, and am pleased that nothing more important needs correction. The John referred to in Dr. Kahl's letter which our friend says caused him perplexity was evidently Jean Baptiste Bernadotte referred to by his name Jean, turned into English, John. I insert the letter (except a few lines) as follows.

J. BAYLEY.

THE LETTER.

" The Royal Library of Stockholm contains a copy of *New Jerusalem, and its Heavenly Doctrines*, translated by C. F. Nordenskold, 1788, and the *True Christian Religion*, translated by Dean Odhner, in 1795. These books, as far as I know, are the first translations of the writings in Swedish. Mr. Deléen did not commence his translations before 1817.

"It is further stated that Mr. Deléen, at his own expense, published all the writings, but the truth is that the Society pro Fide et Charitate, which existed in Sweden from 1795 to 1830, furnished nearly all the means. Other mistakes are made, such as that Dr. Beyer was Greek Professor at Stockholm, when he really was Doctor of Theology at the Gymnasium or High School at Gottenburg. Mr. C. Johansen is called an able clergyman, but was in fact a steel labourer in Eskilstuna. Dr. Kahl, of Lund, is said to be next under the Archbishop of Sweden, when yet there are two degrees of honor between his office and that of a Bishop. Geyer, the national historian, is called a 'thorough receiver of the doctrines,' but when placed on his trial he openly denied his belief in the New Church. It is further stated that in the year 1772 a small society of affectionate receivers was formed by Nordenskiold and Wadstrom, when neither of those gentlemen became acquainted with the writings before 1773."

INDEX.

	PAGE
SAMUEL DAWSON, FIRST LEADER	1
Conversion of his Wife	9
Deep Trial at Last	10
SAMUEL CROMPTON, INVENTOR OF MULE	11
Enormous Increase of Trade	14
Great Procession in his honour	16
OBERLIN, ORIGINATOR OF INFANT SCHOOLS	17
His Wife; His Spiritual Experience	21
Bridge and Road maker	22
Great esteem for Work on H. and H.	26
Celestial Diagram	27
BUCHANAN, INTRODUCER OF CHEAP DAY SCHOOLS	29
Began at New Lanark	30
Westminster Road School, under Brougham	30
Other Early Teachers, all New Church	32
Cheap Day Schools, New Church	33
Sunday Scholars first paid	34
MR. AGNEW, INTRODUCER OF CHEAP SCHOOLS IN THE NORTH OF ENGLAND	37
Promoter of Sunday Schools	41
Mayor of Salford collected 80,000 Children to Sing before the Queen	41
MR. COOKWORTHY, A FRIEND, THE FIRST TRANSLATOR	42
The Caps of his Daughters	45
His Death; Putting off an Old Coat for a New One	48

	PAGE
MR. MOTTRAM, AND FRIENDS OF MR. CLOWES	50
Colportage begun by him	56
Character by Mr. Clowes	56
MR. F. M. HODSON	58
Difficulty of Worshipping with a Service to Three Divine Persons	59
Hat Smelling like an Angel's	60
Excellent Missionary	61
His Hymns	63
MR. GEO. HOWARTH, OF ACCRINGTON	65
Condition of England in 18th Century	66
Great Reader of the Arcana	67
Sunday School and Music	69
Minister sent at the Price	73
120 Teachers	74
MR. BROADFIELD, OF MANCHESTER	78
Left Home at Bridgnorth	80
Go to Heaven Now	82
MR. CORDIN, OF SALFORD	83
Clear Expounder	84
Never mix Scripture with Jokes	87
MR. BOARDMAN, AND MIDDLETON	90
His Neat Cottage and Garden	92
The Frogs and Salt	92
MR. WILD, AND HEYWOOD	95
Common Sense and Cheerfulness	98
Large School	99
MR. DANIEL DUNN, OF LONDON	102
His Essences	105
Support of Orphans	106
His Workmen and Epitaph	107

	PAGE
MR. GLEN AND NEW CHURCH IN AMERICA	109
Receives the Truth on Shipboard	110
Addresses Small Audience in Philadelphia	111
Methodist Ministers in Baltimore receive	116
Died at Demerara	120
JOHNNY APPLESEED	121
Born at Boston and Drest Oddly	122
Took to Planting Apple Trees and Forming Orchards	123
News right fresh from Heaven	127
Warns against the Indians	128
Primrose Christian	129
Loved by Girls and Boys	130
MR. THOS. WILSON, OF FAILSWORTH	132
Threatening Character of Infidelity	133
Checked by Wilson	134
Sink or Swim	138
No Fear of Death	141
JOHN HEYWOOD AND RADCLIFFE	142
Radcliffe Society, begun from Manchester	142
Vestry used for Kitchen	143
Dashing the Little Ones against the Stones	146
THOMAS GEE OF RINGLEY AND KEARSLEY	149
Good Men and Good Women	150
Two Armchair Folk	151
Dictum Factum	153
Mr. Woodman	154
JOB ABBOTT AND MIDLAND COUNTIES	156
Studied Astronomy	159
Council of Three Divine Persons	160
Thorough Consolation	165
His Poems	167

	PAGE
MR. TUTING AND CHURCH IN SCOTLAND. ONE OF EIGHT	169
Mr. Parker, the Wesleyan	170
Mr. Hindmarsh in Scotland	174
Die Hard	175
Gloominess of Calvinism	176
M. RICHER AND NEW CHURCH IN FRANCE	180
The French a Noble People	181
Priests and Pastors who became New Churchmen	182
John Aug. Tulk	183
Alas! they are Disciples of Swedenborg	185
Tollenare and his Timidity	189
The Portals	190
Le Boys des Guays	192
THE NOBLE MOURAVIEFF; FREEDOM OF THE SERFS	198
Religion in Russia very Formal	200
Yet many Thoughtful People	201
Mouravieff met with DOCTRINE OF LIFE	202
Made President of the Committee of Emancipation	205
Happy Departure	209
CARL DELEEN; NEW CHURCH IN SWEDEN	211
Translator and Printer	212
Anti Slave Trade	215
DR. E. TAFEL AND GUSTAV WERNER	220
Dr. Tafel's Piety in Youth	221
Meets with Universal Theology	225
Indefatigable Labours	234
Peaceful Death at Ragatz	238
Werner at Reutlingen	242

	PAGE
THE TWO SENIORS; THE NEW CHURCH IN YORKSHIRE	245
Methodism in Yorkshire	246
New Church at Keighley	247
The Elder Senior at Cooper's Bridge	250
Acquainted with Mr. Clowes	251
Built Chapel and House	252
Built Sunday School and placed it under care of his son, Mr. Joseph Senior	253
The Broken Pitcher	255
Chapel in Leeds bought chiefly by his aid	257
Rev. Mr. Pilkington and Embsay	263
Yorkshire Colportage Association	266
MR. WATSON, THE MODEL DEACON	267
Left early, Head of a Family of Five	269
Secretary of Argyle Square Society	270
Withdrew from Business to serve the Church	271
FRANCIS OLIVER FINCH, ARTIST AND FRIEND OF MUTUAL IMPROVEMENT SOCIETY	274
Great Poetic Feeling	281
MR. BATEMAN AND MR. CROMPTON, FOUNDERS OF NEW CHURCH COLLEGE	282
Mr. Bateman's Great Skill and Kindness as Medical Man	284
Aids in the Erection of Argyle Square	284
Desires to have a N. C. College	285
Obtains the aid of Mr. Crompton	286
After Mr. Crompton's Death rejoiced that the Bequest to the College was to be £10,000	288
The New Church Bible Society	291
HIRAM POWERS, THE GREAT SCULPTOR	292
His Youth in Vermont and Cincinnati; becomes a New Churchman	293

	PAGE
HIRAM POWERS *(continued)*.	
Removal to Washington and Great Success	294
Takes up his Abode at Florence	295
The Greek Slave	296
Universally Esteemed; Faithfulness and Death	300
MR. BECCONSALL, OF PRESTON	301
Mr. Becconsall receives a Tract; the Greatest Truth ever Published	303
Lectures given in the Theatre	304
Mr. Becconsall brought out of Egypt	304
Determines to Build a Church and Minister's House	305
Left Bequests to several Ministers and several Societies	306
Mrs. Becconsall followed up her Husband's Benevolences	307
JOHN FINNIE, ESQ., OF BOWDON	308
Heard N. C. Truth from Mr. Proud	309
Went to Rio Janeiro and was Prosperous	310
Returned Home and Greatly Assisted the Church	314
Passed Peacefully from Earth, Aged 85	317
FLAXMAN, THE WORLD-RENOWNED SCULPTOR	318
Early Reception of N. C. Truth	319
Married Miss Denman	325
Goes to Rome	327
Returns to England, doing ever more and more Splendid Work, chiefly for Cathedrals	330
Becomes Fellow and then Professor in the Royal Academy	332
The Flaxman Gallery	339

EARLY NEW CHURCH WORTHIES.

I.

SAMUEL DAWSON, of Bolton, Lancashire.

THOUGH the Lord our Saviour, in making His Second Coming, has selected as His disciples some men of attainments and position, marked and striking enough to attract attention, yet, as at His First Coming, not many mighty, not many noble, are called. It is doubtless best so.

To mean minds, the inducement to follow the great of the world is so strong, that whatever is sanctioned by people of rank and wealth will command a large following, not for Truth's sake, but from worldly considerations. The loaves and fishes still violently draw the insincere, not for the bread of life, but that they may satisfy their worldly greed, and be filled. The heralds of heavenly truth must therefore have little to offer but truths for their own sacred worth, and because they lead to goodness. Their adherents will increase but slowly, and the hosannahs of the world will be reserved for those who flatter its prejudices, and who induce hope that falsity will not bring evil, and that Divine laws will be effectually evaded at last. For a good while the flock of the Divine Shepherd will be a little flock, but He will still encourage them with His tender consolations : " Fear not, little flock ; it is your Father's good pleasure to give you the kingdom."

The Rev. Thos. Hartley, rector of Winwick, in Northamptonshire, one of the early friends of Wesley and Whitefield, a learned Oxford scholar, was the first clergyman who accepted the new truths of the Second Advent. He personally knew Swedenborg, and translated "Heaven and Hell."

The Rev. John Clowes, rector of St. John's, Manchester, was led very wonderfully to accept the same grand principles, in the very year of Swedenborg's departure into the eternal world—1772.

These were distinguished as Christians, scholars, and clergymen ; from whom other clergymen have received the heavenly teachings of the New Dispensation in a long and widening line to the Rev. Augustus Clissold, and many others at the present day in the Church of England, willing to diffuse the truth under difficulties, if by that means they can reach those who are hungering and thirsting after righteousness, in the forms better suited to a darker age.

Humbler disciples, however, have been used by the Lord to spread the truth around ; devout men, with warm hearts and clear minds, like the disciples of the First Advent, whose wisdom was not that of great learning, but of deep thought, orderly ways, and noble, useful lives ; and men " took knowledge of them, that they had been with Jesus."

My object is to speak of some of these worthies, beginning with the name at the head of this paper, and ending with Flaxman, who, though famous all over the world, as the greatest of sculptors, is but little known as a devout receiver of the truths of the New Jerusalem. I trust my readers will find, as the true stories follow one another, partly from published sources of information, and partly from personal recollection, much will arise that will edify, interest, and encourage. "These things happened unto them for examples, and they are written for our admonition upon whom the ends of the world (age) are come"—the end of the old age, and the beginning of the New (1 Cor. x., 11).

Samuel Dawson was, if not the very first leader of a New Church Society in a worship formed to address the Lord Jesus clearly as the only God of heaven and earth, yet certainly one of those very early ones whose hearts could only be satisfied by avowing, without dubious language, that IN HIM DWELLS ALL THE FULNESS OF THE GODHEAD BODILY, and He alone, Jehovah Jesus, is King of kings and Lord of lords. He was so much respected through his long life, that at its close, at the age of 79, no objection was made by the vicar of Prestwich church to the intimation of his principles on his grave-stone. Any one who will visit the beautiful church-yard of that once lovely village, formerly reckoned four miles from Manchester and now charming suburban district of that great city, may read, on a grave-stone leading to the main entrance to the church, the following striking epitaph:

"To the Memory of Samuel Dawson, of Bolton-le-moors. He was a humble, good, and faithful servant of his Lord and Master: worshipping Jesus Christ as the Only God of heaven and earth, and diligently Making known to his fellow Christians the Heavenly doctrines of the New Jerusalem. He died March 11, 1823, aged 79 years."

Young Dawson was brought up piously by his parents, in the principles of the Established Church, having been born in the year 1744. As a youth he associated himself with a few others to read religious works, and led an altogether exemplary life. From his pious reading, however, his mind was early tinctured with the idea that God was dreadfully angry, both with him and with mankind in general. This distressing idea was, however, somewhat modified by reading a book lent him by a religious friend, Law's "Spirit of Prayer," which led him to see to a certain extent that God was really Love itself, but that the changing aspects in which He is regarded arose from the changing states of the minds of human beings. He was relieved and edified by this, and was induced to read other works of Law, Behmen, and various writers of a mystical character. He derived much profit and delight from these, and was highly pleased to learn that there was a church being erected at the expense of the celebrated Dr. Byrom, a zealous promoter of the views of Law, and designed for a pious young clergyman then at the University, who would illustrate from the pulpit all that was excellent in the theology of the mystical writers.

This church was St. John's, Manchester; the young clergyman was the Rev. John Clowes. He commenced his ministry in 1769, and young Dawson was a regular, devout, and delighted hearer. He listened from Sunday to Sunday to his spiritual teacher, and became more and more spiritual-minded; but after two or three years he found there were some readers of Law and Behmen who seemed to think they were so exalted in spiritual attainments that they need not mind external worship, but stay and read at home, or walk out and meditate. Before giving way much to the persuasions of friends of this class, he thought he would venture to speak to his clergyman on the subject. He was received and listened to in the kindest manner. Mr. Clowes pointed out that the deeper real religion, the more faithful it makes us to our external duties. It is only the natural man, striving for the mastery, and having no taste for spiritual things, that suggests these phantasies, which lead to negligence of the duties of piety, and then to avoiding conversation on spiritual subjects, and then to downright sin. The bottom of it is evil. Mr. Clowes, having explained the necessity of worship and the propriety of spiritual discipline and church order, to the surprise of his visitor added that even the angels of heaven had their constituted times for public worship.

Mr. Dawson, in giving an account of this interview, used to say he forgot for a moment Mr. Clowes' gown and band, and took the liberty of asking how he knew that. He was answered by the remark that the Lord had not entirely ceased to communicate to His servants the knowledge of His Kingdom and the wonders thereof, and this for the purpose of preparing them for a more perfect dispensation. "Is it possible," said Mr. Dawson, "for our Heavenly Father to communicate a more perfect knowledge of the Divine economy than that made known by His Holy Spirit to such men as Mr. Law?" "I will endeavour to explain myself to your apprehension," said his friend, "by a familiar comparison. Suppose a traveller has lost his way in the night time, and finds himself in much embarrassment to pursue his journey homeward, on account of the darkness with which he is surrounded. In the midst of his perplexity the clouds begin to disperse, and the stars make their appearance and give him hope of being enabled finally to reach his home. After some time," continued Mr. Clowes, "he is cheered by the light of the moon, and he travels with much more confidence that he will safely reach his destination. With alacrity in his steps, and his eye towards home, he pursues his journey with gratitude and delight. But how are all these pleasing sensations enhanced when he beholds the sun rising majestically, whilst the moon and the stars, by which his hopes had been cherished in their turn, disappear! Such is exactly the case as to what has been vouchsafed of God in His mercy, and will be displayed to His creatures in the Christian world." "And may I ask," said Mr. Dawson, " the name of him who is so highly favoured an instrument in the hands of the Lord?" In reply to this, his ears were first greeted with the venerable name of Swedenborg. " Well, sir," continued he, "and how may I obtain a sight of what you have raised so great a desire in my mind to behold?" The works of Emanuel Swedenborg, he was informed, had not yet made their appearance in the English language, but they would very soon be translated. " When that is the case," said Mr. Dawson, "I will part with the stars and the moon, to be cheered in my turn with the light of the sun."

This conversation took place probably in 1775. Two years before, in a very marvellous manner, Mr. Clowes himself had come into the possession of the "True Christian Religion" in Latin, at the recommendation of Richard Houghton, Esq., a gentleman of great piety and learning in Liverpool. In the spring of 1773 he got the book, "*Vera Christiana Religio*," but on looking into it felt little disposition to continue its perusal, and placed it away on a shelf. In the autumn of the same year, in the month of October, he was about to pay a visit which for some years he had done annually to a friend in the county of York, a former college pupil. On the evening before he set out he got down the neglected volume, to turn over its pages in a general, desultory way. In doing so the words *Divinum Humanum* several times arrested his eye. He closed the volume, however, and the next day he went off to his friend, the Right Honourable John Smyth, of Heath. "On awaking early one morning, not many days after his arrival," Mr. Clowes relates, "his mind was filled with a tranquillity and heavenly joy such as he had never before experienced. Whilst he lay musing on this strange and to him most delightful harmony in the interiors of his mind, there was made manifest in the same recesses of his spirit what he could call by no other name than a Divine glory surpassing all description, and exciting the most profound adoration. The glory continued during a full hour, allowing him time both to view and analyze it. Sometimes he closed his bodily eyes, and then opened them again, but the glory remained the same. There was no visible form, but only a strong persuasion that the glory proceeded from a visible form, and that this form was no other than the Divine Humanity *(Divinum Humanum)* of Jesus Christ. When the glory disappeared, as it did by degrees, the impression remained with Mr. Clowes all day, and, what was still more remarkable, the next morning the glory was again manifested, but if possible with increased splendour. There now arose in his mind an irresistible desire to return home immediately, in order to enter upon a serious and attentive perusal of the neglected volume. He had intended to remain a week or a fortnight longer, yet he hastened back to Manchester, he says, rather with the impetuosity of a lover than with the sedateness of a man who had no other object of pursuit but to consult the pages of an unknown and hitherto slighted book."

Such is Mr. Clowes' own account of the extraordinary way in which his interest in the New Church

Writings was excited, and having become enraptured by the spiritual treasures found therein contained, he taught Mr. Dawson and others in and around Manchester to receive with avidity the translations as they appeared.

The first works issued were the "Doctrine of Life," and the "Treatise on Influx," published by the estimable Mr. Cookworthy, of Plymouth, a member of the Society of Friends. The next was "Heaven and Hell," by Mr. Hartley, the rector of Winwick; and then followed a series by the Rev. Mr. Clowes himself. As they came one after another, it was to Mr. Dawson a continual feast. His delight would express itself like those of old, who said, "We have seen strange things to-day." He had some difficulty in the account in "Heaven and Hell" that the scenes in the other world are from the spheres of the inhabitants, and correspond to their states. He was very fond of botanising, and had many rare plants in his garden that he might study their natures and uses. One day, when he was out in a field, he came into a state of abstraction, and for some time it seemed as if all his plants were visibly about him. All appeared so real, and continued so long, that he said to himself, if this can happen to me, why can it not be in the other world on a grander scale. So vivid were his spiritual convictions, that he desired to impart the same truths and delights to others.

He attended a meeting of congenial spirits at the house of a friend at Oaken-bottom, about a mile from Bolton. This meeting continued for several years. Others joined from Bolton, and at length it was agreed to have the meeting in Bolton itself, and, finding his teachings always so clear and affectionate, he was solicited to become their leader, which office he faithfully occupied for thirty years.

His wife was rather set against her husband's new views for many years, and being a strong-minded woman sometimes met him on his return home from service rather with a scowl than with a smile. Dawson's Christianity, however, was a patient Christianity. He was pre-eminently a man of peace, and endured long. Their youngest child, a boy I think of about six years of age, sickened and died, and as it was the last it was a bitter trial to the mother. One day, as they sat at tea, the moody, mourning mother fainted and fell on the floor. It was some time before consciousness returned; but when it did, her first words were, "I have seen the child." He asked her to describe it: how it seemed, and how it was dressed; and her account was so like that of Swedenborg in the "Arcana Cælestia," 2296, that he got down the volume and read it to her, and from that day she became as willing to learn as she had before been adverse.

The friends of Mr. Dawson were a very estimable, thoughtful, spiritually-minded company. In my early days it was a great pleasure to visit them. Their eyes would brighten, would glisten, at what they heard. One of them, old Ralph Harrison, was a fine specimen. He would come, as soon as service was over, and exclaim, taking the hand, something like, "Oh, young man, what a beautiful string of pearls you have brought us this morning; how much we thank you!" Mr. Dawson was universally respected. In his later years asthma prevented him almost entirely from quitting the house. Some few kind friends, headed by the benevolent Mr. Samuel Mottram, of Manchester, subscribed annually a sum sufficient to relieve him of care and anxiety. About two months before his departure he had a deep mental conflict which he thus described to a visiting friend: "I have suffered," he said, "the most grievous temptation that ever my Lord permitted to come upon me. I have experienced all the pangs of desperation, and my spiritual foes have spent their utmost rage upon me. But the Lord has triumphed gloriously, and set my feet upon a rock." After that a state of peace set in and his departure was blessed.

II.

SAMUEL CROMPTON,

Inventor of the Wonderful Machine for Spinning Cotton, called the Mule.

WHEN the immense increase of this country in wealth, population, and influence among mankind arising from the stupendous cotton trade is considered, connecting us with America, giving the nation capacity to bear its burdens in the warlike troubles of the early part of the century, and maintaining at the present a population four times as great as it possessed a hundred years ago, it is interesting and suggestive to know that this vast growth of trade was largely owing to the inventions of three humble New Churchmen: Hargreaves, of Standhill, near Blackburn; Highs, of Leigh; and Crompton, of Hall-i'-th'-Wood, the latter an old mansion in a beautiful and romantic region near Bolton.

Hargreaves invented the Spinning Jenny, Highs the Water-frame, and Crompton the Mule, which combined the excellences of the other two. It is with this Crompton especially, a humble, spiritually-minded, excellent, and most ingenious man, with whom we have at present to concern ourselves. He was born at Firwood, lived afterwards at the picturesque old house called Hall-i'-th'-Wood, in which he was making his marvellous inventions, and cultivating his music, in his days of early manhood. There is a fine picture of him with his violin in hand, and his thoughtful face absorbed in meditation.

He received the doctrines from his friend Samuel Dawson of our previous sketch, in early middle life, for at his death, June 26th, 1827, he had been over forty years a New Churchman. His knowledge of the doctrines of the New Jerusalem was obtained from his friend, who was then rejoicing in their full and glorious light, and he at once began practically to carry them out. He made an organ for the little Society at Bolton, of which he was an early member, and composed many beautiful tunes. He was a man of strict integrity, ardent in his attachments, and persevering in all he undertook. His religion was seen in his daily life, which was one ever seeking to perform uses, directed by profound thought. His portrait shows the face of a man deeply meditative, but also a man of order and peace.

From indifference to the attainment of riches, he did not obtain a patent for inventions which have increased the wealth of the country to an incalculable extent. He probably had no idea of the astonishing growth of commerce that would follow in time from his improvements. He had been for some years a worker on Hargreaves' jenny.

Greedy watchers were hanging about when Crompton was known to be scheming his more perfect machines, although he commenced doing so when he was only twenty-one, and it took him five years to complete his mule. The work he produced was so superior, and the wages of those who employed his methods were so increased, that he had to guard his plans from being caught up and carried out before he had matured them himself. In a letter to a friend he says, in regard to the mule, "The date of its being first completed was 1779. At the end of the following year I was under the necessity of making it public, or destroying it, as it was not in my power to keep it (for myself) and work it, and to destroy it was too painful a task, having been four and a half years at least, wherein every moment of time and power of mind, as well as expense, which my other employments would permit, were devoted to this one end, the having good yarn to weave; so that to destroy it I could not."

Being of a retiring and unambitious disposition, he only regretted that public curiosity would not allow him to enjoy what he called his little invention to himself in his garret, and to earn by his own manual labour undisturbed the fruits of his ingenuity and perseverance. The very superior quality of his yarn drew persons from all quarters to ascertain the means whereby he produced it. His first machine was almost entirely of wood, and it had only about twenty or thirty spindles; all the parts of the work were comparatively heavy, but he and others continued to improve, making the several parts in metal, until one machine at the beginning of this century would work 400 spindles, and in 1835 mules of eleven hundred spindles each, or two thousand two hundred the pair, and self-acting, only requiring young girls to join the broken threads, announced its wonderful perfection in its maturity.

The mule, and the other inventions of which, after

the steam engine, it may be considered to be the chief, have increased the population of Lancashire from 297,300 in 1750, to three millions and a half of people, and Yorkshire nearly as many, at the present day. And these people have comforts and advantages of which their forefathers little dreamed. In Crompton's time our manufacturers consumed three millions of pounds of cotton; in 1881 the enormous amount had been reached of fifteen hundred millions; and our readers may conceive faintly the wonderful effect this extent of peaceful, useful trade must have, in inducing friendly feeling and enlarged prosperity all over the world. Although Crompton took out no patent, the gratitude of the manufacturers benefitted was early acknowledged by a present, in the form of a subscription amounting to a hundred guineas. About twenty years afterwards there was another subscription of £400; and in 1812 the manufacturing public petitioned Parliament to recognise the merits of Mr. Crompton, and a grant was made of the sum of £5,000. It was then stated that 70,000 persons were employed on his machines, and they found work for 150,000 weavers. The capital then employed in factories, machinery, and mule-spinning was said to amount to four millions sterling, and in 1825 the amount was said to be four-fifths of the whole capital of the kingdom.

Mr. Crompton's busy, useful life was not without considerable vicissitudes and sorrows. His excellent wife died early, and left him with a numerous small family, and many cares. He embarked in business, and did not succeed; but he paid his creditors every farthing. Inventors are not always successful in the commercial circle. During the remainder of his days he struggled with losses and disappointments; bearing them, however, with Christian patience and fortitude, acknowledged by all who knew him. Chequered by prosperity and adversity, he rejoiced to confess he found the doctrines of the New Church his constant and peculiar support. His only daughter kept his modest house in King Street, Bolton, where he died, leaving her but very poorly provided for. His own means were small, though he had always kind friends who delighted to show how much they appreciated him, and he had always the contented air of being in comfortable circumstances.

His orderly life prevented him probably from having any active illness in his old age. He gently decayed, and without pain faded away. Sustained by the truths he had so long embraced and loved, and which had consoled and strengthened him in all previous trials, he passed away quietly to heaven, almost unnoticed in the town, on Tuesday, June 26th, 1827, in the 74th year of his age.

Soon after his departure, a feeling sprung up in Bolton and the manufacturing districts generally that his genius, his ability, and his worth had not been honoured as they ought to have been, and a desire was felt that something more should be done. This sentiment increased with the growth of the trade which his ingenuity had so much promoted; and at length it was determined there should be a statue erected to his memory. This was at length carried out. A life-size figure, in a sitting, thoughtful posture, on a square stone pedestal, the pedestal about six feet high, was erected in Nelson-square, fronting Bradshaw-gate. One side of the pedestal has a representation of the Hall-i'-th'-Wood, where Crompton lived when he invented the mule; and on the opposite side he is seen as himself working at the mule. It is a fine memento of their townsman, and Bolton now regards his name with homage and respect. September 24th, 1862, when the statue was unveiled, was a great day in Bolton. All the town was *en fête*, and there was a grand procession. Everybody strove to do honour to Crompton. Bands of music played, the trades walked, and the chief people of the town led the procession. The New Church people joined, and testified their respect and love for their brother just gone before.

Little did that modest, excellent man dream that the time would come when his name would be echoed on all sides with acclamation. But, still better than the applause of thousands, was the assurance in his loving Christian heart that his name was written in heaven, and the sweet well-done of his Saviour would be his—"Well-done, good and faithful servant, enter thou into the joy of the Lord."

III.

OBERLIN,

Pastor of the Ban de la Roche.

OUR object as we have stated is to avoid, for this series at least, to present our readers with the biographical sketches of ministers who by their public position became well known; and relate only the lives of those in less conspicuous positions. It might be thought that Oberlin, as he was a pastor, ought not to appear in this company. We think, however, that although we hold he was a New Churchman, and of the first class, yet as he was not technically in the New Church ministry, and his life and virtues probably are not widely known amongst our readers, we may relate his instructive and noble story as that of a New Church Worthy in the early times. We have another reason for placing his history before our readers. We intend to point to the fact that infant schools really orginated in the Ban de la Roche. Afterwards New Churchmen were especially connected with the earliest efforts to teach the very little ones in England to play and learn at the same time.

We desire to some extent to prepare the way by the story of the good Oberlin. The Steinthal, which is the German name for the valley among the mountains about thirty miles from Strasbourg, called in French the Ban de la Roche, was taken in the time of Louis XIV. from Germany and added to the kingdom of France; but as the inhabitants had previously nearly all of them been Protestants, the French, from policy, granted them the free enjoyment of their own religion. Owing to the rude character of the mountain district, and the entire want of roads, the people, though industrious and honest, were very ignorant. As shepherds they had great difficulty to obtain from the mountain sides and the desolate land a poor subsistence, and education was out of the question.

Stouber, a worthy clergyman, the predecessor of Oberlin, relates that when he entered on his duties, in 1750, he enquired if there was not a schoolhouse somewhere, and was conducted to a very mean cottage where a number of children were crowded together with nothing to do, and, in reply to his enquiries for the schoolmaster, he was pointed to a withered old man, who lay on a little bed in one corner of the apartment.

"Are you the schoolmaster, my good friend?" inquired Stouber.

"Yes, sir."

"And what do you teach the children?"

"Nothing, sir."

"Nothing! why, how is that?"

"Because," replied the old man, with characteristic simplicity, "I know nothing myself."

"Why were you then appointed schoolmaster?"

"Why, sir, I had been taking care of the pigs for a great number of years, and when I got too old for that employment they sent me here to take care of the children."

The schools in the other villages were no better, for, if the schoolmasters were not swineherds, they were shepherds, who in the summer followed their flocks over the mountains, and during the winter months only attempted to impart to their little pupils what small knowledge they themselves possessed. Scarcely any could read with fluency, and very few could write at all. Stouber, during seventeen years of conscientious and active ministry, made considerable change for the better, and was then pressed to take the station of pastor to St. Thomas's Church at Strasbourg, which he accepted; and on looking round for a successor it occurred to him that young Oberlin, with whose piety and zeal he was acquainted, would just be the man to succeed him.

He knew young Oberlin was already ordained, and was about to accept the position of military chaplain; this was in 1767. But when he proposed the new position, one wholly uninviting to any one but a true servant of God, who in singleness of heart was ready to undertake anything which he felt was the will of the Lord Jesus, the young minister, after earnest prayer that a blessing might descend upon the flock committed to his charge, accompanied his friend and patron to his post, and arrived at Walbach, the chief village and residence of the pastor, on the 30th of March. He was at this time in the 27th year of his age.

On Oberlin's arrival and settlement at Walbach, he found the parsonage house tolerably commodious, with a courtyard in front and a good garden behind. It stood in a delightful situation, very near the church, and the scene was made beautiful by here and there clumps of pine and other straggling trees. A little acquaintance with the place, its rude inhabitants, and its rough mountains, dells, and rocks, convinced him that, notwithstanding the partial reformation effected by the labours of Mr. Stouber, neither the necessities of his flock, nor the difficulties which were to be overcome, were of an ordinary kind. The people were entirely secluded from the neighbouring districts for want of roads, which, owing to the devastation of war, and decay of population, had been so totally lost that the only mode of communication for the bulk of the parish to the neighbouring towns was across a river, thirty feet wide, by stepping stones, and in the winter along its bed.

The husbandmen were destitute of the most necessary agricultural implements, and had no means of procuring them. The provisions springing from a scanty soil were not sufficient to maintain comfortably even the scanty population; and the oppressive exactions of labouring for their so-called superiors, often without pay, under the old regime, depressed and irritated the spirits of the people.

Confident, however, that strength would be afforded, if rightly sought, Oberlin at once resolved to use all the attainments in religion, philosophy, and science, which he had brought with him from Strasbourg, to the improvement of the parish and of his parishioners. He was so zealous, however, and saw so many things that urgently needed change, that although the more thoughtful and estimable Christians of the parish stood by him, the stupid and prejudiced formed a party against him. They declared that old practices were safe, and whatever was new was pernicious. They resolved, therefore, not to submit to innovation, but to give it their most strenuous and determined resistance. So far did they carry this, that on one occasion soon after his arrival they laid a plan to waylay their new minister, and inflict upon him a severe personal chastisement, judging that such a measure, at the early part of his career, would prevent his future interference.

Sunday was fixed upon for their attempt. Oberlin happily received information of what was contemplated, and preached that day on Christian patience, submitting to surmises, and returning good for evil. After the service the malcontents met at the house of one of their party, and were considering what they had better do, when to their astonishment Oberlin himself opened the door and stood before them. He addressed them with mingled dignity and tenderness, assured them that all he sought was their real and highest good, and added: "If you still think I am doing or intending you any wrong, I have come to deliver myself into your hands, rather than you should be guilty of the meanness of an ambuscade." These simple words produced their intended effect. The peasants, ashamed of their scheme, sincerely begged his forgiveness, and promised never again to entertain a doubt of the sincerity of the motives by which he was actuated, and of his affectionate desire for their welfare.

He next gave himself a worthy wife in whose choice he had prayed to be guided by the Lord, and whose virtues, intelligence, and spiritual-mindedness, were the greatest possible help to him for sixteen years. They were married July 6th, 1768, and she entered the eternal world in 1784. Oberlin always believed she was still with him after death, and counselled him.

One of Oberlin's early projects was to build a bridge over the river, and then to make a road a mile and a half long leading into the highway to Strasbourg. He assembled the people and explained his plans. They were perfectly astonished at the proposition, which appeared simply impracticable. Everyone excused himself, on the plea of other business, from engaging in so stupendous an undertaking. Oberlin endeavoured to refute the objections offered on all sides. The produce of your fields, said he, will then meet with a ready sale abroad. Instead of being imprisoned in your villages nine months out of twelve, you will be enabled to keep up an intercourse with the inhabitants of the neighbouring districts. You will have the opportunity of procuring a number of things, of which you have long stood in need, and your happiness will be augmented and increased by the additional means thus afforded of providing comforts for yourselves and your children. He concluded with this practical appeal. Let all who feel the importance of my plan come and work with me. Then, with pick-axe on his shoulder, he proceeded to the spot to make a beginning, while the astonished peasants, now having learned to trust him, and animated by his example, hastened to fetch their tools and follow. The emulation to assist spread through the whole parish. The increased number of hands rendered an increased number of implements necessary: he procured them from Strasbourg; expenses accumulated: he interested distant friends, and through their aid funds were obtained. Walls were erected to support the earth which was ready to give way; mountain torrents which had hitherto inundated the meadows were diverted into courses sufficient to contain them; perseverance, in short, triumphed over difficulties, and at the commencement of the year 1770 a communication was opened with Strasbourg by means of a new road and a neat wooden bridge thrown across the river. This bridge still bears the name of the Bridge of Charity (Le Pont de Charité). The pastor who on the Sabbath had directed their attention with that earnestness and warmth by which his own soul was animated to the "rest that remaineth for the people of God," was seen on the Monday, pick-axe on his shoulder, at the head of two hundred of his flock, with an energy that neither fatigue nor danger could diminish.

These labours, continued for the spiritual and temporal well-being of his people for a period of sixty years, to the time of his death in 1826, resulted in such a wonderful change in the district that the wilderness might in all respects be said to blossom as the rose. This noble result was acknowledged in 1818 by the Gold Medal of the Royal and Central Agricultural Society of Paris. The presentation was made through M. le Comte François de Neufchateau, who had repeatedly visited the Steinthal and was deputed to this office, and who delivered the gold medal to Oberlin in acknowledgment of the services he had rendered during more than half a century to agriculture in particular, and to mankind in general.

As a coadjutor of the Bible Society, he had taken care that there was a Bible in every house in the district; and as a friend of education, he had diffused such a desire for learning that all the children of due age were well instructed, and he was universally beloved.

But the two special points to which we desire to draw the attention of our readers are, that he was the real originator of Infant Schools; and, secondly, that he was an early receiver of the writings of Swedenborg. Oberlin had observed with concern the disadvantages to which the young children were left while their parents were busily employed in their daily avocations, and the elder children were at school. He laid down a plan for Infant Schools, and carried it into practice in the villages of his large parish, which were the model of those subsequently opened at Paris, and still more recently in this country. He engaged large rooms for them, engaged mistresses, and salaried them at his own expense. Instruction in these schools was mingled with amusement, and whilst enough of discipline was introduced to instil habits of order, a degree of liberty was allowed, that school might be enjoyed by children of two and three years of age. Those of five and six were taught to knit, spin, sew, and read. The mistress would teach them Scripture and natural history by coloured pictures and easy explanations, and vary their exercises by hymns and moral songs, so as to keep them usefully but delightedly occupied. Then came the higher schools and Sunday Schools.

When the Rev. John Henry Smithson was a student in Switzerland, and had been recently introduced to a knowledge of the writings of Swedenborg himself, he paid a visit to the Ban de la Roche, and specially enjoyed his intercourse with the heavenly-minded Oberlin. He relates the circumstances of this visit at considerable length in the *Intellectual Repository* for 1850, from which we extract the conclusion in substance of this paper.

"Oberlin was then in his eighty-fourth year. He was tall and well-proportioned. He could scarcely be said to be bent, his sight was not dim, and he appeared to enjoy the use of his faculties unimpaired. His countenance was very expressive, and full of that energetic appearance which is the characteristic of greatness of soul. In a short time after my arrival dinner was announced, and Oberlin, leading me by the hand, showed me the place at his table reserved for the friend and the stranger, opposite to the seat which he occupied himself.

"The entire household dined together, himself, his friends, and the housekeeper occupying the upper portion; and the servants, and frequently one of the inhabitants of the more distant part of the valley, the lower part of the table. Oberlin embraced this opportunity to instil many solid principles of goodness and virtue into the hearts of his family, his flock, and his guests. After dinner he took me into his library, a large upper room, two sides of which were fitted up with shelves from top to bottom, and well stocked with books in several languages.

"Having received a few explanations from Oberlin respecting the diagrams, models, &c., which I observed in his library, I asked him whether he had read any of the works of Swedenborg. Without replying, he immediately reached a book, and clapping his hand upon it, expressive of great satisfaction, told me that he had had this treasure many years in his library, and that he knew *from his own experience* that everything relating to it was true. This treasure was Swedenborg's work on 'Heaven and Hell.'

"As I had lately become acquainted with the works of Swedenborg," continues Mr. Smithson, "and as Oberlin was almost the only person I had met with who had any knowledge of these writings, I was of course highly delighted to meet with a man whose name was universally honoured, and whose life and character were considered as a bright example of every Christian virtue. The great weight which accompanied the name of this good man, and the approving declaration he had already made respecting one of the most important works of Swedenborg, materially strengthened my convictions of the truth of their claims to universal attention. I accordingly felt the deepest interest in conversing with Oberlin on the subject of Swedenborg's theology, and the amazing spiritual intelligence displayed in his writings.

"I inquired how it happened that he had arrived at convictions so solid respecting the truths contained in the work on 'Heaven and Hell.' He replied that when he first came to reside as pastor among the inhabitants of Steinthal they had many superstitious notions respecting the proximity of the spiritual world, and of the appearance of various objects and phenomena in that world which from time to time were seen by some of the people belonging to his flock. For instance, it was not unusual for a person who had died to appear to some individual in the valley. This gift of second sight, or the opening of the spiritual sight to see objects in a spiritual state of existence, was however confined to a few persons. At first, he said, he was annoyed with the accounts of these things and discouraged them, but circumstances occurred so striking as to stagger his own scepticism, and, being about that time on a visit at Strasbourg, a friend (probably Jung Stilling) recommended him to peruse the work on 'Heaven and Hell.' This work, he informed me, gave him a full and satisfactory explanation of the extraordinary cases occurring in his valley, and which he himself, from evidences which could not be doubted, was constrained to admit. He read the treasure, as he called it, very attentively, and with increasing delight. He no longer doubted the nearness of the spiritual world: yea, he believed that man, by virtue of his immortal mind, is already an inhabitant of the spiritual world, in which, after the death of the material body, he is to continue his existence forever."

The other works which Oberlin possessed, Mr.

Smithson informs us, were the "Divine Love and
Wisdom," the "Divine Providence," and he thinks
the "Earths in the Universe."

"So convinced was Oberlin," Mr. Smithson continues, "of the salutary importance of teaching his
flock concerning Heaven and Hell, and the relation
which man sustains to the spiritual world, that he
formed a chart or map representing heaven, which
he hung up in his church. This celestial diagram,
as it was called, was taken from Solomon's temple,
which in all respects corresponded to heaven.
These correspondences Oberlin had derived from
Swedenborg, and he pointed out to his flock that
according to their humility, piety, fidelity, and their
love of being useful to each other, would be their
elevation either to the first, second, or third heaven.

"His flock were extremely delighted to hear his
remarks concerning heaven; and the manner in
which he explained to them how the love of the
Lord above all things, and the love of our neighbour even better than ourselves, constitutes the life
and soul of the heavenly kingdom, served no doubt
to kindle that celestial fire of mutual love amongst
his people which made them a bright and shining
light to all around them.

"For the numerous instances of remarkable self-denial; of benevolence to the orphan, widow, and
stranger; of liberal contributions from their scanty
means to procure Bibles for those in the surrounding districts who did not possess them, and to purchase articles of clothing and implements of use
for those who were destitute and not able to work
for the want of the necessary means—these facts,
I repeat, when considered in connection with the
general exemption from vice and crime, were striking proofs of something like that spirit of genuine

Christianity which has seldom been witnessed upon earth, but which, as the New Jerusalem Church advances, will not be so great a stranger among men.

"M. Morel, a French writer who composed an excellent life of Oberlin, says: 'Oberlin had much originality in his conceptions, and his most singular ideas bore the impress of a great soul; he attached an emblematical sense to colours. His ardent imagination, nourished by the mystical works of Swedenborg, delighted to bound over the threshold of the tomb, and to expatiate on the mysterious world which awaits the soul when separated from its earthly bonds.'"

Mr. Smithson, from whose interesting account we have been obliged to abbreviate much, concludes by saying: "He taught his flock the way to heaven, and reduced the whole of his religious instruction to two essential points—to the acknowledgment of Jesus as our Heavenly Father, and to the necessity of loving Him by keeping His Divine precepts, as the essential means of salvation. His love and veneration for the Holy Scriptures were very great; he knew that the Word is the medium of conjunction between man and the Lord, and the channel through which all the blessings of salvation are conveyed to the human soul. He spared no pains or labour to distribute the Word of Life, and became one of the earliest correspondents of the British and Foreign Bible Society, as well as one of their most zealous co-operators. He died in the eighty-sixth year of his age, universally admired and beloved.

"On returning to the university, to pursue my studies," says Mr. Smithson, "I reflected much on what I had heard from Oberlin, and resolved to procure all the Writings of Swedenborg, and to study them with profound attention."

IV.

BUCHANAN,

And the Introducers of Infant Schools and Cheap Schools into this Country.

WE have pointed out in our last that Infant Schools had their origin in the heavenly earnestness and wisdom of Oberlin, whose mind scanned the whole of human life, and saw the immense importance of training childhood well. They who would have first-rate plants, or animals, know that their early life must be watched and guarded with care, or no great excellence will be attained; so is it with human beings. Hence in the rough state of things which prevailed before the Lord's Second Advent no wonder that the mass of the people were so violent, and so little valued, as they were, being accounted things for press-gangs, semi-slaves, with the poorest pittance of wages; indeed they were so generally ignorant and neglected that they may be said to have " tumbled up," rather than been brought up and trained to be what the Lord designed them to be, true and noble men and women on earth, and then angel-men and women,

Let any one read Thackeray's description of the time of George II., or any good memoir of that dreary period, and he will feel as the souls under the altar, "How long, O Lord, holy and true, dost thou not judge, and avenge our blood on them that dwell on the earth" (Rev. vi., 10). The Lord did judge in the world of spirits, where final judgments take place; and soon new and brighter influences began to pour into the world.

Men began to care for the children; Infant Schools, Sunday Schools, cheap Day Schools, took their rise, and rapidly multiplied. It was as if the Lord was felt to have said, Train them for Me; and good men everywhere felt the impulse, and went to work. We need not wonder that those whose hearts the Lord had touched with the great truths that God is Love itself and Wisdom itself, were among the foremost to initiate these principles into practice. We have seen how this was with Oberlin. The name at the head of this article, Buchanan, was the first associated with an Infant School in this country. He had been, I think I have heard, at New Lanark, where Robert Owen had established an Infant School in Scotland. The English school was commenced at Westminster about 1820, and was supported chiefly by Mr. Brougham, afterward the renowned Lord Brougham. He was at first the entire supporter of this school; but the master, Buchanan, was a New Churchman, attending the place of worship of the Rev. Thos. Goyder, in St. George's Fields. The second school, begun in a few months afterwards, was that of Mr. Wilderspin, at Spitalfields, also a New Churchman, connected with the same congregation, at the sole expense of Joseph Wilson, Esq. This Mr. Wilderspin did much to spread the Infant School system. He wrote an admirable book on the subject, and delivered many lectures in which he described many droll things in relation to the difficulties of the management of the little ones at first. Quite a number of very young children were taken in the first day, and for an hour or so they got on pretty well, with repeating and singing little amusing songs; but the children got tired of sitting still; some yawned and some began to cry. The disorder was becoming great, and the master and his wife were getting to their wits' end, when the thought came into his mind that he would put his wife's cap on and dance up the room. This manœuvre succeeded to perfection. The young disciples were charmed, and paid the utmost attention to see what would come next. He then marshalled the children to march after him, and thus alter the position, and after a time to settle again, and so introduced change and variety. Thus was evolved a plan of part work, part play, mixed with music, and there was a great success.

It was urged by Mr. Wilderspin, " that the expense of sending two convicts to New South Wales would support an Infant School, of 200 children, a year. Thus, supposing each child to continue in the school five years, sixty useful members might be introduced into society for the sum which it costs to send two injurious members out of it; there surely, then, cannot be a more profitable as well as benevolent mode of employing some portion of the finances of the nation." On the necessity of such schools, Mr. Wilderspin wrote : " We find by sad experience that children can very early learn vice. While in their cradle they will watch our motions and notice our actions, and be those actions good or bad they will copy them, and manifest them in their own conduct as soon as they are able. How extremely cautious, then, ought we to be, in whatever we do or say before children, how zealous ought we to be in checking the very first appearance of evil in the infant mind! But how can this be done without taking them out of the streets? Will the parents do it? Many cannot. The father goes to his daily labour in the morning before the children are out of bed, and probably does not return until the children are in bed again at night. The mother, in many cases, goes out also because the father's earnings will not support the family. In this case, if they were so disposed to instruct their children, they cannot do it. What is the consequence? The children are intrusted to the care of some girl, whose parents, probably, are still poorer, and who are glad to let her earn something towards her support. I know numbers who go out in this way before they are twelve years old. These children are not qualified to check the first appearance of evil in their little charge, poor things. They have received no education themselves but what they acquired in the streets, and this is readily taught to those placed under their care. It consists in general of deceit, lying, pilfering, and extreme filthiness." Mr. Wilderspin evidently proved the necessity of Infant Schools, and several other New Churchmen entered upon the occupation of teachers.

Mr. D. G. Goyder, then quite a young man, afterwards the Rev. Dr. Goyder, in his autobiography, informs us he was early induced to leave London to undertake an Infant School at Bristol; Mr. Chalklen was for some years an Infant School teacher; thus showing how early and how earnestly the New Church had to do with the introduction of this admirable loving system of training the young, whose parents, from occupation and other reasons, were so little able to discharge properly the important duty of teaching childhood.

The effect of Infant Schools and Sunday Schools, so good as far as they went, yet so limited in the amount of education they gave, was to induce a strong desire for good and cheap Day Schools. Our friends led the way in this respect also, and curiously enough the same society from which the Infant School men started, in 1820, commenced the first of the special cheap Day Schools to which we now refer. It was the society of the New Church in Waterloo Road, presided over by the Rev. Thomas Goyder. They began a school in 1821, and called it the New Jerusalem Church Free School. Mr. Grainger was the master, an admirable teacher, and an excellent man. For many years it was very prosperous, and did most gratifying work. It declined only after many years, the society to which it was attached having removed elsewhere. The building was given up and sold. These schools were not exactly free schools; there was a small payment of two-pence per week, and there was a system of circular classes and medals to promote emulation among the scholars, which made them very efficient, and the schools scenes of activity and excellent order. The boy who won the greatest number of medals in a week was head of his class to begin the next week. Schools on this system were much sought after by respectable artisans for their children. They found their children rapidly improved, and they preferred to send them and pay for them, to sending them to the National Schools then existing, and at which they paid nothing. The working people generally thought they were worth nothing, and they were not much mistaken.

The National Schools to which we are referring were commenced by Dr. Bell and Mr. Lancaster, of the Society of Friends, in 1811, and were free; but they were conducted with so little good-will under the auspices of the clergy, great numbers of whom disliked them altogether, and probably in the majority of cases committed them to the parish clerks, that the result was, they were little valued by the people. There was no compulsion requiring the children to attend, and the result was general neglect. Parents also, being themselves extremely ignorant, saw very little good from their children attending, and when they were persuaded by patronizing friends to send them they supposed they were conferring a favour in letting their children go. This feeling had also prevailed for a time in the early days of Sunday Schools. I have known places where children were paid a penny a Sunday to induce them to attend, and at least in one instance the mothers came and struck for some time for two-pence. This was the case at Sabden, near Pendle Hill.

In the schools commenced by our friends the feeling was entirely different. Such was the heartiness in teaching, such was the interest taken in them by New Church people, and such the excellent system of these circular classes, that the schools were soon filled and numbers waiting for vacancies that they might be admitted. In the second report of the London school, published in 1824, it is stated that two excellent examinations of the pupils had taken place, conducted by the Rev. Samuel Noble, at which a considerable number of friends were present, who expressed themselves fully satisfied with the progress which the children had evidently made, a progress which elicited from the examining minister unqualified praise, and his warm recommendation of the institution to all receivers of the heavenly doctrines. This, and other schools soon commenced in other parts of the church, to which we intend to call attention, were greatly assisted by a bequest recently left by Mr.

Cheap Day Schools. 35

Chester, of Dover, and administered by the General Conference, for the spread of education.

The Committee closed their report with the following excellent sentiments : "The Committee, grateful for the privilege of being instruments of promoting so glorious a cause, wish to impress upon the subscribers that the school of which they are the supporters cannot fail to be of especial service to the rising generation; but whether this will be perceptible on a small or on a large portion of society depends primarily on that Providence whose tender mercies are over all His works, and to whose goodness we are indebted for all the means, mental and physical, through which has been accomplished the little we have done. But, while we render up the praise to Him to whom all praise is justly due, let us not forget that the measure of utility depends, derivatively, upon our own exertions. Wherefore, let us not upon any occasion, when we cannot accomplish what we wish, neglect to do what we can, but let us go on, actively performing uses to those around us, in the full confidence that, while we keep within the means provided for us by our Heavenly Father, He will not fail to grant His blessing upon our exertions."

V.

Mr. AGNEW,

And Cheap Day Schools in Manchester, Salford, and the North.

THE Cheap and Good Day School system having been commenced, and seen to be successful, in London, excited attention in Manchester.

Indeed, the excellent Mr. Thomas Jones, of London, brother of the Rev. Richd. Jones, of Peter Street, Manchester, wrote to Mr. Agnew in 1824, and described the success of the school in London as so gratifying, and promising so much good both for the children and the Church, that Mr. Agnew became very zealous that a similar school should be established in Manchester, and called a meeting for the purpose of promoting that object. The minutes of that meeting in 1824, and subsequent proceedings, I possess in the hand-writing of my dear and life-long friend, Thos. Agnew, Esq., the founder of the great well-known artistic firm of Thos. Agnew and Sons, of London and Manchester.

Mr. Agnew was chief promoter, and was chosen secretary, an office he held for very many years. I give the minutes of the first meeting, as the names and circumstances will be interesting to a wide circle of friends, especially to friends advanced in age, to whom the memories of the men concerned, all gone to their eternal homes, will be full of tender recollection.

"Meeting of the Members of the New Church in Manchester and Salford, held in the Lecture Room, Peter Street, Decr. 3rd, 1824. Rev. R. Jones in the chair.

"The following Resolution, proposed by Mr. Agnew, and seconded by Mr. Goadsby, passed unanimously :

"'That this meeting, considering it of the greatest importance to instruct the youthful mind in the principles and doctrines of the New Church, is of opinion that a Day School, founded for this specific purpose, would be highly beneficial to the rising generation in this neighbourhood, and extensively useful to the Church at large.'

"Proposed by Mr. Lockett; seconded by Mr. Goadsby:

"'That a Committee from the two Societies, with power to add to their number, be appointed, to consider the means of carrying the foregoing resolution into effect, and to report thereon to a public meeting.'

"Passed unanimously:

"'That the following gentlemen form the Committee: John Prince, Ed. Preston, F. Goadsby, John Barge, John Holgate, T. Agnew, Will. Lockett, Wm. Newbery; and that four be competent to act.'

"RICHD. JONES, *President.*"

The Committee thus appointed intended to erect a separate building for their school, but found some difficulty in carrying out this plan, and after much consideration accepted the Sunday School room belonging to the Temple, Salford; and in June, 1827, their school commenced, under Mr. Joseph Moss, a gentleman of Burton-upon-Trent, who had visited London to observe the system of the school there.

Mr. Moss was an excellent man, a first-rate teacher, and an earnest New Churchman. The school was very soon a complete success. In twelve months it was so well filled that it was resolved to have another school in the Lecture Room adjoining Peter Street Church, and Mr. Moss was transferred there, another master being chosen for Salford. Both schools were greatly sought after, and overflowing with scholars, for very many years. Two-pence per week was charged, and afterwards three-pence and four-pence, and paid willingly. Mr. Agnew was secretary, and Mr. Goadsby treasurer. Companion schools for girls were soon provided, both in Salford and Manchester.

Mr. Moss, though an exceedingly kind man, was a very rigid disciplinarian; and though his school was always distinguished in all scholastic respects, sometimes held up by the Inspectors of Schools as the most eminent for order and excellence in the kingdom, and always in the first line, it was never of the use in attracting young minds to the truths of the New Jerusalem that its early supporters had hoped.

The same may be said of almost all the other Day Schools of the Church, with some modifications. Where they were in close connection with the Sunday Schools, so that the scholars could be kept in association with the Church as Sunday scholars and teachers, a permanent attachment was effected. Where this was not the case, little was heard of the children after school period was over. Subsequently a large and noble school-room was erected on the ground adjoining Peter Street Church, chiefly by the generosity, zeal, and influence of my never-to-be-forgotten, lifelong companion and friend, dear John Broadfield, one of the best of New Church Christians and men, where it still maintained or increased its high character, under Mr. Scotson, now under the City School Board.

Often have I heard Old Mr. Barge exult in the multitudes of young minds which would be attached to the Church, and make up for those whose prejudices prevented them from receiving its bright and glorious truths; but this was a kindly illusion. Where the rational faculty has not laid hold of the truth, and implanted it in a good heart, it has little fixity. Like the seed on the wayside, false views, like voracious birds, destroy it, or under the hot passions of self-love, the scorching sun of the bad man, it presently withers away.

One unexpected result came out of these schools. Many of the young men, who became teachers or assistant teachers, became clever laymen, or competent and highly respected and beloved ministers. The Rev. Mr. Boys, Rev. Mr. Mackereth, Mr. Johnson, of Wigan, and many others, were and are of this class.

But the chief benefit of these schools was that they led the way and formed the model of the good Cheap Day Schools. First one religious body, and then another, adopted these schools, until at length the time came when Mr. Forster could carry his great bill and extend the system over the nation. Supplemented by the compulsory enactment, and the good-will of the vast majority of the working classes, this grand system is providing for each child that elementary instruction for the mind as essential to its well-being as food for the body.

The New Church led the way in this great work. Mr. Agnew, who took the lead in the introduction of these admirable institutions in the North of England, had a most amiable disposition and an intense love of children. He had long fostered the Sunday School of the Temple, and was greatly beloved both by teachers and scholars.

His presence with the Rev. Mr. Hindmarsh at the annual treats of the school, when they were taken to Dunham Park in the packet on the Bridgewater Canal, was a time of great enjoyment.

He greatly popularised the school by taking untiring pains to train a select number of scholars to recite dialogues and appropriate pieces in poetry and prose.

He placed the children on an ornamented platform, surmounted by a striking picture of little Samuel kneeling, and he usually got an original opening address. The following was obtained, in 1819, from the Rev. Mr. Proud, and as I believe it has never been printed, I insert it here, as it may still be useful elsewhere.

I believe I was the little boy, with whom he took great pains, that it should be said effectively. At the commencement all the children rose.

OPENING ADDRESS.

Your little children now before you rise,
To offer up their humble sacrifice ;
We rise—we bow before our ev'ry friend,
And pray our artless strains you will attend.
Young as we are, we know that much is due
To friends benevolent, like each of you.
Our infant minds, with little science bless'd,
In feeble language praise must be expressed :
But poor and weak, as infant language, prove
To you our bosoms glow with ardent love !
Some few years past, we're taught to understand,
No Sunday Schools appear'd in Britain's land.
Then children poor, distress'd, untaught must be,
And doom'd to ignorance and misery.
The honest parent mourned his children's state,
And looked with sorrow to their future fate,
For wild they ran in sin and folly's ways,
And no kind hand to bless their youthful days ;
But, trained to vice, to ignorance, and evil,
Strangers to all that's virtuous, moral, civil,
They spent their days as many sinners do—
No God they honoured, and no God they knew !
But now, behold ! what num'rous schools appear,
To chase from lab'ring poor the falling tear !
Look up, my fellow children, turn your eyes
And see the Sunday School for us arise :
Our bless'd asylum in the days of youth,
To guide our feet in learning, science, truth :
To well instruct us what we need to know,
And make us virtuous Christians here below.
Kind friends, kind teachers, how shall we repay
Your gen'rous aid—our gratitude display !
For thanks and praises dwell upon our tongue :
We feel the mercy, though we are so young ;

> We forward look, and see with raptur'd eyes
> Our blessings when to manhood we arise !
> Then will our minds, by your instruction giv'n,
> Be well prepared to take the path to heav'n—
> Then virtuous servants, masters, we shall prove,
> Respected in whatever state we move—
> Live not as heathens, but as Christians live,
> Faithful to men, to God due rev'rence give !
> Trained up in pure Religion's sacred laws,
> And firm to our Jehovah-Jesu's cause,
> We shall, with you, arise to heav'n above,
> And live for ever in that world of Love !
> Oh, may we there our benefactors view,
> And be a crown of joy to each of you !
> While we behold you take your vast reward,
> And highly honour'd by your Sov'reign Lord,
> May we, the children of your love and care,
> Be well prepar'd in time to meet you there ;
> Then rise with joy, through your instruction giv'n,
> And happy live in that eternal heav'n !

November 28th, 1819. J. P.

The great interest Mr. Agnew felt in universal education, and especially in Sunday Schools, received its supreme enjoyment when the Queen and Prince Albert visited Manchester and Salford, in 1850. Mr. Agnew was Mayor of Salford that year, and he arranged that the royal visitors should have a sight possible only in Lancashire, then pre-eminently the land of Sunday Schools.

In Peel Park, which he had been mainly instrumental in obtaining for the town, and furnishing with an admirable Museum, he assembled 80,000 Sunday Scholars to sing before Her Majesty, and to have the pleasure for once of seeing the Queen.

It was a great day of delight probably for the Sovereign, certainly for the schools, and, I have good reason to know, for the benevolent New Churchman, Mr. Agnew.

VI.

Mr. WILLIAM COOKWORTHY, of Plymouth,

The first Translator, in conjunction with Rev. T. Hartley, Rector of Winwick, Northamptonshire, of Swedenborg's works, "The Doctrine of Life," "Treatise on Influx," and "Heaven and Hell."

THE memoir of this admirable servant of the Lord is so well given by Mr. Clowes *(Intellectual Repository, 1825)*, from a manuscript submitted to him, that I cannot do better than, with some unimportant abbreviations, present it to the reader:

Mr. William Cookworthy was born as one of the Society of Friends, at Kingsbridge, in Devonshire, in the year 1704, and was the son of William and Erith Cookworthy, who had six other children, three sons and three daughters, all younger than himself.

At the age of fourteen he lost his father, who was engaged in the weaving business, and, though an industrious man, left his family with but a slender provision for their maintenance.

On that event, young William was bound an apprentice to a chemist and druggist in London, and pursued his course to the metropolis on foot. So scanty were his means, that he had only a camlet coat for Sunday wear, and, as a poor apprentice boy, was but little noticed, except in being occasionally invited to the house of a distant relative. Yet was his heart thankful, having had early religious impressions from his excellent mother, a woman whose tenderness of spirit commanded, not merely the respect of her neighbours of fortune and influence, but their cordial aid in her zealous efforts to do good. On recurring in after years to this period of separation from his family, and contrasting the comforts he then enjoyed with the solitude and privations of his apprenticeship, his heart would be repeatedly melted with gratitude for the over-ruling care of Him who is the Father of the fatherless. On such occasions he was wont to exclaim, with the patriarch Jacob, "Oh, GOD of my father Abraham, and GOD of my father Isaac, the LORD which saidst unto me, Return unto thy country, and to thy kindred, and I will deal well with thee: I am not worthy of the least of all the mercies, and of all the truth, which thou hast showed unto thy servant; for with my staff I passed over this Jordan, and now I am become two bands."

From the termination of his apprenticeship to the time of entering on the duties of married life, little is remembered. It is, however, known that he enriched his mind with the stores of science and polite literature, for both of which his relish was keen, and his capacity well adapted. Thus qualified, his company was eagerly sought in the most accomplished society. He was well acquainted with, and was himself one of the literati who, at that time, flourished at Plymouth. Northcote, a bookseller, father of the painter, the celebrated Dr. Huxham; Mudge, father of the late Col. Mudge, and others of the same cast, constituted a society, intercourse with whom must have been a highly intellectual treat.

Soon after his thirtieth year he was married, to his heart's content, to Sarah Berry, the youngest daughter of a respectable Somersetshire family, of the same religious persuasion. The issue of the family were five daughters, the two youngest of whom were twins, who were deprived of their mother when only a year old.

On his wife's death, which occurred in his 41st or 42nd year, he withdrew from Plymouth, and lived in seclusion at Lowe for twelve months. Still his character maintained its lofty fearlessness and courteous integrity. On his return to Plymouth he met his old acquaintance as usual, and again resorted to the meetings of that little knot of literary friends with whom he had before associated. Indeed, so far were his new habits from secluding him from the rest of the world, that he cultivated an intimate acquaintance with some of the first gentlemen and most scientific men of the day. Smeaton, the engineer, was a regular inmate of his house, while engaged in erecting the Eddystone lighthouse; Captain Cook, Dr. Solander, and Sir Joseph Banks were his guests, before they sailed from Plymouth on the Captain's first voyage to the Southern Sea; and to Thomas Pitt, afterwards the first Lord Camelford, and to the gallant Jervis, afterwards Earl St. Vincent, he was united by the closest ties of friendship.

By one of these two accomplished men, probably the latter, it was observed that whoever was in Mr. Cookworthy's company never came out of it without being the better or the wiser for having been in it. Such were the charms of his conversation that when his mouth was opened all were listeners; and though his fondness for chemical subjects would lead him occasionally into details interesting only to persons skilled like himself, yet even then his object was to improve others, or promote science, and not to display his own superiority in the discussion of such subjects.

The effect produced on his mind by the writings of Swedenborg was, beyond all question, salutary. As an acknowledged minister, and as what is technically termed a consistent *friend*, he could scarcely be expected to be altogether free from the *esprit du corps* which, in past times, was more prevalent in the religious society to which he belonged; a society which, whatever may be said of it in other respects, has undoubtedly made rapid advances of late years in the exercise of an enlarged and liberal spirit. Under such circumstances, a temper naturally ardent and hasty would occasionally break out into petty acts of assault on the caps of his daughters, all of whom inherited their father's relish for good society, and some had no ambition to appear more forbidding than their neighbours. Not that his hostility to a smart cap bore any resemblance in degree or kind to the church-prostrating wrath of a John Knox; yet it is nevertheless certain that, now and then, a propensity to destroy had the upper hand in him. But after he had imbibed the doctrines of Swedenborg this propensity subsided; Christian forbearance prevailed; his temper was in every respect purified and sweetened; and of faith, hope, and charity, all which graces he possessed in abundance, he fully verified the Apostolic declaration that "charity is the greatest."

On his first opening one of Swedenborg's works, the book was soon thrown down in a fit of disgust. From some cause or other, not now remembered, he was induced to make another trial; and, whether the inspiration of the heavenly nature of conjugial love was congenial to his own feelings; or the doctrine concerning heaven, as a kingdom of active usefulness, appeared rational and scriptural; or, above all, the unfolding of the true nature and attributes of the sole object of Divine worship flashed conviction on his mind; it is certain that, from that time forward, he became gradually more and more convinced of the soundness of the views which the Swedish theologian had taken of scriptural truths. Whether he gave full credence to all the Memorable Relations is not known with equal certainty. Possibly he might adopt a remark which has been made by another reader: " What I do understand, I find to be excellent; therefore what I do not understand I conclude to be so too."

So convinced, however, did he become of the truth and utility of the works, that he translated from the original Latin two smaller works, and then prepared for publication the treatise on "Heaven and Hell," under the revision of Thomas Hartley, a pious clergyman of the Church of England, in Northamptonshire.

Hartley was a man of the same affectionate disposition, and the same enlarged views of religion; yet, from a nervousness of constitution, more inclined to shrink from society and discussion. They corresponded for some time before they were personally acquainted, until the repeated interchange of sentiment had produced such a union of soul that, when they met for the first time, they flew into each other's arms as if they had been old acquaintances.

Shortly before Swedenborg's death they both visited him at his lodgings in Clerkenwell. The interview must have been interesting, but the particulars of it are not recorded, except that it was impossible to avoid noticing the remarkable innocence and simplicity of Swedenborg, and how, on inviting him to dine with them, he politely excused himself, adding that his dinner was already prepared, which proved to be a simple meal of bread and milk.

The new views of religion which opened on Mr

Cookworthy's mind did not relax the ties of affection which bound him to the Society of Friends. This was also the case with Mr. Leadbeater, of Chester, who published an edition of the "True Christian Religion," in three volumes; and Dr. Abbot, of Blackburn, and many others of the Society of Friends who received the doctrines.

He did not confine himself within that narrow pale which his more rigid, though perhaps equally conscientious, but less enlightened brethren might deem essential; and when in London his valued acquaintance at the west-end of the town had as strong attractions for him as those of a more sombre cast.

At all times he entered fully into the lively sallies and innocent enjoyments of youth; and preserving to the last the cheerfulness, and the fresh and warm feelings of his younger days, he was a happy illustration of what has been aptly termed "a green old age."

The closing scene of his life has been frequently related; but as it is desirable that things should be twice told rather than that one circumstance of importance should be forgotten, it may be proper to mention that when Dr. Gasking called on him one day as a professional man, as well as a friend, and asked him how he was, he replied: "I'll tell thee how I am, Gasking—no doubts—no fears—but a full and certain assurance that I am going *where the wicked cease from troubling and the weary are at rest.*" On Dr. Gasking's return to the parlour, the usual enquiry took place. "How do you find my father?" "Find him," said the doctor, "So as I would give all I am worth in the world to change places with him."

During the early part of his life he had looked at death with something like dread, not from a fear of bodily suffering, but from the awfulness of that great change; but when the hour arrived which was evidently to remove him from things terrestrial, and when his hands and feet were already cold, he said to one of his daughters who was in attendance on him, "And is this death, which I so long dreaded? This great, this mighty change! What is it? Why, ceasing to breathe, that is all!"

In the course of the preceding day he asked his medical attendant how long he thought he could live? After a pause, the apothecary replied, "Why, sir, I should hope you might live four-and-twenty hours." "Hope, dost thou say?" was his answer, "and is that a subject worth a hope?"

With his family round his death-bed, he is stated to have expressed himself to the following effect: "I must say, with the Apostle, 'Little children, love one another,' hate everything that is in the least contrary to love in your life and in your conduct to one another. What shall I say to mankind? That if they feared God they would be happy. Tell them your father did not love 'dying sayings,' yet this you may add, that he says the Lord God Almighty is love, and nothing but love to His whole creation."

Near his close he said "death was like putting off an old coat to put on a new one." He passed away quietly, in his own house, on the 17th October, 1780. His funeral was attended by marks of public respect. All the shops were shut in the streets through which the procession passed, and the principal gentlemen of Plymouth, after the immediate relatives and friends, followed the body to the grave.

His candour marked itself by an immediate acknowledgment of error or mistake. He considered it beneath a man to hold an opinion with obstinacy, when convinced of its incorrectness; and therefore, when so convinced, he gave up his own as willingly as he first embraced it.

After an interview with Cookworthy, Captain Jervis one day returned to his ship, and going to the cabin of the chaplain, his intimate friend, called to awake him, saying, "Gardener, you must awake, for I have had such a day with Mr. Cookworthy as you must hear of before I can sleep." He then began, in animated language, to describe the delight he had felt, when Gardener (who related the circumstance) began to enlarge on the pleasure of a life dedicated to religion and virtue. "Hold your tongue," said the Captain abruptly, "If I delight in hearing Mr. Cookworthy's instruction, I did not come to receive a sermon from you; I came to make you participate in my pleasure."

To sum up all in a few words—as a *minister*, he was clear, pathetic, engaging, persuasive, beyond all language, and indefatigably assiduous; as a *man* and a *Christian*, he excelled in literature, still more in science, and most of all in religion.

Through heavenly meekness, conscious innocence, and integrity, he bore unmerited censure with the greatest contentment. Steady and indefatigable in the prosecution of laudable and religious purposes, he seldom failed of success.

VII.

Mr. MOTTRAM,

And the Immediate Friends of Mr. Clowes.

SOME forty years ago, passing near St. John's, Manchester, and seeing one of the doors of the church open, I felt a desire to go in and look at the two beautiful tablets: one by Flaxman, erected in 1820, to celebrate the 50th year of the Rev. J. Clowes' ministry; and the other by Westmacott, to commemorate his departure for the visible enjoyment of the eternal world, in the year 1831, at 88 years of age, after a ministry of 62 years. Flaxman was an especial and esteemed New Church friend of Mr. Clowes, and produced an exquisite representation of the venerable rector addressing three generations, children, parents, and grandparents, shown in a group of ten figures. The other was done by Westmacott, and the idea of Flaxman was carried out by the other distinguished sculptor, who represented the rector in his last hours, with the same three generations gathered at his couch.

After surveying, as I had done on former occasions, those lovely and interesting works of art, the aged female who acted as apparitor of the church came near, and I said, "Did you know Mr. Clowes at all, and the people who attended the church in his time?" "Oh, yes, sir," she replied, "I knew him and them very well; those were good people; they were heavenly people, sir. There are no such people come here now. It was quite happiness to be near them, sir. It is quite different now."

I was aware that after Mr. Clowes' departure a change had gradually taken place, by the prevalence of old church doctrines through his successor, and a more dogmatic state, even to the removal of the books explanatory of spiritual things he had written for children, from the Sunday School and its library. I was not, therefore, much surprised to learn that there was a considerable change in the spirit of the church altogether.

I then recalled my own recollections of these truly estimable gentlemen. They were most kind, gentle, spiritually-minded people. There was Mr. Shelmerdine, who acted as a sort of secretary to Mr. Clowes, especially in his communications with the Manchester Printing Society, established in 1782 to print and circulate the Writings of Swedenborg as Mr. Clowes translated them, and also such works as he wrote in their defence or elucidation.

This Society was much earlier than the one in London now called the Swedenborg Society, British and Foreign, which was established in 1810. Then there was Mr. Ollivant, the founder of the large silversmith business at the corner of St. Mary's Gate, leading into St. Ann's Square. He was a model of the good old English gentleman, upright, pious, exact in all his duties, true and charitable, with whom you would never think of associating anything not genuine or honourable.

The New Church books were not issued and kept at the bookshops of the regular trade, but were stored gratuitously in a portion of the establishment of Messrs. Hutchison and Mallelieu, admirable and worthy men, probably the most extensive ironmongers' in the town, situated in Cateaton Street.

One of the young men who himself valued the New Church works attended to the customers for them, and to the other business when not so engaged. One of my earliest friends, Mr. Thomas Leeming, a thoughtful, earnest, and loving New Churchman, had this duty for many years; and in his appearance, and in his whole demeanour, was a most suitable agent for the purpose. The country people, coming into the town with their work, on the market days, and seeking more of the heavenly instruction which they valued, would enter the shop and address one of the miscellaneous shopmen with, "Please, sir, I want one of the heavenly doctrines of the New Jerusalem."

The shopman, inclined for a little good-humoured banter, would reply, "Oh, I'm not the heavenly man. Yonder gentleman will do your heavenly business. That's your man. He'll make all right for you."

The country friend would go to Mr. Leeming, and be sure to be received in a kind and gentle manner, with a courteous word or two, and served with the book he required. Thus the work was done for many years. Mr. Leeming was also the librarian at the Temple on the Sundays, and the books were kept in the most perfect neatness and order.

Then there was Mr. Banning, the respected postmaster of Liverpool, for a long series of years a constant correspondent of Mr. Clowes, and universally respected and esteemed as a Christian gentleman.

His son was afterwards a curate under the Rev. Mr. Hornby, a special friend of Mr. Clowes, and became later the incumbent of a district church at Croft formed out of the extensive parish of Winwick, presided over by Mr. Hornby. This younger Mr. Banning I once heard preach in his church a most admirable sermon, on the text, "By their fruits ye shall know them," full of New Church wisdom, in which also he condemned in the most decided way all trusting to salvation by faith alone, and insisted with great force on the necessity of uniting charity to faith. On making inquiry among the most intelligent looking members of his congregation, I was sorry to find how little his most excellent remarks had been understood and appreciated.

He had explained beautifully the gradual growth of a tree from seed or young plant, by the operation of the light and heat of the sun, and the action of air and rain, until there appear first the green leaves, then the delicate blossom, and at last the fruit. The fruit too he showed had a bitter, unpleasant flavour at first; only getting a delicious quality with maturity.

So, he said, was it with the tree of religion in the human mind. It began with instruction from the Word of the Lord. The seed, he said, quoting the Gospel, is the Word of God (Luke viii., 11). The Sun is the Lord. His love and wisdom are the light and heat. As you look up to the Lord in prayer and spiritual mindedness His light and heat are shining upon you. The air is His Spirit, infusing into the soul His strength and help; and the rain is the refreshing of true doctrine, which you get on the Sabbath from time to time. The leaves are true thoughts from the letter of the Bible; the blossoms more heavenly thoughts from the spirit of the Bible. The fruits, He said, are good works, and their flavour at first is tainted with self-merit, and only with their progress in humility and experience do good men mature, and their works attain to the right flavour of good, done from grateful love, without any self-righteousness.

I was charmed with the discourse, but, so far as I was able to ascertain, the congregation present while it was delivered carried but very little away. I said, at last, to one of them on leaving, "Don't you think that was very excellent about uniting charity to faith?" "Oh, yes," he said, "he is very charitable. He gives many a shilling to the sick, and sometimes physic too." From this, and similar experiences, I was led to conclude that the position of a gentleman who had been able to receive the truths of the New Church, still ministering in the old, must often be very unsatisfactory. If he aimed at placing the truth very plainly and definitely before them, contrasting it clearly with its opposite, he would arouse the prejudices of many and appear to be opposing much that is wrong in the Litany and elsewhere. If he clothed his views in general and indefinite language, they would not be roused to think, but would assist, as the French call it, by being there happy and contented while, as they trust, the right sort of thing is going on.

A sense of something of this kind, felt a few years ago, no doubt induced many persons to send letters to the papers suggesting that the writers thought it would be profitable to go to church to say their prayers, as they said, and leave before the sermon.

Such persons could have little perception of the infinite value and beauty of truth, or the force of the Lord's words, "Ye shall know the TRUTH; and the TRUTH shall make you free (John viii., 32).

The Rev. Mr. Clowes, though disapproving of the movement to form separate Societies, yet regarded with kindness and encouragement the small companies that formed in several towns around Manchester, for those who feared the Lord spake often one to another. He visited them occasionally, and addressed them seated in a chair, either in a private house, a schoolroom or a barn, and from these visits occurring about once in six weeks, at some of the places our friends were denominated " six-weeks folk." His visits in this way were always greatly prized at Radcliffe, Bolton, Ringley, Ramsbottom, and one or two other places, and remembered with admiration.

Another of the greatly valued friends of Mr. Clowes was Samuel Mottram, Esq., who not only exemplified the spiritual wisdom then being given to mankind, but was especially generous in affording aid in a great variety of ways. He and Mr. Clowes were greatly attached to each other by the principles which yielded both such heavenly delight. In the first of these papers we noticed the annual help he afforded for years, in the late old age of good Samuel Dawson. Mr. Mottram was a constant visitor at the house of Mr. Clowes, and many are the stories told of their brotherly affection for each other. It was scarcely possible for Mr. Mottram to come across and enjoy any good thing, but he would wish directly that Mr. Clowes should also participate in it.

Mr. Mottram was one of the earliest members of the Printing Society, and very ingenious in suggesting means by which the translated works, and especially the pamphlets and tracts of his friend Mr. Clowes, should be placed within the reach of as many as possible. I am inclined to believe that colportage which has been in recent years so admirably useful in connection with the Bible Society all over Europe, and the New Church Colportage that has done such excellent work amongst us, especially in Lancashire and Yorkshire, was first started by Mr. Mottram.

He devised, and caused to be constructed, a number of covered hand-barrows, with various divisions for holding the publications of the Society, and especially the books for young people written by Mr. Clowes: "The Young Prince," "The Rainbow," "The Mysterious Ladder," "The Golden Wedding-ring," "The Parables and Miracles," all attractive as well as of a deeply instructive character.

Mr. Mottram employed a number of young men at his own expense, and under his direction, with these barrows, to go through Lancashire, and some of the adjoining counties, to sell the works; and, where it could be done with discretion, to lend or to give them.

In this way, it is believed, thousands of these publications were circulated, and good was done to an extent only to be estimated in the eternal world.

He was a diligent attender at the meetings, including the Hawkestone Meeting, as long as his health would permit; and his presence aided the heavenly cheerfulness which pervailed at them. His generous support to the small Societies, and the useful charities of Manchester and Salford, especially those connected with education, made his name to be long remembered with warm affection.

Mr. Clowes wrote his obituary for the *Intellectual Repository* for 1816, p. 126, which closes with the following testimony to the excellent Samuel Mottram, whose name heads this paper:

"Notwithstanding, therefore, his departure as to bodily presence, he will still remain, through the recollection of his excellencies, virtually present with all who loved him, while the brightness of his example will still continue to promote the uses in which he delighted; so that the regret which his friends may feel from the apparent loss of him, is more than compensated by the conviction, that in truth and reality they have suffered no loss, but are rather become gainers by having now an additional friend in heaven, who by his influence is ever prompting them to virtuous energies, and whom they may hope soon to meet again in those happy mansions where God will wipe away all tears from their eyes." Amen.

VIII.

Mr. FRANCIS MARCELLUS HODSON.

WE have spoken of the excellent, heavenly-minded men who, in immediate association with the Rev. John Clowes, formed the leading portion of the company which, under the name of a "Society of Gentlemen," were the centre in Manchester for publishing the Writings of Swedenborg, and those of Mr. Clowes in elucidation of them.

These held a monthly meeting, which they called "The Coffee Meeting," for spiritual edification chiefly, but also to direct any business to be transacted in relation to their publications.

Mr. Clowes met with them, and a very reverent and sacred atmosphere pervaded such meetings.

There grew at St. John's a feeling, even among many of the most serious and devout, that the incongruity between the New Doctrines and the wording of the Liturgy of the Church of England in the prayers, with the unscriptural addition, "for Christ's sake," and especially the invocations of the Litany, "O Holy and Blessed Trinity, three persons and one God," were injurious to that simplicity and truthfulness of mind which are essential to full and happy

Mr. Francis Marcellus Hodson. 59

worship of the Lord. This feeling increased, until a considerable number determined to have a place of worship and a service in which the Lord Jesus Christ was directly adored, without any obscurity from the semi-idolatry of the dark ages.

A curate of St. John's, the Rev. Wm. Cowherd, much encouraged this sentiment, and offered to be their minister; and the circumstance of the New Churchmen in London having arrived at a similar conclusion in 1787 and opened a chapel in Great Eastcheap on the 27th of January, 1788, giving their reasons to the brethren generally, increased their determination, and they erected a commodious church in Peter Street, Manchester, which was opened August 11th, 1793, by the Rev. J. Proud.

Mr. Clowes thought the movement was premature, and there was much discussion on the subject, oral and printed, but conducted in a Christian spirit, and events have fully justified those who would not utter in their worship what they did not believe in their hearts. The brethren who separated took their own course, and those who were of a different opinion still attended St. John's. Both sides continued to meet in "The Coffee Meeting," and to support the publication of the works.

One of the most active of the separated friends was the gentleman whose name heads this paper, Mr. Francis Marcellus Hodson, the father of the late Mrs. Bayley. He resided in Quay Street, very near to St. John's Church, and was very intimate with Mr. Clowes. Mr. Hodson was a calico-printer, in business, when the trade was comparatively new. He and his excellent wife had been pious Methodists; at length read the works as translated by Mr. Clowes, and were attracted to his ministry.

When Mr. Clowes visited Mr. Hodson's house, or

"The Coffee Meeting" was held there, the children looked on it as the visit of an angel. Powder was worn then, and considered especially proper in a clergyman. One of the brothers, when both were very young, called his sister, then a little girl, to smell at Mr. Clowes' hat, and see if it did not smell just like an angel's. Their next-door neighbour was Peter Clare, of the Society of Friends, subsequently one of the main supporters of the triumphant movement for the abolition of slavery in the West Indies. Mr. Hodson was very earnest, studied deeply the works as they appeared, and was an eloquent and affectionate preacher. In a short time, the Rev. Mr. Cowherd, though the first minister at Peter Street, evinced an eccentric and intolerant spirit. Instead of thoroughly mastering the spiritual unfoldings by the Lord through Swedenborg, he diverged right and left. He spoke of heaven as being in the sun. He became an early vegetarian, and abstained from wine; and instead of leaving every one to decide on such subjects according to his conscience and sanitary convictions, he made a religion of them. He refused the sacrament to all who did not perfectly conform in these matters.

He soon, however, quitted Peter Street, and built a separate chapel for himself, in King Street, Salford, erecting a tomb in the front for his burial, inserting upon it, after his own name, the sad inscription, which I have often seen:

"All feared, none loved, and few understood."

He was succeeded at Peter Street by the Rev. Mr. Dean, of Blackburn, also a minister of the Church of England, who received the doctrines in a general way, was a preacher of considerable ability, and zealous; but rather superficial as a student. He was invited to London after hardly two years, and soon exhausted himself wherever he went.

On the departure of Mr. Dean from Peter Street, the Society invited Mr. Hodson, and Mr. R. Jones, afterwards the Rev. Richard Jones, a most pious and saintly man, to become joint ministers of the Church, about the year 1800. They undertook to supply as well, on alternate Sundays, a small Society at Radcliffe, six miles from Manchester.

Mr. Jones found this labour too great for him, and for some time he left Mr. Hodson to minister alone at Peter Street, where his ability, and the interesting character of his discourses, strengthened the Society in every way. This was in 1802. He had the habit of taking texts of which the common reader could make nothing, and bringing out their Divine wisdom with extraordinary brilliancy.

Hence, he was acceptable wherever he went. He was very instrumental in encouraging the friends at Radcliffe to erect their first chapel, and his labours were most welcome to the good people there. Their eyes would glisten as he preached, and no one was more helpful to the church at Radcliffe in the early days than Francis Marcellus Hodson. The call for Mr. Hodson, with his special abilities for that work, to visit the places in the country was so great, that he resolved to deliver up Peter Street to Mr. Jones, and devote himself to that use. He was a poet, and frequently, after having delivered an interesting and impressive sermon, he would give out an excellent new hymn he had composed on the subject, which would be sung with affectionate warmth by the congregation. He was of great assistance at Accrington in their early days, and each Sunday rode over the twenty miles from Manchester, to perform the service of the day.

He opened their first chapel in 1807, and took

for his text the verse respecting finding a bird's nest (Deut. xxii., 6). He drew from the injunction to "take the young bird to thee, and let the old dam go," a brilliant lesson, to take new truths to the soul, and let the Old Dispensation go.

He was always known afterwards with affection by the population generally as "The Bird's-Nest Fellow." Whenever it was known that "The Bird's-Nest Fellow" would be there, the chapel would be certain to be full.

In 1818 he had a strong feeling that there ought to be other places of worship in Manchester, in districts not near enough to be served by either the church in Peter Street or the one in Salford. He took a small chapel in Ancoats Road in 1819, and collected his hymns and added some new ones, to be used in the worship there. This constituted their hymn-book. The Society had some success, but the exact duration of the continuance of worship there I am unable to state. He was induced, however, to give it up to go to Hull, to a chapel where the friends were without a minister. This chapel with an unfortunate name (it was called Dagger Lane Chapel) was quite made famous for a time by the sermons of Mr. Hodson.

He gave sermons to the sailors, on quitting for their whaling voyages; sermons on ships, seas, storms, and calms; and became remarkably popular. His advancing age, and the unwillingness of his family to leave Manchester, led him reluctantly to resign that very promising field of labour, and, as it turned out, to come home and die, in 1828, at the age of 66.

He was a most exact and accurate arranger of a sermon; quite a large number of his sketches came at one time into my hands, and they were remarkably clear, and were always very neatly written.

His hymns, of which we have six in our present hymn-book, are full of pious and beautiful feeling, and disclose special felicity in introducing passages of Scripture with admirable effect. See hymns 2 and 189, in our present collection, as specimens. He wrote some very appropriate hymns for Sunday School recitals and Charity Sermons. There are more of his hymns quite worthy to have been adopted in our present hymn-book, only of course a limit was indispensable. One, however, I was sorry was not continued, it is so grand, and with a spirited tune and a large congregation I have often heard it with majestic effect:

"*For the Lord God Omnipotent reigneth.*"—Rev. xix., 5, 6.

1. Hark, a voice in the sky, Proclaiming on high,
   Through all the ethereal plains,
   Ye servants of God, Now publish abroad
   That the Lord, the Omnipotent reigns!

2. Oh, sing to His praise, In celestial lays;
   Tune your harps to the loftiest strains;
   To Him whom ye fear, With rapture draw near,
   The Lord, the Omnipotent reigns!

3. As the voice of a host, On the heavenly coast,
   Many waters the music maintain;
   Mighty thunders proclaim His ineffable name,
   And announce His Omnipotent reign!

4. In the concert of praise, Which to Jesus they raise,
   Hallelujah fills all the glad strains;
   Small and great they all join, In the anthem Divine,
   The Lord, the Omnipotent reigns!

5. May I mingle among The sanctified throng,
   And to theirs join my own feeble strains;
   My tribute of praise In eternity raise,
   And sing the Omnipotent reigns!

He commenced a little book on Correspondences for Children, on an ingenious plan, which it is a pity he had not time to carry out, for he would have been sure to do it well. It was to have a picture at the top of the left-hand page, say the Sun, a little descriptive poem under it, and on the right-hand side question and answer showing the correspondence and its applications.

Taking him all in all, we may truly say that one of the early worthies who largely diffused Divine Truth in his time, was Francis Marcellus Hodson.

IX.

Mr. GEORGE HAWORTH,

And the Accrington Society.

SO corrupt and demoralised had society generally become in the last century, that the clergy of the Church of England in this country were loose in their habits, to an extent scarcely credible at the present day.

The journals of Wesley and the early Methodists, Thackeray in his "Early Georges," and S. C. Hall in his "Retrospect of a Long Life," abound with evidence and illustrations of this state of things, which continued very much even to the commencement of the present century. Peers and Prime Ministers would drink two or three bottles of wine to dinner, and a party would commonly end by all lying under the table, except such as were carried upstairs. Princesses, and ladies of the highest rank, would interlard their conversation with oaths which now would shock us from an ignorant mechanic. In my youth, old men at Accrington and elsewhere have told me, that almost every church within ten miles round in their early days had a clergyman more or less subject to drunkenness. Happily an immense change has been wrought, which we must all hope will go on, until the idea of a minister making free with intoxicating liquors, except as a necessity or as medicine, will be a thing regarded as impossible.

In parishes afflicted with clergymen such as we have mentioned, there would sometimes be a few pious people who would meet together and read the Bible, and pray with each other for heavenly blessings, when they could obtain no assistance from their official spiritual adviser.

This was the case at Accrington in the year 1800. A few met together for mutual edification, including Joseph Cronshaw, the grown-up son of the parish clerk. They invited their clergyman to meet with them, but he refused. They heard, however, that there was a pious and spiritually-minded clergyman at St. Paul's, Blackburn, four miles away, Mr. Dean, and they sent a deputation to invite him to meet with them, with which he was kind enough to comply. They were delighted with his explanations, and his Christian demeanour, and after several visits they learned that he, as well as the Rev. Mr. Clowes, of Manchester, was a reader of the Writings of Swedenborg. He placed some of these in their hands, and they were eagerly read and approved.

This gentleman, whom we have mentioned in a previous article, visited them occasionally until he went to take the ministry in the New Church at Peter Street, Manchester. A Rev. Mr. Gardner also came at times to commune with them, and strengthened them about the same period.

In 1801, Mr. George Haworth, the brother of Mr.

Adam Haworth, more recently and widely known, who had been living away from Accrington, but whose father had kept a school in that small town, returned and took the school on the death of his father. The young man, by trade a printer and bookbinder, was of a vigorous mind, fond of investigation, who by reading the works of such writers as Volney, Voltaire, and Paine, had landed in the desert of deism.

Becoming more settled in life, and his spiritual cravings unsatisfied by hugging a lamp without a light, he turned his attention to the doctrines of the New Church, which his father had previously accepted, and found there a New Heaven and a New Earth. He began to read with eagerness the translated works of Swedenborg, and then the originals, and the works of Mr. Clowes. He soon ventured to speak to the other friends with whom he met weekly, and gradually came to be looked upon as their leader, though another worthy man, named Garsden, for a while was felt to be a very edifying helper too.

In the first three years of his awakened interest in the New Church writings he is said to have read the "Arcana Cælestia" through *five* times, and it continued to be his favourite work. During his life, besides desultory reading, he is said to have perused it systematically through *thirteen times*. It was from this habit, he was always full of spiritual matter, and the Rev. D. Howarth, who had been well acquainted with Mr. G. Haworth, on several occasions observed to me that the latter had the readiest perception of the spiritual sense of any part of the Divine Word, taken off-hand, of any gentleman he ever knew.

Encouraged by the zeal, earnestness, and wisdom of Mr. Haworth, the friends ventured on building a small place of worship, in 1805, so constructed that it might if necessary be turned into a cottage. They found themselves so augmented in numbers, that they erected a larger place, but with the same cautious feeling, so shaped that if needful it could be made into two cottages. This latter was opened, as we have elsewhere related, in 1807, and sufficed for the whole term of Mr. G. Haworth's leadership, nearly twenty years.

A minister's house was built next door during his life, and the basement room was used as a Sunday School.

Mr. Haworth's clear expositions, his vigorous defence of the doctrines, and his abilities as a preacher, which were of a superior kind, sustained and increased the society; but the chapel, which was twelve yards square inside, was quite sufficient for their accommodation during his life. No gallery was needed until 1829, in the ministry of the Rev. D. George Goyder, afterwards the Rev. Dr. Goyder, who was located at Accrington for about three years.

It is an interesting circumstance that when the New Church doctrines are unfolded in a neighbourhood, they attract certain minds that seem to have been waiting for them, and are awakened by their divine light; but after they have obtained a certain footing and progress, and the novelty has worn off, the power of apathy, custom, and prejudice make a dead weight against them, and their progress is very slow.

The number of members during the whole period of Mr. G. Haworth's leadership was never more than thirty. At the end of Mr. Goyder's time (1831), though the attendance had much increased,

Music Cultivated.

the members were still only about thirty, and when the present writer took the Society, in 1835, the members had but slowly advanced to forty-three.

The Sunday School had, however, much increased. In the procession of Sunday Scholars to celebrate the Coronation of George the Fourth, in the year 1820, the New Church Sunday School, with its sixty scholars, was the smallest in number of the various schools present.

Three teachers, two young calico-printers and an engraver, Bradshaw, West, and Dixon, in their years of early zeal, thought that this was not at all the proper condition as to numbers. They resolved to give up all recreation, *for this one thing*. They would teach a Night School one or two nights a week. They addressed the scholars, and promised a halfpenny to every scholar who brought a new pupil. They made the teaching and singing agreeable, and in six months they changed the number from sixty to two hundred. Their Sunday School now numbers nearly 1,000. They gave a great start to the Society.

The cultivation of music had for some years been a great feature in the Society, under the direction of one of the members, Mr. John Pickup, a man thoroughly well read in the doctrines, of steady and powerful character, and at the same time of great musical ability and solid worth in every respect. He was the author of several very popular hymns and tunes. The New Jerusalem Choir, of Accrington, under him, was renowned far and wide, and in great request on public occasions. His house too was one of the chief places where friends would meet to talk about the truths of the church, which they called "having a camp."

He kept a provision shop, and the customers

were sure their articles would be genuine if they had them from him. He was a long time before he would countenance coffee in which there was any chicory. I question if he ever did. He would sell them coffee, and he would sell them chicory, but separate, so that the people knew absolutely what they bought. From the New Church principles, the clear and straightforward preaching of the leader, Mr. Geo. Haworth, and the sterling worth of the most prominent people, the character of the Society for uprightness was high. The members were made overlookers and managers, and were placed in positions of trust and responsibility, and this became later a great element of progress. Good old Joseph Cronshaw, a warm friend of music, humble, earnest, excellent in every way, with his loving wife and large, admirable, virtuous family, was a grand cement of the Society. And there were an increasing number of others, too numerous to mention, adorned with every excellence, whose names are embalmed in the memories of the present generation, but too recently to be mentioned here. There could not possibly be better teachers than the Grimshaws, Cunliffes, Barnes, Rileys, Bridges, Greenhulghs, Kenyons, and many others. Some had not missed their classes in School, or their place in Church, for seven, ten, or twenty years.

From these circumstances, when from the great fatigues of a missionary journey of many weeks, he took to Scotland, at the request and at the expense of the Manchester Missionary Society, Mr. Haworth, whose health had long been feeble, became seriously ill, and at length he departed this life, in 1823, at the early age of 48, the Society kept well together.

His life and death had been to them all of inestimable value. As a preacher, his abilities were of a very superior kind. His intellect was clear, and of firm grasp. The logical management of his discourse was close and connected. He was fertile in illustrations from analogy, grounded in the works of God, elucidating his subjects by rational argument, and supporting his positions by scriptural evidence. On doctrinal points he was acute, and he would often lecture on these subjects from the apostolical writings, because he considered the epistles to constitute the Bible of the common professors of religion. He always spoke extemporaneously.

The writings of the Rev. John Clowes he valued very highly, and the Gospel of Luke, illustrated and edited by that gentleman, was his death-bed companion.

He himself interleaved a quarto Bible, and wherever he found an explanation of any passage in the Writings of Swedenborg, he inserted it verbatim against its proper chapter and verse. This work he always considered to be of great utility.

He had received a knowledge of Latin and Greek under the instruction of his father, and in his after studies he applied himself to Hebrew, his esteem for which increased with his attainments, and he considered a knowledge of that language the greatest auxiliary to the understanding and explanation of the Holy Word.

Like his Master, he had some deep troubles towards the end of his pilgrimage. To an intimate friend he said, shortly before his career on earth was ended, "I have suffered much in body and mind. The devil, within these few days, has given me a severe handling, but it is now over." He conversed with his friends until within a few moments of breathing his last. He offered up a few ejaculatory sentences to his God and Saviour, and passed away in calmness and peace.

From 1823 to 1828 the Society was assisted by the Manchester Missionary Society, one of the members reading a sermon, chiefly from the works of Mr. Clowes, when they were without a supply. They endeavoured to obtain a minister by requesting Conference to send them one, stating their ability to contribute to his comfort to the extent of £16 per annum. The Conference was unable to find a suitable person at the time. It must have been during this period that, as the old men have related the matter to me, a person resident at Newcastle-on-Tyne, having learned their application to Conference, and being pretty confident of his own qualifications, resolved to walk across the country, and offer himself.

There are occasionally persons well disposed, but not very capable of true self-knowledge, who for want of humility will push themselves forward, and this was one. The friends learned afterwards that he was a man fond of arguing; religious disputation was commoner in public-houses at that time than it now is. He presented himself at the Chapel House on Saturday afternoon, where Mrs. Haworth, the mother of the late leader, still resided, and told her his errand. He said he was known in Newcastle as "The Bright Star of the North." Mrs. H. sent round to some of the committee, and gave the visitor some refreshment. In due time a committee meeting was assembled, and the visitor stated his views and wishes; he desired to be their minister, and he was satisfied he was the right man.

It was evident that when he set off on his journey he was very barely clad, and his three days' tramp had probably not brightened his appearance. His worn habiliments, the committee thought, were rather unusually threadbare, but some of them muttered to the others that the Conference had probably *sent them one at the price.* Nevertheless, they decided he should be lodged, and he could preach the next morning. This he did, but the service and the sermon were such that the committee concluded they would give him a small sum they collected among themselves, and wish him God-speed in his journey home; but not trouble him further, not even in the afternoon.

The Rev. D. G. Goyder ministered in Accrington nearly three years, and under a deafness, becoming gradually worse, and other difficulties, laboured hard for the good of the church, with a fair amount of success; but at length an increasing family compelled his removal to Hull, where a somewhat larger stipend offered a more liberal supply of comforts. In his time a new gallery was erected, to meet the demand for seats.

About this time Mr. Adam Haworth, brother of their former leader, Mr. George Haworth, returned from Valparaiso, South America, where he had realised a respectable fortune as agent for a great calico-printing house, and though he had been many years away from the church, his early attachment to it revived on coming to England, and especially on returning to his native town; and he gave himself so devotedly to spiritual things that he began to speak freely, and he was invited to become their leader. He passed four useful years among them, and was extremely serviceable both in the pulpit and in private life. His health, however, required change, he thought, and he went for a time to reside in Paisley, then in Jersey, having strongly united with the Society he was leaving to request the present writer to give himself to the ministry in that Society, which he did in 1835.

From that time, by the blessing of the Lord, during twenty years, very great prosperity attended the schools, the church, and the town. Several severe controversies took place from attacks made on the New Church, but ending with great success to the party attacked. A large new school was erected, and filled; a branch school was built two miles away, and also filled. Societies were commenced and established in several neighbouring towns, Haslingden, Warren Lane, Blackburn, Preston, Burnley, and Clitheroe, and were aided and encouraged from Accrington. One or two became weak and ceased, but the rest are doing well. A splendid New Church was erected, the largest and handsomest of the buildings in the kingdom dedicated to the service of the New Jerusalem Church. A more numerous membership than any other Society continues to be a blessing to the church and the town, by promoting glory to the Lord our Saviour, and goodwill towards men.

Many favouring circumstances have contributed to the progress of the New Church at Accrington, but the one predominating all others has been the appreciation of the Society all along of the fact that, not only has the Sunday School been one of the grandest results of the Lord's Second Advent, but is the right hand of New Church operation.

The leading families have encouraged their Sunday School with visits and liberal support; their sons and daughters have been steady and excellent teachers. One hundred and twenty teachers have willingly given their time to their classes, and from the young people, as junior members, have sprung Mutual Improvement Societies and supporters of all that is good, cultivators of thought and music, and excellent members of the church. The teachers have taught themselves in teaching others.

Long may this example continue, not only to strengthen the church in that town and neighbourhood, but to be a beacon to light other Societies to the grand lesson—LOOK WELL TO YOUR SUNDAY SCHOOLS, AND SPARE NO LABOUR IN YOUR STEADY, LOVING CARE AND HELP.

X.

Mr. BROADFIELD,

And the Society at Peter Street, Manchester.

WE have related the circumstances associated with the erection of Peter Street Church, and the difficulties that arose early from the waywardness of the clergyman they brought from St. John's, the Rev. Mr. Cowherd, just as the first apostles had uncertainties and disagreements which early brought them into trouble. The new congregation at Peter Street had also many excellent men, gentle, spiritually-minded, good every way. The Holgates, Atkinsons, Harrisons, Princes, Foxes, Murrays, Locketts, excellent people who would sit round delighted while Mr. Jones would give his monthly lectures to the young men, of whom the writer was one.

Not of this earliest group; but soon after, through his marriage with his admirable partner in life, who had been connected with Peter Street many years earlier, as an intelligent member, and a portion of the choir, Mr. Broadfield became known to me.

His affectionate nature soon led to a warm attachment, and the same characteristic caused him to imbibe the principles of the Church with great avidity. He accompanied me in my first missionary journey through Yorkshire. And while I preached in kitchens and barns, or chapels, he revelled in spiritual delight. That was more than fifty years ago, before there was any chapel at Embsay. His business led him to make a round once a week, on Monday, and he usually ended by calling upon me to speak upon the truths mutually interesting, and exchange ideas on passing events. I was then unmarried, and my housekeeper, not a New Churchwoman, but a kind-hearted body, knew him as the " gentleman with the large watch-key."

If anything had prevented me from being at home when he called she would soon let me know, with a smile on her face, that the gentleman with the large watch-key had been, expressed his regret, and left his kind regards. He was diligent in business, fervent in spirit, serving the Lord. Assisted by his invaluable wife, who was quite a mother in Israel, they became prosperous; and the more they prospered, the more liberal they became, not only to the Church in their own Society, but to all round, and all the institutions. In the Charity Sermon time, in spring and early summer, the friends would be sure to be cheered by the presence of Mr. and Mrs. Broadfield. And, when they saw their kind, cheerful, smiling faces, they were certain they would have a good collection.

He was one of the most humble, as well as the most kind and generous men I ever knew. There was no self assertion about him. He would wait, while a thing was being discussed fully on both sides; and then, very modestly, but practically, state the view which commended itself to him, and offer to bear a generous part.

As the doctrines grew with him, they pervaded his whole being, and at length, having attained a moderate sufficiency, he withdrew from business, leaving it to his sons, with the full acquiescence of dear Mrs. Broadfield, that he might devote himself to assist the church, the schools, and works of benevolence generally. His life thenceforward for twenty years was devoted diligently to doing good. For many, many years the two had been the New Church in business; thenceforward, they were the New Church walking about, wherever good was to be done, doing good.

For more than fifty years, when he passed to his higher home, in 1876, he had been a loving and consistent member of the society. Through great part of Mr. Jones's ministry he was a constant attendant, through the whole of Mr. Smithson's, and onwards for many years. He had been for very many years a member of the committee, Trustee of the Church, Trustee of Conference; and he represented the Society in Conference TWENTY-NINE TIMES. He was a steady supporter of the Day Schools, and from the beginning on the Committee. He was the constant helper of the Sunday School, and all its departments of use. He was the special active manager of the Provident Saving Society, and the leader of the Band of Hope. He was ever ready to promote with purse and influence every needful improvement in school or church, to the last.

As I addressed to the Society words of consolation at the conclusion of his career, every one evidently felt the manifest simple justice of the remarks then made, and which now I cannot do better than repeat. "He was the general peacemaker. In the conduct of affairs, even in a religious society, differences will sometimes arise. Zeal for the opinions we regard as correct, and are persuaded are important, will sometimes be pushed to angularity, and a disregard for the equally cherished opinions of others; in all such cases within his sphere he was ever ready with the sweet persuasiveness of charity, allaying feeling, and inducing consideration and peace.

"He was especially the comforter of the Society. If any one were sick, or in trouble, and he heard of it, he would not be long before he was there. With words of sympathy, consolation, and aid so far as might be, he was sure to do his best to cheer and to lead the sufferer to his Heavenly Father, the Saviour, and thus aid to bind up the brokenhearted, and to comfort those that mourned. Indeed standing among you, surrounded by this great audience, consisting of acquaintances and friends in the Church who have come to evince their esteem and admiration for his virtues, and having known him intimately for almost fifty years without one unkind expression or one shadow having come over our friendship in all that time, I cannot but look round and feel as if every man, woman, and child of this Society, from every portion of the building, almost from every flag and pew here, which he prized with fond affection, there would come a sweet memory, a fragrant recollection of the mutual friend, the loving, good John Broadfield."

He had to leave his home in Bridgenorth, where there was little opening for business, a mother whom he tenderly loved, and who tenderly loved him, to come quite a youth to Manchester, and he felt dreadfully lonely. He had a severe fever in his early manhood, and seemed still more tried and alone. But Divine Providence so overruled these things, that they led to connections that were just the right thing, and to the conviction ever after that—ALL IS FOR THE BEST.

He would relate to you how apparent evils had been often turned to real good, how crosses had been surmounted by crowns, how in his own career things that had seemed most untoward had turned out to be the very best that could have been done, and so he had learned to the fullest extent to be assured that THE LORD WILL PROVIDE.

He could realise the history of Joseph when rejected by his brethren, and left in the pit, to be devoured by wild beasts, even when sold as a slave, and his character temporarily destroyed by calumny. He learned in due time that this was the way to a sacred mission for the safety of his family and a nation—ALL WAS FOR THE BEST.

Of course troubles will sometimes occur. This is a world of discipline, and afflictions, like blessings, have their uses. If they come, let them come, and let us humbly try to profit by them. But let us not forestall them. If they won't come, let us not try to fetch them, and strive to drag them in by unwise anticipation.

Sufficient for the day is the evil thereof, rest in the Lord. Take the sweet messenger Hope, and hear her gentle whisper: "Unto the upright there ariseth a light in the darkness." Hope, trust, wait—ALL IS FOR THE BEST.

Duty and trust, as he would explain, must go together. We must do everything a case demands, as if success entirely depended upon ourselves;

and then trust as if we entirely depended upon the Lord, and are sure that He will make all right.

He was very great upon duty, and doing your best. He was himself in business, and at all times A HARD WORKER. "Do your duty," he would say, "a little more if you like, but not less. Always do your duty."

> He prayeth well, who loveth well,
> Both man, and bird, and beast.
> He prayeth best, who loveth best
> All things both great and small ;
> For the dear God who loveth us,
> He made and loves them all.

Another axiom great with Mr. Broadfield, and of supreme value, was—" BE HAPPY NOW."

Often have I heard him, long years ago, impressing this doctrine upon some complaining soul, well-disposed, but weak in faith. "You think you would be happy if you had so much, or when you are in such and such circumstances, which you hope to attain in seven years. But you should be grateful for the blessings you have; don't mind what you have not. Whatever you really want for the future, the Lord will provide. But don't wait for that--BE HAPPY NOW." And this would be said with such kindly earnestness, that he helped many a sad soul to lay aside half its burden, and go away with a lighter heart. The steps of a good man are ordered by the Lord. If ordered by Him, they must be ordered in the very best way. What varieties of weather the trees have to pass through, from the early bud to the ripened fruit—the sunshine and the storm, the frost and the mellowing warmth. But it is all ordered by the Lord, and at length comes the matured and luscious fruit. How much of the keen energy of winter is needed to divide the clods, and prepare the kindly soil of spring. It is all right, and we should be thankful for the winter, as well as for the summer. So the good man progresses through trouble and triumph, through mourning and comfort, and thus attains Christian perfection. Let us take then our dear friend Broadfield's maxim, and BE HAPPY NOW.

"Thus," he would add, "we GO TO HEAVEN now, by being heavenly." My last visit to him was about a month before his departure. Being in the neighbourhood, and learning that his illness was very serious, I went over to see him. It was a privilege to pass a little time with him, when his weakness was so great that he could receive only those who stood in very close relation either of family or friendship. As I was leaving he said: "My dear friend, we have been close friends a very long time. There is just one thing I want to mention. I have been considering how many blessings I am surrounded by on earth; and then there is the other side. I have been thinking if I had to determine whether I should go or stay by moving my finger, how I should do; and I have concluded I could not do it. I LEAVE IT ALL WITH THE LORD."

His last word, I believe, was "Mary," as if he felt the presence of her who had been so meet a help for him on earth, and was charged by the Lord to receive him on entering the inner world of being. Perhaps he saw her; I have good reason to believe in many instances such glimpses have been permitted for the comfort of good people, toward the last.

> Blest is the man who dies in peace,
> And gently yields his soul to rest;
> Who gains from earth the kind release,
> Leaning upon his Saviour's breast.

XI.

MR. WILLIAM CORDIN, of Salford, Manchester; CHILDREN the Astronomer; and JOHN THE BEGGAR.

THE manner of Mr. Hindmarsh's being induced to remove from London, in 1811, and settle for thirteen years in Lancashire, is related with copious particulars in his admirable "History of the Rise and Progress of the New Jerusalem Church," pp. 203 and elsewhere. He was prevailed upon to come and assist the Rev. Wm. Cowherd in a project to translate and print the philosophical works of Swedenborg; but in three months he was convinced that he must separate from a spirit so turbulent and dogmatic as that of Mr. C., if he sought for progress and peace in heavenly things. He was about to return to London, but several worthy people, including Messrs. Barge, Goadsby, and Joseph Lockett, urged him to commence a new Society, and they would assist heartily.

He made a beginning in a room in Clarence Street, Princess Street, and for two years public worship, preaching and lectures were continued in this modest accommodation; and the attendance was so encouraging that in 1813 the Temple was erected in Bolton Street, Salford, and opened by Mr. Hindmarsh on Sept. 19th the same year.

Some years after, I was induced as a youth to attend, and recollect quite well the clear and interesting sermons and addresses of Mr. Hindmarsh, and his kind, intellectual and venerable appearance. I remember the sorrow of the greater portion of the congregation when advancing age made it necessary that Mr. Hindmarsh should retire from the labours of the ministry, in 1823, and live in a very quiet way at Milton, near Gravesend, where the upright stone over his remains may be very distinctly seen.

The Rev. D. Howarth, who succeeded Mr. Hindmarsh, instituted a weekly meeting for considering the doctrines, at first taking the work on "Heaven and Hell," chapter by chapter; then subjects chosen from the Word, and illustrating and explaining them. Mr. Howarth was an admirable expounder, and he was assisted by several intelligent friends who could speak well; Mr. John Atkinson, Mr. Leeming, Mr. D. Taylor, but by far the clearest and most forcible of those speakers was the gentleman whose name is at the head of this paper—MR. WM. CORDIN.

He was a friend of Mr. Howarth, and of my father; and through him a portion of my family was led to the Temple. He had a clearness of perception, and a power of placing a subject before his audience in the most lucid and telling manner. His gentlemanly and amiable bearing made him especially a man to be esteemed and beloved by young men; and when he had explained and enforced a subject, there was little more to be said. It was as clear as daylight. Meetings of this character are of great value to a Society. A certain number of intelligent speakers should attend to keep up the interest, and never let it flag. There are always young people, and there are always novitiates. At such meetings explanations can be afforded and doubts removed; and all who attend are strengthened. It is good to have a break in the middle of the week, to raise the mind into the element of spiritual thought.

Such weekly meetings are also training places for young speakers, giving them the opportunity of acquiring readiness in giving their thoughts and impressions on spiritual subjects; and with such men as Mr. Cordin to assist, it is like a school of the prophets.

Mr. Cordin was also a valued missionary for the small country Societies. He was welcome everywhere.

In a Manchester Missionary Report for 1823, the year in which Mr. Hindmarsh returned to the south, there is a letter from Mr. Cordin, in which he writes : " Feeling confident that every circumstance calculated to promote the interests of the New Church will be received by you with pleasure, I venture to lay before you the following particulars. About two years ago, our indefatigable and respected friend, Mr. R. Boardman, began to visit a family of receivers of the writings of Emanuel Swedenborg who reside at Rhodes, a small village near Middleton, for the purpose of conversing with them on the doctrines of the New Church; and being desirous that the public might be benefited by his visits, as well as the family at whose house he visited, he proposed that regular service should be performed once a month, and that strangers should be invited. The plan was accordingly adopted, and has since been continued; a great number of persons attend regularly at the meetings, and I have no doubt much good will result from these labours of our worthy friend. On the 13th instant, at the request of Mr. Boardman, I paid a visit to the place of meeting at Rhodes, and found the room crowded with persons anxiously waiting to hear the doctrines of the New Jerusalem Church again preached. There were upwards of forty persons present, and many more were desirous to hear, but they could not gain admission. After service about thirty persons remained, with whom I had some interesting conversation, and all of them seemed well satisfied. I distributed about 120 tracts that had previously been supplied by the Manchester Printing Society, which were very thankfully received. From the marked attention which the audience paid to the subjects, and the lively interest they manifested, I have reason to believe that a considerable impression was made upon their minds, and that a society is likely to be permanently established in that neighbourhood."

For some years Mr. Cordin was engaged in that work for which he was so admirably fitted, and I and many other young men enjoyed an interesting, edifying friendship with him, until declining health interfered with his active labours.

I was privileged to be often at his bedside, and to read him selections from the "Arcana." He would often enlarge upon them, in a manner most valuable to me as a young man.

On one occasion, when a young friend had been with me to make arrangements for the then annual meeting at Eccles, and in conversation had lightly used an expression of Scripture, in joking language, on casually mentioning this to him, Mr. Cordin drew my attention very feelingly to what is said by Swedenborg in A.C. 582 and 1878, which he requested me to read; and cautioned me against ever using the Word lightly, in a way I never forgot. "The Word," he said, "is the appointed source of comfort to us, in all our distresses; but if light jokes are associated with it in conversation, when the passages come to mind the lightness comes also, and weakens the power to console. How sad it would be now, when the Word is my constant consolation, if when comforting passages are suggested, frivolous jests were to come too." This caution I have always felt to have been valuable to me through life.

"There are," says Swedenborg, "some who in the life of the body had despised the Word, and some who, by a *ludicrous application of Scripture phrases in common discourse,* had abused it; some too who had imagined the Word to be of no consequence but to keep the vulgar in awe, some who had plasphemed the Word, and some who had profaned. The lot of those in the other life is miserable, of every one according to the quality and degree of his contempt, derision, blasphemy, and profanation. For, as was observed above, the Word is esteemed so holy in the heavens, that it is as it were heaven to those that dwell there. Wherefore, as in the other life there is a communion of the thoughts of all, it is not possible for such spirits to be in company with the angels, but they are separated."

When he passed away a most admirable guide and helper was lost to the Temple and the country Societies, but in the memory of a very few of our oldest friends will still linger a tender recollection of excellent William Cordin.

MR. CHILDREN THE ASTRONOMER.—About the same time of my life, I met a gentleman whose career, as related to me by himself, led me to appreciate the many wonderful and little-known ways by which Divine Providence acts in the introduction and spread of truth in unlikely places. It is written, "I will bring the blind by a way that they know not; I will lead them in paths they have not known; I will make darkness light before them, and crooked things straight."

This Mr. Children was a lecturer on the solar system, with illustrations by the magic lantern. His route was chiefly, as I understood him, in the parishes and small towns on the east and south coasts. He had pursued his career for many years, and the course he laid down for himself was as follows. He requested from the clergyman of each place where he sought to give his lectures the use of the national or parish school. There was rarely any difficulty in obtaining permission. When he had completed his series, he ascertained the sum he had realised, and he made it a point of conscience to give away in the parish or small town as many of the smaller works of Swedenborg as a quarter of his receipts would purchase. He commenced his distribution with presenting one to the clergyman himself.

In this way a large diffusion of truth, in a very quiet manner, must have been effected; and a fragrance must have been felt by many an appreciative soul, like that of the sweet violets which, hidden under the plants of larger growth, shed their sweet sphere around.

Still more peculiar, and unlikely, is the influence

of a singular person whom some of the very aged people whom I knew in the early days of my ministry informed me was the one from whom they received their first impressions of New Church truth. His name was John Saxon, and they called him John the Beggar. He was an aged man—a sort of Edie Ochiltree person, who wandered from place to place in North Lancashire, chiefly I believe in the district known as the Forest of Rossendale. He was past the period of steady manual labour, but was a spiritually-minded man, and was welcomed by the poor cottagers of many poor districts for a night's rest. He paid for their hospitality by holding a meeting where their neighbours could assemble, and he would give them a little sermon and exhort them to live for heaven. He would explain the days of the week as stages of the regenerate life, and go over Monday, Tuesday, Wednesday, and so on, in a very edifying manner, and tell the people that God formed the week into seven days that they might never forget these heavenly things. On other occasions he would explain the meaning of sun, moon, and stars, and show how these also are intended to invite the soul to things higher than themselves—to a sun that will never go down, and a moon that will not withdraw itself, when the Lord shall be our everlasting light, and our God our glory, and the days of our mourning be ended.

In this way, many a humble old man has told me he received his first inward impressions from this old pilgrim, John the Beggar.

XII.

Mr. RICHARD BOARDMAN,

And the Middleton Society.

IN 1828, at the annual meeting of friends from the various adjacent towns, on the Friday in Whit-week, which was held in the somewhat humble room in which the Society at Middleton held its worship, the Rev. Richd. Jones in the chair, and the subject the twentieth chapter of John; after many excellent speeches had been delivered, each speaker selecting the particular verse which impressed him especially as affording matter for edification, the worthy Chairman said he noticed a young friend present who sometimes addressed them at the monthly lecture to the young men, and he thought he might say on this occasion some things that the elder friends would like to hear.

The young man, thus kindly introduced, then eighteen years of age, took the 17th verse of the chapter for his theme, and was kindly listened to, and is the writer of the present article. This was his first really public address.

Thus was his acquaintance made with the New

Church at Middleton, and with the pious and most estimable leader, Richard Boardman. He was then an aged man, gentle, wise, and good. He had received the doctrines by reading the work on "Heaven and Hell," in 1785, and after a period of doubt and anxious thought, his eyes were opened, and heavenly light streamed in. He had much intercourse, both on the Sabbath and week evenings, direct with Mr. Clowes himself, and was a living example of the worth of the new truths he embraced. He delighted to speak in phrases borrowed, perhaps unconsciously, from his teacher, and impress his hearers with what he called THE LESSONS OF ETERNAL TRUTH.

He was rather above the middle height, with a thoughtful, intelligent face, somewhat slender, dignified, and solemn, yet kind and cheerful. His whole conversation was on heavenly things, and it was a rich spiritual treat to spend, as I was often enabled to do, a few hours in his company.

Middleton being only six miles from Manchester, the Society claimed and obtained considerable help from the friends in Manchester. Their place of worship, in the upper part of Wood Street, has been mentioned. It was a rather humble room over two cottages, approached by open wooden steps outside. This had sufficed for many years, since 1798; and many an earnest soul, among them David Howarth, afterwards the Rev. D. Howarth, had received his spiritual nourishment there.

Mr. Boardman's cottage, for he was a working weaver, where the visiting ministers stayed between the services, was a model of order, neatness, cleanliness, and comfort. The walls were chiefly decorated with needlework by his daughters. There was a neat garden behind, and not very distant a pond well supplied with frogs, which in autumn made a loud murmuring croaking noise, which was followed in due time by a steady march of hundreds of them, engaged in emigration. They would come over the field, through the hedges, up the garden, and if not guarded against into the houses; as they did in the time of Pharoah, when his pride had to be humbled by these ugly croaking pests.

To defend themselves the cottagers placed a good layer of salt across their back-door sills, and, thus met, the army of frogs turned away.

Here I learned for the first time the beautiful illustration of the law of correspondence afforded by the action of salt on frogs. The croaking of the frogs representing the noisy opposition of false reasoning against the truth; salt, representing the affection for truth, will soon compel the frogs to depart, or will destroy them. The Lord said, "Have salt in yourselves, and peace with one another."

When troubled by the murmuring and grumbling of short-sighted discontent, how much wiser than incessant complaining would it be, to pray for some more of the heavenly salt of affection for Divine Truth; that our faith might be increased, and our confidence in the behests of Infinite Love and Wisdom might be settled into perfect peace.

The steady virtues of the Boardman family, and of the Middleton friends generally, led to great respect among their neighbours; and the assistance of the friends in Manchester and Salford, which was freely rendered, encouraged the Society to determine on building a becoming chapel for themselves. Mr. Ogden resided at Middleton, and was of considerable service at that time. A young

New Churchman, Mr. Brooksbank, from Holme, in Yorkshire, settled in Manchester, and in company with Mr. Boardman collected quite a handsome amount to help them, and frequently came to preach for them, and thus aided them not a little. They had been subscribing a penny per week for twelve years before they built their chapel.

When the new place of worship was opened, which would seat 300 persons, on the 24th of June, 1834, Mr. Brooksbank arranged for a course of lectures on the leading doctrines, to be delivered by himself and the present writer. He led off, and attended the second. He was delighted with the interest and attention that were excited, and good-humouredly insisted that there was no use for him to come any more, and the lectures must be completed without him; and so it was. At that time there was scarcely a house from Middleton to Blakeley, and returning alone, in the dark hours after ten, was a walk not the most agreeable part of the labour. The Society continued steadily to increase, and in due time built a very commodious schoolroom, which enabled them to exercise themselves as Sunday School teachers, and to keep, through the scholars, an intercourse with a large number of families, and to influence hundreds of young people of the working classes for good.

As soon as they were able, they commenced day schools on the Manchester system, and assisted by Conference. This was in 1859, and with able teachers the schools have been flourishing and most useful. There must, with these varied means of use, be a very large number of people in Middleton with whom New Church principles are more or less influential. With the present excellent, intelligent, and zealous minister, the Rev. W. Westall, the Church in Middleton will flourish more and more, and be a beacon for good to a wide district around.

Mr. Boardman continued with the Society until the year 1845, when he passed to his eternal home, esteemed and beloved by all who knew him, aged 81. His aged wife, who had been a help-meet both in natural and spiritual things, followed him in twenty-five days. The Rev. D. Howarth, in writing of him, says of Mr. Boardman: He performed the ministerial duty as leader of his little flock gratuitously for nearly *forty years*, with great benefit to the Society and credit to himself.

Mr. Boardman was also a zealous labourer during nine years in the Manchester Missionary Institution, from the commencement of its present plan of local operations; and for many years the missionaries who visited the Middleton Society were hospitably entertained under his roof and at his own expense.

In all his efforts as a teacher of the truths of doctrine, our friend was especially watchful to lead to the good of life by his own example.

From his first reception of the doctrines of the New Church, to the time of being incapacitated by infirmities common to advanced age, his life was one continued scene of actual usefulness in the service of God, and in promoting the eternal as well as temporal interests of his fellow-man. His practical motto was the Saviour's emphatic declaration, "If ye know these things, happy are ye if ye do them," and no doubt he has now begun to realise somewhat of the fulness of its promised never-ending blessedness.

XIII.

MR. JOHN WILD,

And the Heywood Society.

THE Society of the Lord's New Church in the town of Heywood, eight miles north of Manchester, from the faithful and long-continued labours of its able, pious, and venerable minister, its large and well-conducted schools, and the admirable and respected characters of the friends in general—preëminently so of some of them—has become a power in the town for good. In my early days, fifty years ago, it was a place that impressed me least favourably of all the small towns of Lancashire which I was in the habit of occasionally visiting.

It was a long, straggling, ill-formed village, rather than town, crowded with beershops.

Of all the places which were injured by the injudicious act of the Duke of Wellington, to spread these low drink houses for the working classes over the kingdom, Heywood struck me as about the poorest specimen.

On a Sunday morning the people might be seen untidy, lounging in their shirt-sleeves about the front of their not very neat cottages and at the end of their streets; not at all beautiful specimens of the intelligent operatives of the British Public.

Now, the scene is entirely different. It is a respectable, orderly, corporate, well-regulated town, with, I trust, a noble future. The character of its houses has greatly changed for the better. Its streets are regular and well-paved, it has many excellent public buildings, and commodious, goodly mansions of well-to-do tradesmen. Heywood has, now, the air altogether of an intelligent community, pleasant to visit.

Much of this estimable progress is due to the existence and growth of the New Church Society and schools in Heywood, and their efficiency owes very much to the steady, persevering worth of some of the early members, especially of Mr. John Ashworth, a man of a quiet celestial genius, and Mr. John Wild, a man more of a spiritual, but of a most useful class.

I have selected the latter as the subject for our consideration, because he came more to the front in the visible progress and efficiency of the Society.

The Society was formed of six persons, in 1812. And as Middleton had a Society from 1798, and is only two and a half miles away, I have always concluded that the doctrines got to Heywood from Middleton. I have often walked the distance from one to the other, myself.

The first name that appeared in any document connected with the Heywood Society is Robert Crabtree, as leader, in the Minutes of 1818. Two years after (1820) appears John Wild, tin-worker.

He was one of the original six, and was true and

steady to the Society in all its vicissitudes. His position was then one of those quick-witted working men, earnest, religious, energetic, and persevering, by whom the cotton-trade was advancing with colossal strides.

About this time he was married, at the age of twenty-three, and with a modest commencement with which to begin housekeeping, of which he has with a merry face given me the figures, but which I should not like to mention, for it was an exceptional case, not always to be followed. He, however, and his excellent partner in life, with whom he had great happiness, and reared a goodly family, had the qualities of diligence and thought, by which property is made, and the prudence and thrift by which to take care of it. He soon rose to comfort, and then to affluence. Mr. Wild took warmly to the principles of the Church, and was ready at all times to defend them.

He became familiar with his Bible, and generally for years had one in his pocket; so that it became well-known that the cause of the New Jerusalem Church would take no harm if John Wild was there.

Next to the care of his own household, the Heywood Society was the object of his heartiest love and devotion. For forty years he was an active member: for twelve years he was treasurer, and for thirteen years he was leader and preacher.

He was for many years an active teacher in the Sunday School, and always its zealous friend. He assisted as a preacher in connection with the Manchester Missionary Society, and was very acceptable. His hearty, cheerful face and spirit were always welcome.

The Heywood Society altered the position of its

place of worship several times. It began in Church Lane, then moved to a place called Coach-turning; after to Gooding-lane, and subsequently to their present site, in 1837, Church Street, probably the same road in which they began, with its name a little dignified in harmony with its improved condition. They had now built their *first modest chapel*, at whose opening I assisted, and I believe at every enlargement since, or school foundation or erection, I have been privileged to rejoice with them, and render any little aid I could.

Mr. Wild was always there, and always helping, but so as always to leave plenty of room for other zealous souls to help also. He never came so much to the front, as to keep others back. There were many rising young men, who both had the will and the ability to take a due part in aiding the Society; and Mr. Wild never did so much as to discourage them.

Indeed, if there was one special quality that was peculiarly manifest in Mr. Wild, it was COMMON SENSE. He was embodied COMMON SENSE.

He saw the immense importance of Sunday Schools in removing the dense ignorance of the common people, and he did all he could to foster in the Society enthusiasm for their Sunday School. Like Accrington, the Society at Heywood has diligently supported and fostered its Sunday School, and the most efficient members have arisen from its scholars and teachers.

Another manifestation of the sound Common Sense of Mr. Wild was his urging of the necessity, as soon as they had obtained a place of worship of their own, that they should have a regular pastor.

Missionary visits he thought might do very well

while things were not fully fixed in a Society; but when it had shown its capacity to grow, and taken a fair stand, there must be a regular shepherd, as the Lord said in the case of Peter, to feed both lambs and sheep. Hence he urged the invitation to Mr. Storry, then an earnest young man at Pickering, in Yorkshire, zealous for the heavenly doctrines, and in 1837 that connection was formed at Heywood, with an interval only of a few years' removal to Dalton, when in the absence of Mr. Storry, Mr. Parry, the Rev. J. B. Kennerley, and the Rev. R. Eddleston occupied the pulpit, until the ministry of the Rev. R. Storry was resumed, to the great satisfaction of all parties.

When cheap day schools, on the London and Manchester plan, had been shown to be valuable, the opening of one in Heywood was greatly encouraged by Mr. Wild, and in 1846 he was determined they should have a large and noble school. There were a great number of short-timers from his own factories, and with other children besides he saw there was room for something commodious, and he went vigorously to work for a supply.

The laying of the first stone made a great day. The Rev. Mr. Storry presented a silver trowel to Mr. Wild on Good Friday, the day chosen; and in doing so he stated that "Mr. Wild's services to the Society extended over nearly the entire period of its history. They were indebted to him for the liberal contributions and active assistance he had rendered in the secular affairs of the Church, and still more for his untiring zeal and useful labours for many years as their leader."

Mr. Wild, in reply, said that "his connection with the Society had been a source of comfort to himself, and attended therefore with its own reward. He was, nevertheless, glad to receive this assurance of the affection of his brethren, and hoped that the spirit of mutual love which existed in the Society would long continue." He then dwelt at some length on the beauties of the New Jerusalem, and the superior excellence of her doctrines.

I was present, as usual, and took part in the general joy. The school is now one of the most commodious in the Church, with admirable teachers and nearly 700 scholars. The Church at Heywood was enlarged and beautified from time to time during Mr. Wild's life-time, and always with his liberal concurrence and assistance. He would sometimes shed tears of joy at the progress and success of the Church he so dearly loved. The last enlargement and decoration of the Church, at whose re-opening I was as usual called on to assist, recalled the many happy seasons I had taken part in, with my dear and good old friend, then an angel, excellent John Wild.

He was highly esteemed on the Manchester Exchange, which he had attended for more than thirty years, as a leading manufacturer, and a man of cool, sound judgment. He was on the Exchange, when a stroke of apoplexy occurred which, after two days, terminated his journey of life in this lower world. This was in March, 1859.

In his obituary it is truly stated: "In every relation of life Mr. Wild was held in the highest respect. He was, under God, the architect of his own fortunes, and rose to a highly influential position in his own neighbourhood. As a large employer of labour, few men ever had the respect, and even love, of his servants to a greater extent. He knew the struggles and sorrows of the poor, and always sympathised with them. Nothing could speak more touchingly on this subject than the reverential and sorrowful countenances of the hundreds of his townspeople who lined the streets as the funeral procession passed along to the place of interment. All were affected, many were in tears. For many years he took an active part in parochial affairs; and though at public meetings he sometimes thought it his duty to tell the people hard and disagreeable truths, he never lost their esteem. Persons of every shade of political and religious belief resorted to him as a friend and adviser in times of difficulty and trouble. He was a clear-headed, intelligent man of the world, and his advice was valuable. In this respect he will be long remembered with gratitude by those who received the benefits of his assistance."

At the commencement of this sketch it was observed that another excellent, affectionate man, to whom the Heywood Society owed very much, was Mr. John Ashworth. He had been connected with the Society all his thoughtful life; and was for many years a Sunday School teacher, and lovingly aided with Mr. Wild in doing all they could for the general prosperity. "They were lovely and pleasant in their lives, and in their deaths they were not divided."

With a very short illness, Mr. Ashworth passed away only a week before Mr. Wild's departure, and the latter had been conversing on the Exchange, on his interest in the funeral sermon on his friend the Sunday before, when his own summons came, emphasizing the great truth: "Be ye also READY, for ye know not the hour when the Son of Man cometh."

XIV.

Mr. DANIEL DUNN,

And the Church in London.

IN my early visits to London, to spend a short time with the good old man whose name is at the head of this sketch was an enjoyment to me, and seemed ever pleasant to him. His house was half-way down Pentonville Hill. He was tall and impressive in appearance, though beginning to stoop from age, kind and genial in his manner, always delighted with spiritual things, and rich with the experience of long-life. Everyone seemed then to know of "Dunn's Essences," but everyone did not know that Mr. Dunn was an aged New Churchman.

He gave you the idea of an Old Prophet more than any man I ever knew. Wise and worthy sayings were constantly dropped from him. A sketch of him can therefore hardly fail to be useful and interesting.

Mr. Dunn was born at Netherton, near Dudley, Nov. 26th, 1773. His father and mother were strong-minded, excellent people, but not joined with any religious body. The old gentleman was wont to say that his father's creed was the one which our Lord furnished: "To do unto others as you would they should do unto you;" and he practised this doctrine in his life. His mother was a very notable housewife, and excellent woman, who always strove to inculcate in him the love of work. The old gentleman delighted to tell that his mother used to say to him, "I know thou wilt work, Danny, and father will make thee work, but I want to see thee like it." And the young man did like it, and continued to like work to the very last, as long as he could use his head and his fingers.

Mr. Dunn received the doctrines of the New Church when he was a young man working at Dudley, at 23 years of age. He was working with a pious young man named Piper at a church, and Piper pleased young Dunn from the delight he seemed to have in making the communion table, and doing his very best to it, because it was for the worship of the Lord. Young Dunn had obtained from the conversation of an old man previously, the true idea of the Lord Jesus Christ being the only God, and the trinity of Father, Son, and Holy Spirit being in Him. On speaking of this with Piper, the latter told him that these views were, he believed, preached in Birmingham by a minister named Proud, and they were something new. The two young men determined to go to Birmingham, eleven miles, and hear this remarkable preacher; and they went on foot there and back on the Sunday.

They were delighted with what they heard, and from that time continued to attend regularly, still walking the distance, and ever charming the way by conversation on the great things which the preacher had opened to their eagerly receptive minds. This continued for about three years, until young Dunn undertook a situation that removed him from that part of the country. Wherever he went he continued to read the writings of the New Church, to associate with the receivers of them, and to exemplify them in his life.

He settled in London about sixty years ago, and since that time he has been connected with all the movements of the New Church in London. He attended Friar Street, and his name was the third entered on its list of members; and subsequently, when the Friar Street Society joined with others and formed the Society in Argyle Square, he was a member and attendant there until increasing infirmities confined him to his house. Then his room became a resort of intelligent friends who delighted in New Church conversation; and the wise and cheerful sayings of Mr. Dunn were the delight of many who loved to call upon him, and led not a few to associate themselves to the New Church in outward worship, when he could no longer lead them externally thither.

Mr. Dunn was extremely ingenious, inventive, and practical. He was originally a scythe maker, but afterwards turned to the nail trade. He soon saw the importance of improving the nails for horse-shoes, and invented a nail which became well known in the trade, both in this country and in America, as Dunn's nail. He subsequently invented many other contrivances, having several different patents; and a great number of improvements which he gave to the world from the love of use, without any patent at all. He was the associate of John Isaac Hawkins, and many other scientific minds. Some fifty years ago his mind was turned to the idea of extracting the essence from hops, in consequence of the large export trade in the article and its bulk. A considerable business was attained, but Mr. Dunn felt somewhat uneasy at his time being taken up entirely with what was not altogether free from unpleasant associations. He had too much to do with brewers.

Some one suggested to him to try tea and coffee. He did so, and succeeded admirably, and went from one thing to another with his extracts and essences until he came to cocoa. This greatly delighted him, for he felt that in the preparations of cocoa there was a most nutritious, healthy, and pleasant addition to England's beverages; and he went on improving that to the utmost, and it became in his hands a great and important business, to which he attended as long as health and strength permitted.

He used to say when he turned his attention to it that chocolate was only an article of luxury, enjoyed by the rich; but it was an excellent article of food, and he was determined to bring it within the reach of the poor. He first made it soluble, and continued his attention to it until a comparatively short time before his death. He ever sought in his manufactory to preserve everything pure and genuine, so that New Church principle might run through his trade. At one time so many adulterations were introduced into the business by unprincipled imitators and rivals, that Mr. Dunn's business was in great danger from cheapness, induced by spurious ingredients; but Mr. Dunn held on his way unswerving; and after a time the genuineness of his business triumphed, and he achieved a complete success in trade as well as in principle.

The benevolence of Mr. Dunn shone conspicuously in his life during its entire length after boyhood. When he was in his teens he commenced the first Sunday School in Netherton, and although his income was only £60 per annum, he spent £10 a year upon this Sunday School. Though three times married, he never was blessed with any children of his own; but, nevertheless, his house was never without a child in it, either an orphan or the child of some poor friend adopted and brought up by him. It is said the number of such children is over FORTY. Many of them are now in good positions. Other children he sent to boarding schools, and he also educated at day schools a considerable number.

When his workmen's wives brought an addition to their families, it was a common thing with Mr. Dunn, on the new comer being announced, to send a sovereign and a kind word to the mother. One female, on the day of his funeral, named that she had received thus seven sovereigns, and a relative four from the same kind hand. When a young man got married his considerate master always gave a kind present to assist the young couple in their house furnishing.

The result of such a life was in old age a tenderness of character, a sweetness of disposition, a grateful regard for the Lord Jesus Christ his Heavenly Father, most striking and touching to notice. His voice would tremble with emotion when he spoke of the goodness of the Lord. He never seemed as if he could speak with tenderness deep enough of the Divine mercy, and tears would flow down his benevolent face when he contrasted, as he sometimes did, the goodness and pity of the Lord with the folly and evil of man.

His circle of friends and work-people was numerous, and from the words and countenances of all on the day of his funeral, at which I officiated, was evident the feeling that pervaded them all.

Thus ended, at nearly ninety years of age, the life in this world of one of the very salt of the earth, one of the world's best and greatest.

His remains were interred at Highgate, on the 15th May, 1862. His workmen followed, and where they could bore the coffin, and many there were whom he had befriended in early life, many of his own work-people who loved and wept for him as a father, many old friends who had walked with him in the paths of heavenly wisdom, many who had taken sweet counsel with him, and to them all it was evident his memory was fragrant with tender recollections, and the feelings of all seemed to say, "Let me die the death of the righteous, and let my last end be like his."

In the Highgate Cemetery, where may be seen the tomb of Mr. Noble, and where have been laid the remains of many New Church brothers and sisters, on a square block of marble, the emblem of his character, may be read the following epitaph on the worthy subject of our sketch:

"If thou wilt enter into life, keep the Commandments."
DANIEL DUNN,
Entered the Spiritual World May 8th, 1862, in his 89th year.

In early life a diligent student of the
WORD OF GOD,
He became convinced of the Sole Supreme Divinity of the
LORD JESUS CHRIST as
"God Manifest in the Flesh" (1 Tim. iii. 16),
"The Only Wise God our Saviour" (Jude 25),
"In whom dwells all the fulness of the Godhead bodily"
(Col. ii. 9).
He therefore addressed his worship to Him alone, and

zealously kept His commandments, turning many to righteousness by well-timed precept, and still more by the example of his own holy life.

Pious in Youth,
Earnest and Upright in Manhood,
Devout and Childlike in Age,

He was a worthy pattern of the faithful Christian to whom Heaven is not merely a glorious prospect, but a cherished and present Possession.

To perpetuate the memory of their venerable and esteemed employer,

HIS WORKMEN,

With the assistance of their friends, have erected this block of marble, in testimony of their admiration of his upright conduct and Christian benevolence towards them, during a long series of years; and of their respect for him as a Master, and their love for him as a Friend.

XV.

Mr. GLEN,

And the Introduction of the New Church into America.

This year is the hundredth since the first tidings of the Second Coming of the Lord were declared in Philadelphia. The opening of the higher truths of His Word, and by their means all things being made new by the Lord, were announced by James Glen in 1784.

The circumstances were interesting and remarkable, and the Hand of Divine Providence may be recognised very plainly, now we look back at the chain of events, and see how the different links were then connected one with the other in a marvellous manner.

Mr. Glen was a Scotch gentleman who had been to purchase an estate in Demarara, British Guiana, South America, in 1783; himself then about 33 years of age, a man of a pious and admirable character, of brilliant intellectual powers, and great learning, especially in the original languages of the Sacred Scriptures.

Having purchased a plantation, Mr. Glen was returning home to make his final arrangements, and was gratified to find in the captain of the ship a highly intelligent companion. They had many interesting conversations, and at length, noticing Mr. Glen was of a free and open disposition, not narrowed by religious prejudices, the captain told him he had a very remarkable book on board, written in Latin, by a very extraordinary man. It was entitled " De Cœlo et Inferno "—the work on " Heaven and Hell "—which he commended to Mr. Glen's favourable attention.

As he read the work, Mr. Glen became all astonishment, first at the nature of the information the book conveys, and secondly at the goodness of Divine providence which had unexpectedly brought him into so peculiar a situation that, when he had the time to ponder much over Divine things, such a book was offered for his perusal. While sailing on the surface of the great deep of waters beneath him, his eyes were opened to behold an abyss of truths above and around him. Mr. Glen declared he had now arrived at the happiest period of his life, which thus brought to his view the glories of the heavenly state, and the stupendous realities of the eternal world.

Mr. Glen was in London, when he saw the advertisement by Mr. Hindmarsh, announcing a meeting to be commenced in a Chamber of the Inner Temple, near Fleet Street, on Thursday, December 19th, 1783. He went, and was delighted to find the few zealous friends gathered together, who were equally charmed to hear of his gladness at the views of the Divine Truth, of which he had to speak. At the same meeting, the Rev. Joshua Gilpin, a young clergyman of great piety and uncommon ability, was introduced by Mr. Hindmarsh, as a warm receiver, who afterwards became a curate of Fletcher the saintly Vicar of Madeley, and probably introduced to the vicar and Mrs. Fletcher the writings of Swedenborg, which it is certain they in due time learned highly to esteem.

When Mr. Glen returned to America, in 1784, instead of going direct to Demarara, he was led by his zeal for the New Truths to land in Philadelphia, the city named from Brotherly Love, to deliver some lectures on the new views he so highly prized. The place was certainly very appropriately named, since Philadelphia meant the same as John. And John, by his representation among the Apostles, and by his character, was the fit emblem of Brotherly Love. "I, John," said the Apostle, "saw the New Jerusalem coming down from God out of heaven." The Johns are the only ones who can truly and fully see the New Jerusalem descend.

It is to be hoped there were many Johns in Philadelphia, where, it is interesting to notice, the New Church Convention HAS BEEN ASSEMBLED THIS YEAR, after a century of growth; and with a great result, visible and invisible, since the time Mr. Glen first addressed a very small audience there, in Bell's Auction Room, in Third Street, on the Science of Correspondence, in June 1784.

He travelled through various parts of Pensylvania, Virginia, and Kentucky, as a herald doing what he could to make the Truth known; but it was the day of very small things. All seeds are small. Mr. Glen, before leaving England, had packed a box of books, partly at his own expense, and partly contributed by the good-will of others. This box was to come after him, but did not reach Philadelphia until he had left the city. It was, however, taken in by Mr. Bell, in whose room Mr. Glen had lectured, who shortly after died. Mr. Bell's effects were sold, and these books among them. At that time there were already translated into English part of the first volume of the "Arcana," done at the expense of Swedenborg himself, in 1750; the "Doctrine of Life," translated by Cookworthy, in 1763; the "Heaven and Hell," prepared and published by Cookworthy and Hartley, in 1778; and the "True Christian Religion," translated by Mr. Clowes, and published in 1781. The "Brief Exposition" had also been published at this time.

How many of these works were in the box sent to Mr. Glen I am not aware, but at the sale Mr. Bailey, printer to the State of Pensylvania, and one of the deacons of the Presbyterian Church in Pine Street, Philadelphia, bought some, and with his wife was led to read and heartily to embrace the important and sublime truths they contained. Some of the descendants of the Baileys are now active and esteemed members of the church in Philadelphia.

A Miss Barclay, who resided in Mr. Bell's family, a pious and intelligent lady, embraced the doctrines, and united with the rest to form at first a small company for reading the works containing the heavenly doctrines. These were soon joined by others, and Mr. Bailey wrote to Mr. Hindmarsh for more books, which were immediately sent, and some he reprinted and circulated at his own expense.

Judge Young, of Greensburgh, reprinted the "True Christian Religion," in 1788, and the celebrated Dr. Benj. Franklin was one of the subscribers for the book.

Several remarkable visitors or emigrants settled in Philadelphia about the same time, thus increasing the focus of New Church light and love in the United States.

The Rev. Jacob Duché, head pastor of the Episcopal Church in Philadelphia, had been compelled to leave the city during the War of Independence, and he decided to reside in London until peace was concluded. He was in London Chaplain and Secretary of the Orphan Asylum, and one of the most popular preachers of the day. He received the Heavenly Doctrines, and became a valued friend of Mr. Hartley and Mr. Clowes. He and his family returned to Philadelphia soon after the visit of Mr. Glen, and so added an important element to the little company. Soon after, a greatly valued and excellent clergyman, the Rev. Wm. Hill, who translated the six volumes of the "Apocalypse Explained," emigrated to America, and in a short time married the eldest daughter of the Rev. Mr. Duché, who after many years of happy married life returned to this country, and was greatly beloved for her most amiable and Christian character, and as the widow of the Rev. W. Hill. She died in Edinburgh, in December, 1836.

Miss Bailey, in a letter to C. Raquet, Esq., in 1837, mentions that about this early time, from the year 1789 to 1794, they were visited by several interesting foreigners, among whom were Col. Julius Van Rohr, a Swede, who had seen Swedenborg and knew his family. He possessed all his writings, theological and philosophical. There was also Mr. Chalmer, or Charing, a Danish gentleman, in some diplomatic capacity, who had also seen Swedenborg, and highly valued his works.

Thus all was arranged by Divine Providence to comfort and strengthen the small flock in the New World, so that the two great branches of the English-speaking people might equally rejoice in the New Light, and extend its radiation by those good works which enable men to glorify their Father in the heavens. From these small beginnings a visible New Church Society was commenced in Philadelphia, and in a short time another in Bedford, in the same state (Pensylvania), to which the excellent Miss Barclay had removed to reside with her brother. Her intelligent and spiritual conversations led to the establishment of a Society, which ever held her memory in tenderest regard. Baltimore preceded Philadelphia in having a distinct place of worship and separate society, for in 1792 the Rev. James Wilmer, of the Church of England, cordially embraced the doctrines and led the way in a regular church.

In the year 1798 two ministers belonging to the Methodist Episcopal Church in Baltimore, having received the principles of the New Jerusalem Church, separated themselves from their former connection, and published their reasons for this step in a vigorous farewell address to the Episcopal Methodists of Baltimore. Their names were Adam Fonerden and John Hargrove.

They addressed their farewell to the Rev. John Harper, resident minister, and the members of the Episcopal Church in Baltimore. The American Methodists have bishops. We extract a portion of their address:

"As a very important change has taken place in our sentiments respecting an article of the Christian creed, which in our view is one of the most essential, and which, if erroneous, of consequence must have its influence upon all other doctrines which flow from it, or are connected with it; and as we already feel that this change will subject us in future to considerable embarrassment, or what is far worse, unfaithfulness in our public ministration and services; we have therefore, after the most solemn and serious consideration of the subject and its consequences, both with respect to the welfare of the church to which until now we have been connected, as well as that of our own souls, come to this conclusion: That it is best for us peaceably and quietly to withdraw ourselves and resign our membership in the Methodist Episcopal Church, that we may more consistently enjoy our present religious sentiments in a state of perfect freedom, and act accordingly. Upon a retrospect of our general conduct amongst you for thirty years past, we trust none of you can find just cause to suspect our sincerity when we declare to you, that no base considerations of any kind have influenced us, but that we do in our hearts believe that it is now required of us to take this unexpected and unpopular step—a step not unattended, on our parts, with much regret."

They proceed further to say: "We conceive it may be consistent with our present duty, calmly and meekly to mention that the leading article in which we differ from you is the doctrine of the Trinity, concerning which we beg leave to say that we think this doctrine as generally apprehended to be neither consistent with, nor reconcileable to Scripture or reason, to wit, that the Trinity in the Godhead consists of three distinct Divine Persons, each of whom separately, and by himself, is very and eternal God. On the contrary, we believe that the Lord Jesus Christ, in whom dwells all the fulness of the Godhead—who is the Everlasting Father as well as the Son, who hath declared that He and the Father are One, and that he that seeth Him seeth the Father—is the true and only God of heaven and earth, and that in Him is a Divine Trinity of Father, Son, and Holy Ghost: that the Divinity within Him is the Father, the Humanity is the Son, and the Divine Proceeding thence is the Holy Ghost, constituting one adorable and gracious object of Christian worship."

Our space compels us to be brief, but the address was signed Baltimore, June 5th, 1798.—Adam Fonerden, John Hargrove.

Mr. Hargrove now openly preached the new doctrines in a chapel hired for the purpose, in conjunction with Mr. Ralph Mather, a gentleman who had also been a Methodist, and often in England had preached the doctrines in the open air when he became a New Churchman, and now had emigrated and settled in Baltimore. A temple was in a short time erected, and Mr. Hargrove for many years lived to preach the truths he loved with great success.

He appears to have been much esteemed, for on the 26th of December, 1802, he preached at the Capitol in the city of Washington, before the President and Congress, on the leading doctrines of the New Jerusalem. The sermon was printed. In 1804 he preached again before both Houses of Congress, on the Second Coming of Christ and the Last Judgment, which was also published.

In 1816, the first temple was erected in Philadelphia, and a Sunday School commenced, under the ministry of the Rev. Mr. Carll, whom at a later period I saw in this country. The same year a Society was formed in New York, and societies and ministers of various religious bodies who received the welcome light showed themselves in various parts of the States, with wonderful activity and vigour, and soon surrounded themselves with earnest disciples. Church of England ministers, Methodist ministers, Presbyterian ministers, Unitarian ministers dotted all up and down hailed the New Light, and declared their conviction that God is Love, and Jesus Christ is God. Our space will not suffer us to expand upon this attractive theme, but the commencement of the Boston Society, which took place in 1818, and which is related by the Rev. Mr. Carll in the American *New Church Repository* for October, 1818, is so intrinsically interesting, and pioneered such important results, that we are sure our readers would not wish us to pass it over :

"Steam Boat, Fulton, August 21st, 1818. My dear Friend and Brother,—At the conclusion of my last I promised you an account of the state of our Society, as well as our proceedings, in the town of Boston. We arrived there on the afternoon of Wednesday, and, as you may well suppose, were most joyfully received by our friends, who had for some time been expecting us. We went immediately to Dr. M——'s, the only one whose dwelling was known to us, where he received us with his accustomed urbanity and politeness, and soon introduced us to our other friends. The afternoon of Saturday was appointed for the organisation of the Society, the place of meeting Dr. M——'s. The ceremony of organisation was preceded by the baptism of those adults, nine in number, who had never before received that sacred ordinance, as it was considered more orderly to receive this rite previous to signing the articles of faith. The articles of faith of the Lord's New Church, as contained in the Philadelphia Liturgy, were then distinctly read and signed by all present; the whole concluded with a prayer that the Lord would bless what had been thus auspiciously begun, and that the brother who had been appointed by the united voice of the Society as their Leader would be strengthened and supported in the fulfilment of the pleasing duties assigned him. The Society has much reason to rejoice that the Lord has raised up for them a young man of such pious inclinations and promising abilities, to conduct the solemnities of their worship; and the church at large have to hope from his future labours in the Lord's New Vineyard. On Lord's Day a public meeting, which had been previously announced, was held in Boylston Hall, a spacious room, elegantly and conveniently furnished, and calculated to contain about a thousand people. At an early hour the house was filled, and the worship conducted according to the form used in the temple at Philadelphia. The service of the morning was concluded by the celebration of the Holy Supper, of which twenty-six of our own members partook, and several others who were unknown to us. My dear friend, this was a most affecting and interesting spectacle, to behold so many to whom the opportunity had never, with the exception of one or two, been afforded of sitting round a table spread by the Lord Himself, and dedicated to Him alone. The devotions were rendered more solemn by the tones of an excellent organ, which was touched with great taste by a gentleman amateur, who volunteered his services in the morning, and by Dr. Jackson in the afternoon. The two discourses, which were the first of the New Dispensation, avowedly such, ever delivered in Boston, were listened to with much respect and attention by numerous audiences, and there was a manifest desire evinced of hearing more. Indeed, there appears to be a void in the hearts of many here, which nothing but a Redeemer such as the New Church has to declare, an Almighty Saviour, can fill and fully satisfy. In the evening we had a meeting of the members at Dr. M——'s, where, after a farewell sermon and hymn, we parted with those feelings of pain which flow from the separation of hearts united by Christian love and affection, which were mingled, however, with the pleasing assurance that it was only a temporary separation."

The young man who was chosen as Leader was Thomas Worcester, afterwards Dr. Worcester, who was so highly efficient in the Lord's hands in leading the Society onwards to numbers, efficiency, and influence of the most remarkable kind. Boston increased so as at present it has not only the greatest number of members of any New Church Society in the world, but became the mother of twenty other Societies in the State of Massachusetts, of which it is the capital.

Since that time numbers of earnest and devoted men have laboured with admirable love and energy, Hurdus, Field, Sewall, Reed, Seward, Hibbard, Barrett, Goddard, Giles, and many others, with some little differences in their course of action, but all promoting that knowledge and love of our blessed Lord Jesus, which is to cover the earth as the waters cover the sea.

Mr. Glen, with whose name we started, came several times to England, and took part in the early movements of the Church here. His name appears at the meetings for commencing a separate organisation, and also at that for establishing the ministry; but he finally settled in Demarara, and was loved and esteemed there until his death, on the 9th of September, 1814, at the age of 64.

XVI.

JOHNNY APPLESEED,

Who Made a great part of his Religion to Spread the New Church and Plant Apple-trees in the Western States of America.

THE story of the worthy New Church Christian, Jonathan Chapman, A PIONEER HERO, which we are about to relate, is abbreviated from *Harper's New Monthly Magazine* for November, 1871.

He was a man who in other and darker ages would have made a hermit of the desert, like St. Antony in A.D. 305, who was devoted to his sense of duty, but considered it saintly to keep himself unwashed for twenty years together; or a St. Francis d' Assisi in A.D. 1209, who not only loved birds and fishes, but deemed it right to preach to them.

Our hero desired above all things the spirit of love, but he prayed also for the truth, and for power to diffuse the truth, as constantly inculcated in the Word, though much overlooked: "I have not concealed thy loving-kindness and thy TRUTH from the great congregation" (Ps. xl, 10); "Behold,

Thou desirest TRUTH in the inward parts" (Ps. li., 7); "Send out thy light and thy TRUTH, let them lead me to thy holy hill, and to thy tabernacles" (Ps. xliii., 3); "Ye shall know the TRUTH, and the TRUTH shall make you free" (John viii., 32).

For more than fifty years, his religion consisted of self-denial as far as his personal comforts were concerned, spreading through the far west of America the cultivation of apple-trees, and the knowledge of New Church truth as "NEWS RIGHT FRESH FROM HEAVEN."

Chapman was born in Boston, in 1775, and probably became acquainted with the works of Swedenborg from some of the early New Churchmen of that famous city. In personal appearance Chapman is said to have been a small, wiry man, full of restless activity; he had long dark hair, a scanty beard which he never shaved, and keen black eyes that sparkled with peculiar brightness. His dress was of the oddest description. Generally, even in the coldest weather, he went barefooted. But sometimes for his long journeys he would make himself a rude pair of sandals; at other times he would wear any cast-off foot covering, a boot on one foot, a shoe on the other. He had always money to purchase shoes, but he did not care to do so. On one occasion, in an unusually cold November, while he was travelling barefooted through mud and snow, a settler who happened to possess a pair of shoes which were too small for him, forced their acceptance on Johnny, declaring it was sinful for a human being to travel with naked feet in such weather.

A few days afterwards the donor met Johnny in the village that has since become the thriving city of Mansfield, plodding along contentedly, with

his feet bare and half-frozen. With some degree
of anger, he enquired for the cause of such foolish
conduct, and received for reply that Appleseed had
overtaken a poor barefooted family moving westward, and as they appeared in much greater need
of clothing than he was, he had given them the
shoes.

His dress was generally composed of cast-off
clothing that he had taken in payment for apple-
trees. In his later years he seems to have thought
that even this kind of second-hand raiment was
too luxurious, as his principal garment was made
of a coffee-sack, in which he cut holes for his head
and arms, and pronounced it a very serviceable
cloak, and as good clothing us any man need wear.

These eccentricities must be regarded, not as
matters for imitation, but as illustrations of the
judgment even good and wise men sometimes need
to guard themselves against the tendency to run
into extremes.

The first reliable trace we have of our modest
hero is that in the Territory of Ohio, in 1801, he
was forming orchards, with a horse-load of apple
seeds, in various places on and about the borders
of Sicking Creek, the first orchard thus originated
being on the farm of Isaac Stadden, in what is now
known as Sicking County, in the State of Ohio.
During the succeeding five years, though he was
following the same strange but useful occupation,
we have no authentic account of his movements,
until we reach a pleasant spring day in 1806, when
a pioneer settler in Jefferson County, Ohio, noticed
a peculiar craft with a remarkable occupant and a
curious cargo, slowly dropping down with the cur-
rent of the Ohio river. It was Johnny Appleseed,
by which name Jonathan Chapman was afterwards

known in every log cabin from the Ohio river to
the northern lakes, and westward to the prairies of
what is now the State of Indiana. With two ca-
noes lashed together, he was transporting a load
of apple seeds to the western frontier, for the purpose of planting orchards on the farthest verge of
white settlements. A long and toilsome journey
it was, as a glance at the map will show, and must
have occupied a great deal of time, as the lonely
traveller stopped at every inviting spot to plant the
seeds, and form his infant nurseries. These are
the first authenticated facts in the history of Jonathan Chapman.

The seeds he gathered from the cider presses of
Western Pensylvania. His canoe voyage in 1806
appears to have been the only occasion on which
he adopted that method of transport; all his subsequent journeys were made on foot. Securely
packed, the seeds were conveyed sometimes on
the back of a horse, not unfrequently on his own
shoulders, either on a part of the old Indian trail
that led from Port Duquesne to Detroit, by way of
Fort Sandusky, or over the second route through
the wilderness of Ohio, which would require him
to traverse a distance of one hundred and sixty
miles in a west north-west direction, to reach the
Black Fork of the Mohican.

This region, although it is now densely populated,
still possesses a romantic beauty that railroads
and bustling towns cannot obliterate, a country of
forest clad hills and green valleys through which
numerous bright streams flow on their way to the
Ohio; but when Johnny Appleseed reached some
lonely cabin, he would find himself in a veritable
wilderness. Johnny would shoulder his bag of
apple-seeds, and with bare feet penetrate to some

remote spot that combined picturesqueness and fertility of soil, and there he would plant his seeds, place a slight enclosure around the place, and leave them to grow until the trees were large enough to be transplanted by the settlers who in the meantime would have made their clearings in the vicinity. The sites chosen by him are many of them well known, and are such as an artist or a poet would select—open places that border the creeks, rich secluded spots hemmed in by giant trees, picturesque now, but fifty years ago they must have been ten-fold more so. Theoretically he was as methodical in matters of business as any merchant. In addition to their picturesqueness, the locations of his nurseries were all fixed with a view to a probable demand for the trees by the time they had attained sufficient growth for transplanting.

He would *give* them to those who could not pay for them. Generally, however, he sold them for corn meal, or a small sum, or a note payable when he applied, or at an indefinite period. When this was accomplished he seemed to think that the transaction was completed in a business-like way, and if the giver of the note did not attend to its payment, most likely the holder of it would not trouble much about its collection. His own expenses for food and clothing were so very limited, that he was frequently in possession of MORE MONEY THAN HE CARED TO KEEP, and it was disposed of to some poor family whom the ague had prostrated, or the accidents of border life had impoverished, or for the wintering of infirm horses.

Wherever Johnny saw or heard of an animal being abused, he would purchase it, and give it to some more humane settler, on condition that it should be cared for and kindly treated. It frequently happened that the long journey into the wilderness would cause the new settlers to be encumbered with lame and broken-down horses that were turned loose to die. In the autumn Johnny would make a diligent search for all such animals, and gather them up; he would bargain for their food and shelter until the next spring, when he would lead them away to some good pasture for the summer. If they recovered so as to be capable of working, he would not sell them, but lend or give them away, stipulating for their good usage.

He had a most profound reverence for the writings of Swedenborg, and always carried a few volumes with him. These he was very anxious should be read by everyone, and he was probably not only the first colporteur in the wilderness of Ohio, but, as he had no Tract Society to furnish him supplies, he certainly devised an original method of multiplying one book into a number.

He divided a volume into several parts, and of course " Heaven and Hell" would easily arrange itself to this treatment, and he would leave a portion at one cabin and a portion at another, and continue this process as though the work had come out in serial numbers. By this plan he furnished reading for several people at the same time.

It was his custom, when he had been welcomed to stay for the night in some hospitable log-house, to lie down on the floor, and after asking if his friends would like to hear him read a portion of the New Testament, then he would give them some "NEWS RIGHT FRESH FROM HEAVEN."

A lady who knew him in his later years, writes in the following terms of one of these domiciliary readings to the poor settlers of self-sacrificing

Johnny Appleseed: "We can hear him read now, just as he did that summer day, when we were busy upstairs quilting. His was a strange eloquence at times, and he was undoubtedly a man of genius. What a scene is presented to our imagination! The interior of a primitive cabin; the wide open fire-place, where a few sticks are burning beneath the iron pot in which the evening meal is cooking; around the fire-place the sturdy settler, with his wife and children, listening with reverential awe to the "news right fresh from heaven;" and, reclining on the floor, this wanderer clothed in rags, but glowing with faith and love and with the gifts of genius and eloquence, who believes with the faith of apostles and martyrs that God has appointed him to preach the Gospel of love and plant apple-seeds that shall produce orchards for the benefit of men, women, and little children whom he had never seen. If there is a sublimer faith, or a more genuine eloquence, in richly decorated cathedrals, and under brocade vestments, it would be worthy a long journey to find it."

Next to his advocacy of his religious views, his enthusiasm for the cultivation of apple-trees in what he termed the only proper way, that is, from the seed, was the absorbing subject of his life.

Upon this, as upon religion, he was eloquent in his appeals. He would describe the growing and ripening fruit as such a beautiful gift of the Almighty, with words that became pictures, until his hearers could almost see its manifold forms of loveliness present before them. To his eloquence on this subject, as well as to his actual labours in planting nurseries, the country over which he travelled for so many years is largely indebted for its numerous orchards.

Though so strangely clad, and wandering through forests and morasses, suddenly appearing in the white settlements and Indian villages, he was always treated with the greatest respect by the rudest frontier settlers. By the Indians he was regarded as a great Medicine-man. There must have been some real force of goodness dwelling in him, manifest in his looks, and pervading his words, for even the boys of the settlements never jeered at him.

He had a great affection for little girls, always having pieces of ribbon and gay calico to give to his little favourites. Many a grandmother in Ohio and Indiana can remember the presents she received when a child from homeless Johnny Appleseed.

When he consented to eat with any family, he would never sit down to table until he was assured there was an ample supply for the children. His sympathy for their youthful troubles, and his kindness toward them, made him friends among all the juveniles of the borders.

In the unhappy war of 1812, between Great Britain and the United States, when the former made the cruel mistake of subsidising the Indians to assist them, and the frontier settlements were assailed and their inhabitants tortured and slaughtered by the savage allies of England, Johnny Appleseed continued his wanderings, and was never molested by the roving bands of hostile Indians.

On many occasions his impunity enabled him to learn where an attack was intended, and he spared no toil or pains to warn the settlers to shelter in their block-houses before the savages could attack them.

In the most cruel part of this danger Johnny

travelled day and night warning the people. He
visited every cabin and delivered this message:
"The spirit of the Lord is upon me, and He has
anointed me to blow the trumpet in the wilderness, and sound an alarm in the forest; for behold,
the tribes of the heathen are round about your
doors, and a devouring flame followeth after them."

The aged man who narrated this incident said
that he could feel even now the thrill that was
caused by this announcement of the wild-looking
herald of danger, who aroused the family on a
bright moonlight midnight with his piercing voice.
Refusing all offers of food, and all rest, he traversed
the border day and night until he had warned
EVERY SETTLER of the approaching peril.

Appleseed was not without a vein of drollery
in his character. Towards the latter portion of
his career in Ohio a missionary found his way to
the village of Mansfield, and preached to an open-air congregation. The discourse was tedious, and
the preacher, though tolerably showy in his own
dress, held forth with much Pharisaic leaven on
the sin of extravagance as showing itself among
the people in the carnal vanities of calico and
stone tea. "Where now," he said, "is there a man
who, like the primitive Christians, is travelling to
heaven bare-footed and clad in coarse raiment?"
This he repeated beyond reasonable endurance.
Johnny rose from the log on which he was reclining, and advancing to the speaker, he placed one
of his bare feet on the stump of the tree which
served for a pulpit, and pointing to his coffee-sack garment, he quietly said, "HERE'S YOUR PRIMITIVE CHRISTIAN!"

The well-clothed missionary hesitated, stammered, and dismissed the congregation. Johnny's personal appearance was far more primitive than the preacher was inclined to copy.

In 1838, thirty years after his appearance at Sicking Creek, Johnny noticed that civilisation, wealth, and population were pressing into the wilderness of Ohio. Hitherto he had easily kept just in advance of the wave of settlement; but now towns and churches were making their appearance, and even at long intervals the stage-driver's horn broke the silence of the grand old forests, and he felt that his work was done in the region in which he had laboured so long. He visited every house, and took a solemn farewell of all the families. The little girls who had been delighted with his gifts of calico and ribbons had become sober matrons, and the boys who had wondered at what he could bear were heads of families. With parting words of loving admonition he left them and turned his steps steadily toward the setting sun. During the succeeding nine years he pursued his avocation on the western border of Ohio and in Indiana.

In the summer of 1847, when his labours had literally borne fruit over A HUNDRED THOUSAND square miles of territory, a space twice the size of Great Britain, he entered the home of a settler and was, as usual, warmly welcomed. He declined to eat with the family, but accepted some bread and milk, which he partook of sitting on the doorstep and gazing on the setting sun. Later in the evening he delivered his "news right fresh from heaven," and read the Beatitudes. Declining other accommodation, he slept as usual on the floor, and in the early morning he was found with his features all aglow with a supernal light, and his body so near death that his tongue refused its office.

The physician, who was hastily summoned, pronounced him dying, but added he had never seen a man in so placid a state at the approach of death. At seventy-two years of age, forty-six of which had been devoted to his self-imposed mission, he ripened into death, as naturally and beautifully as the seeds of his own planting had grown into fibre, bud, and blossom, and the matured fruit.

Thus died one of the memorable men of the pioneer times, who never inflicted pain or knew an enemy. A man of strange habits, in whom there dwelt a comprehensive love, that reached with one hand downward to the lowest forms of life, and with the other upward to the very throne of God. A labouring, self-denying, and yet most happy man —happy in living, as he believed, as pleased the Lord. A benefactor of his race, homeless, solitary, ragged, he trod the thorny earth intent only on making the wilderness fruitful. Now, no man knoweth of his sepulchre; but his deeds will live in the fragrance of the apple-blossoms he loved so well.

XVII.

THOMAS WILSON, of Failsworth,

An Early Shield amongst the People against Infidelity.

AFTER the excitement of the great French War had sunk down, in 1815, and the wild expenditure of money for war purposes had collapsed into depression of trade and VERY BAD TIMES, the spirit of disaffection became very general indeed, and the wide spread of ill-will to Church and State disposed the people, especially in Lancashire and Yorkshire, to gather readily, and listen in great numbers, to infidel lecturers.

The clergy, probably from conscious weakness, were very timid, and did not appear and reply to these people; and the result was that largely the populace were like sheep without a shepherd, and unbelieving orators were to a great extent regarded as invincible. Two lecturers who became very notable at that time, in the North of England, between 1820 and 1840, were Richard Carlile, and an apostate clergyman, the Rev. Robt. Taylor, who styled himself the "Devil's Chaplain."

These people would defy the clergy, and invite ministers and the professors of religion to come and discuss with them openly; and as no one appeared, for a time, it seemed to many that religion was not defensible.

The speakers on such occasions were listened to by hundreds and thousands, and in the unhappy state of the times, and with many glaring political abuses and absurdities unreformed, infidelity made rapid strides. They would scoff at God, the Bible, and the most sacred themes.

At length a New Churchman, Mr. Thomas Wilson, in the vicinity of Manchester, a silkweaver, at Woodhouses near Failsworth, began to attend these infidel meetings, and discuss on new grounds the statements made there. He showed that the lecturers could be perplexed and defeated when they were properly met.

This was hailed with welcome by religious people in general, and after some time, whenever an infidel champion appeared in Lancashire, Mr. Wilson would come, to the delight of the friends of religion, examine his statements, and show that they had no force at all against religion if properly understood.

When I was quite a young man, at the Temple, Salford, it was announced that the greatly lauded infidel, R. Carlile, of London, and Thomas Wilson were to have a full discussion at Middleton, on scepticism. It was to take place in the open air, on the parsonage ground near the parish church. I went, with a company of young religious New Churchmen from Manchester, to listen to the debate, and was somewhat disappointed when the parish constable appeared, after two speeches only on each side had been delivered, and stopped the meeting. However, I had an opportunity of noticing and forming an opinion of the two speakers. Carlile was a gentleman somewhat below the middle height, moderately intelligent in his appearance, fluent and flippant, but with no signs of depth of thought. Wilson was tall, over six feet, manly, massive, and evidently thoughtful; with great quiet and good-humoured force and depth indicated in his whole appearance.

He spoke calmly and slowly, evidently with great deliberation, and clearness of perception. He aimed chiefly to show that the position of an unbeliever has no rational basis.

He would say the IDEA of God exists, and has existed everywhere with human beings. It is either taught by NATURE, OR IT IS NOT. If taught by nature, the unbeliever must admit its truth, because NATURE is in his estimation the TEACHER OF TRUTH. If it is not taught by nature, then it must be derived from a CAUSE ABOVE NATURE, THAT IS, GOD. And, therefore, the existence of the idea of God proves that God exists, and that He has given a revelation, since THAT IDEA HAS BEEN REVEALED. If the sceptic replied that the idea of God was born in the imagination; and, like many other imaginary things, might be false; Mr. Wilson would reply that the imagination never created anything. It could only picture, it might be clearly, or it might be dimly or obscurely, what did REALLY EXIST.

Imagination, Mr. Wilson would say, could picture an animal with the limbs of a lion, the body of a deer, the wings of an eagle, and the head of an elephant. But every one of these parts existed.

He would call upon his antagonist to imagine an animal of parts which were none of them anywhere to be found. A man could not imagine a thing which neither in whole nor in parts had an existence.

Very droll attempts would be made sometimes to reply to this, but were easily discomfited by Mr. Wilson, and he would show they were only using the old absurdity, which infidels themselves ridicule in Christians of the old church as ridiculous and impossible, namely, to CREATE SOMETHING OUT OF NOTHING.

He would add : Nothing, cannot be conceived. Wrong implies that there is a right, a bad thing implies there is a good, error in religion implies there is a RIGHT IN RELIGION. At other times, Mr. Wilson would show that it was a necessity of the human mind to conclude that every effect must have A CAUSE, and that every REAL CAUSE must be adequate to produce the effect. He would illustrate this by the case of a little child, who was told to lift an object greatly too large and too heavy for its power. The child would at once say, I CAN'T. This would imply two things. The object could not lift itself; and, secondly, it could only be lifted by one who had the power to do it.

He would proceed to show that men, and all things around them in the universe, are effects ; not a man has made himself, nor a single thing produced itself.

These things, he would say, could not be the eternal cause ; for they are all effects, and none of them, as can easily be shown, have existed from eternity. But there must be AN ETERNAL CAUSE. Had there ever been NOTHING, nothing would still have been. For in NOTHING there is no maker, and nothing out of which to make anything. Everything too, he would add, is the product of intelligence; for it makes a man intelligent when he studies and perceives something of their beauty and order.

Everything also, when we understand it rightly, has a good object to serve; even wild beasts show us the cruelty of wild passions, and so are subservient to use.

Hence there must be Wisdom, Order, and Benevolence, and these Infinite in the Eternal Cause, and these are the essence of Humanity, and therefore the Eternal Cause must be an Infinite Divine Man in first principles; and when it was required, by the necessity of His creatures, His love, which had caused Him to give His Word, as it was needed to manifest His Truth, would cause Him in fulness to reveal himself, when that was needed, and be the Word made flesh, Jesus Christ, the Divine Man in last principles—the First and the Last.

The clear, steady, and cogent way in which these rational and yet spiritual views were put forth and illustrated by a man of the working classes, respected by all who knew him, with no gainful or professional object to serve, but only for the sake of truth and the good of all, gave him such weight, that often when an infidel speaker would observe him to enter the room the lecturer would bring his discourse to a close, and plead some engagement to conclude the proceedings.

Mr. Wilson, in his early manhood, had carefully read the writings of the unbelievers, Voltaire, Volney, Paine, and others chiefly known and read at that time, and for a while thought there was much truth in them; but profounder reflection, and the principles of the New Church, manifested their utter weakness, and filled him with a sacred courage to meet unbelievers everywhere and overthrow them.

When he was twenty-one, he was taking a Sunday walk in the neighbourhood of Blakeley, a village we have mentioned in a previous sketch, where his family resided. A friend who was going to assist in the New Church choir at some special service of Mr. Boardman, invited him to accompany him, and he would have a musical treat. He went, and enjoyed the music; but the sweet, earnest wisdom of good Richard Boardman was a greater treat still. He went again and again, without the inducement to hear the music, and began to read book after book, until he became a New Churchman; and in due time he had the happiness of finding his father, a shrewd, intellectual man, whom I also knew well at a later period, and his sister also, equally delighted in his books and equally convinced with himself.

In 1811, when Wilson was twenty-three, the family removed to Woodhouses, near Failsworth, many miles more distant from Middleton, but they continued to attend Middleton with tolerable regularity.

He soon after this commenced his discussions with open assailants of the truth wherever they came across his path, and first in his own village of Woodhouses, which contained quite a hotbed of them. He convinced and interested a certain number, and commenced a reading meeting among them, first in his own house, to study the writings of Swedenborg.

This meeting continued for ten years. His fame for clearness and ability in dealing with infidels became well known, and one Sunday, in 1824, he appeared at Middleton after the service had begun, and was observed by Mr. Boardman, who conceived the idea that the time was come to draw his young friend out, and without further ado announced that "Thomas Wilson will preach in this place of worship to-night"; and then went on with his discourse.

At the end of the service, Wilson walked up to the good old man, and enquired in his smiling, humorous, quiet way, "Do you know what you've said this morning?" "Oh, yes," replied the other, with a smile, "I said Thomas Wilson will preach to-night, and so he will."

Wilson had come unprepared, but he preached his first sermon that night; it was on the Trinity, and was much appreciated. I have had the story from both worthy men, and I don't know which enjoyed it most, but Wilson added, "You see I was thrown into the water to sink or swim, and I've been doing my best ever since."

In 1829, Mr. Wilson delivered a course of six lectures at Failsworth, a few miles from Woodhouses, and these interested a number of people, some of them worthy members of the Wesleyan Society, and they were led to read, and ultimately to determine to form a New Church Society and to begin with a Sunday School.

The friends at Woodhouses had outgrown the private house in which they had so long met, and obtained permission to occupy the village school, where I once preached to them. This was in 1839.

In 1841, the New Church people in both places united to have a definite position of their own in Failsworth, and Mr. Thomas Robinson, an earnest, sincere, worthy New Churchman, nephew of Mr. Wilson, had begun to be very useful among them.

The school was opened on the 15th of September, 1841, and I had the pleasure of officiating on the occasion. In a few years their steady working together filled their school to overflowing, and they determined to have a larger building, and to have it erected at their own expense, with the assistance of their friends. This was in 1847. And on this occasion I was permitted again to aid and encourage them, and was delighted to find they had done so well. Their Sunday School contained, according to their last report, 377 scholars and 52 teachers. In 1849 they commenced a Day School, and with a noble school house, and excellent teachers, it has flourished also, and numbers 490 children.

The Failsworth Society has contained among its members an interesting body of sincere, plodding, worthy Christians, steady and kindly disposed, who have done a great amount of spiritual work. They are men worthy of all esteem, but their success and their comfort would have been largely augmented if they had had a true, active, spiritually-minded man as their minister years ago.

They have hundreds upon hundreds of children and young people about them, but they report only 59 members. They have abundance of raw material for a Society ready to their hand, but it wants forming, directing, and guiding by a shepherd whom all would respect and love. He would find a group of steady, excellent New Churchmen, who would be shoulders, arms, and hands for him; but he must be a pastor after the Lord's heart, who would feed them with knowledge and understanding.

Nothing can be a substitute for the Divine arrangement of the ministry. The Lord guides and aids men through men, whom He fills with His Spirit for the purpose, and who become, not hirelings, but true shepherds, laying down their lives for the sheep.

One of the worthy old members, John Rydings, the poet, whom I knew well and highly esteemed, wrote of Thomas Wilson, when, at the Lord's time, in November, 1850, aged 62, HE WENT HOME, these very expressive lines, full of genuine feeling :

> "Behold New Salem's happy state,
> Her grandeur, how Divinely great."
> Oh, yes, his love for her was strong,
> And, for her welfare, he has laboured long :
> Thousands of miles, all weathers, day and night,
> On foot he's gone to spread her holy light.
> She was his favourite theme ; where'er he went,
> To strengthen her, his last, best strength was spent ;
> Her powerful truths his armoury supplied,
> And fighting in her glorious cause he died.

We close our sketch of the noble and venerable Thomas Wilson, whose career and its results at Failsworth we have very briefly described, with the concluding remarks given in the obituary account prefixed to his published lectures. Of him, it was said by the Rev. D. Howarth: "Last, though not least in importance, is the fact that our friend endeavoured to make the doctrines and truths of the Word HIS RULE OF LIFE, and the success of his endeavours was strikingly manifest in the fact, that neither in life nor in death had he any fear of death. In the full vigour of health, he would sometimes speak to the following effect, when the subject was being named : Death is not worth thinking about ; life is the only thing worthy of thought. If we think rightly of life, we need have no concern about death. In the last short illness, indeed the only illness of moment he ever suffered, a friend called to see him, and while speaking of the course of lectures Mr. Wilson was then engaged in delivering at Hulme (Manchester), hinted that he thought he was overworking himself for the church, and would thus shorten his days. His reply was in effect: 'I think much good may be done at this crisis, by making known the doctrines of the New Church, by lectures, discussions, or otherwise, as there is now great agitation in the Christian world, and if, by trying to accomplish this good, I should shorten my life a few years, I do not see that it matters much.' In less than two days afterwards the final summons from his Lord and Master arrived, and then, with the most peaceful composure, he said, 'Now I am just ready to go,' and immediately breathed his last."

His remains were interred in the same grave as his father's, at the New Jerusalem Temple, Middleton, in connection with the Society through which they, when living, had received those doctrines in the dissemination of which they had done almost more than the ordinary share of duty.

XVIII.

JOHN HEYWOOD,

And the Radcliffe Society.

IN previous sketches we have stated the very early period in which readers of the New Church Writings, and receivers of New Church truth, are known to have existed at Radcliffe, a place six miles from Manchester.

In 1783, a Society was formed, and a few years afterwards a small place of worship was erected for Divine service, according to the heavenly doctrines of the New Jerusalem. Mr. Robert Ashworth, of Radcliffe, Mr. Ogden, Mr. Pickstone, Mr. Bradshaw, Mr. Booth, and Mr. John Heywood, were among the promoters and steady supporters of the place; and a warm, zealous, brotherly affection distinguished the members one among another.

Mr. Jones and Mr. Hodson supplied the pulpit alternately in the early days, and later, the missionaries of the Manchester Missionary Society, with James Booth as leader.

The chapel would contain about two hundred people; there was a vestry behind, and a room over the vestry, from which the minister entered the pulpit through a door in the wall. The music was aided by violins, large and small, assisted by clarionets, and quite an effective band was produced. Half the congregation, probably, sometimes came from places three or four miles distant, often more, and that they might stay at both services they would bring some provision that would serve for dinner. The vestry was used for kitchen and dining-room. And, at their meal, they would often divide with one another, and so make a repast with variety. One old gentleman that came invariably from Ringley, whom I knew for years, and up to the age of ninety, old James Holt, always brought an apple-dumpling, usually formed of one apple. Great simplicity, kindliness, and intelligence prevailed among them, and frequently there was much interesting conversation.

Old John Bradshaw, who had much to do with Mr. Clowes, Mr. Cowherd, Mr. Clowes' curate, and others in the early times, used to mention incidents which illustrated the different dispositions of these gentlemen.

Old Bradshaw had a tolerably strong will of his own, and stood and walked very upright indeed. He had been, as he thought, insulted and harshly treated by some one, whom otherwise he respected, but to whom he would not for a moment give way. He would never submit.

When his excitement was at the highest, he trudged off with his grievances to Manchester, to Mr. Clowes.

He was kindly received, and desired to explain the circumstances; which he did fully, but vehemently; and which Mr. Clowes heard with silent care and patience.

The old man stood quite stiff while he expatiated upon his case. At length he ended, and Mr. Clowes saw he was partly right, and partly wrong, but was making too much of his grievance. Mr. Clowes got up, and gently laid one hand on the arm of his visitor, and the other on the middle of his back, and said gently, "John, can you stoop?"

The question seemed so different from the stately speech the visitor expected, that it excited his good humour; and then Mr. Clowes pointed out where he might give way a little, and explain a little, and restore the old friendship with advantage, and sent him home with a lighter, kindlier heart.

Mr. Cowherd, on the other hand, had a harsh and haughty spirit. He considered the business of the priest was to lay down the law, and of the people obediently to submit. He was opposed to Mr. Clowes' desire to translate the works of Swedenborg out of Latin into English, that the people might read, themselves, the spiritual and beautiful things therein contained, so necessary and serviceable to their regenerate life.

Mr. Cowherd considered that the clergy should read such things in the Latin, and unfold them to the people, and the people should listen and obey.

Mr. Bradshaw thought that this keeping of the works of Swedenborg to themselves would be entirely wrong, and he would go and remonstrate with Mr. Cowherd, whom he knew very well. I had the story from the old man himself.

He said he was received cheerfully at first, but when he told his errand and stated his case, Mr. Cowherd became quite excited, and told him he considered it was a most impudent thing for him, a layman, and an ignorant countryman into the bargain, to come and instruct him, an ordained clergyman and a priest of the Lord.

Mr. Cowherd became so excited and violent at what he considered the impertinence of a mere layman, that he threatened to put him out of the room by the shoulders; but the other rose briskly and assumed an attitude of defence, declaring if Mr. C. put a hand upon him it would be worse for him, and so ended the interview, and John Bradshaw returned home.

The Radcliffe Society was noted during the many years of its early existence for two things, the genuine, steady character of its members for orderly, good lives; and secondly, the delight that was expressed in their bright eyes and cheerful faces, as they sat listening to the delivery of truth in the sermons.

Very prominent and very lively amongst them was the good old man, John Heywood, whose name is at the head of this paper, and who was extremely useful in leading the singing. He was quite as earnest in listening to and appreciating the truth in the discourses, as he was in seeing that the hymns and anthems were duly effective under his direction, which is not always quite the case.

In the chat after a discourse, when I had been officiating on one occasion, he named a conversation he had been having the week before with an old lady, a neighbour, who said she liked the New Church people for some things; they were very kind, neighbourly folk, but she could not do with their spiritual sense of the Bible. She thought people should take the Bible just as it said, and do just as it told them.

"Dear me," said old John, "do you think so,

Mary? And when are you going to begin? Because belike some of us had better be getting out of the way. You know, it says in th' Psalms, 'Happy shall he be, that taketh and dasheth thy little ones against the stones" (Ps. cxxxvii., 9).

The old man suited the action to the word, and startled his motherly old friend as he imitated dashing the children with violence against the stones.

"Oh, no, John," she said, "that must have another meaning. What does it mean, do you think?"

He then explained that Babylon in Scripture signified a haughty, domineering spirit in religion, making religion the means of ruling. The little ones of Babylon mean the beginnings of such spiritual pride, and we should destroy them by the truths of the Bible, which are God's stones, before they become too strong for us.

A small Sunday School was commenced in a cottage at Rhodes, fifty years ago, four miles at least from his home—probably five. The time came for them to have a charity sermon, and this worthy old man went week after week to teach and train the scholars in the music of their hymns; he came to me one evening seven miles to request me to go and preach for them, which he thought would help them. All this after his day's work was over, and on foot. I consented of course, and preached in the low room; being on a stool, my head as nearly as possible touched the ceiling, and the apartment was so crammed up with people that it was as nearly as possible like preaching in an oven. However, it was all very satisfactory to them, and when after service I expressed my delight at seeing their faithful labour, another old gentleman, the superintendent, remarked, "Oh, yes. But it's all right. We serve a GOOD MASTER; He pays us as we go on."

Such was the style of men of which the Radcliffe Society consisted. I visited them at one time pretty frequently, and on many occasions preached their annual charity sermons, which they have invariably on Whit-Sunday.

I had the pleasure of making the acquaintance of Dr. Philip P. Carpenter, the Unitarian minister at Whitefield, close to Radcliffe, who was a most excellent and spiritually-minded man. He became quite interested in New Church truth. He invited me subsequently to preach for him; and later, when he took the ministry at Warrington in the chapel formerly used by Dr. Priestley, when he, Dr. Aitken, and Mrs. Barbauld carried on the Warrington Academy, Philip Carpenter often urged me to come and preach there, which on several occasions I did. He not only became a New Churchman, but spread quite a New Church element throughout the congregation. When he went to America, in the interests of conchological science, he was followed by the Rev. Dixon Porter, at Warrington, who also adored the Lord Jesus as the manifested and only God.

The edition of the "Heaven and Hell" which is called "The Future Life," was commenced by Dr. P. P. Carpenter, and only passed to others when he was leaving for America. I have no doubt the favourable disposition which induced Dr. Carpenter to look into New Church principles was aided by the general esteem induced by the excellent character of the friends at Radcliffe.

When Mr. Boys became their minister, in 1840, the Radcliffe Society had lived and grown in the atmosphere of New Church principles, and consisted of 98 members, and had a Sunday School of 240 scholars and 50 teachers.

They have pursued their way steadily, quietly, but earnestly, and under the same respected and venerable pastor, with the help recently of my dear young friend Mr. Stonestreet, there are now 219 members, a school of 333 scholars, and 51 teachers. They have also a day school of 298 scholars.

They have built a beautiful church, instead of their former homely place of worship; they are as solid, as influential for good, as they ever were, and have an offshoot in the Society at Besses bidding fair, under the vigorous ministry of the Rev. Mr. Tansley, to be as successful and diffusive of goodness and truth as a New Church Society can possibly be.

XIX.

THOMAS GEE, of Ringley Brow

And the Society at Kearsley, near Bolton.

IN the quarterly tea-meetings which were regularly held at Salford, Manchester, during the early years of Mr. Howarth's ministry, who became pastor in 1824, as successor to the Rev. Robt. Hindmarsh, friends from the country were often present and addressed the company assembled with great good feeling, and sometimes with much interest and intelligence.

One of the most constant and welcome of these was the good old man whose name heads this sketch. He was one of the small company that had met in a quiet way in a small back room on Ringley Brow to edify one another, and occasionally to receive a missionary visit. Mr. Clowes used for many years to visit them, two or three times a year. I once preached for them, and found them very well informed in the doctrines, and excellent, spiritually-minded men; but not very pressing to give the truths they rejoiced in to mankind in general.

When old Thomas Gee spoke, his remarks were always urgently persuasive to a good life; and he was most careful never to forget the lady portion of his audience. "Oh, my dear friends," he would say, "we must become good men and good women, or we cannot be what the Lord wants us to be."

The old gentleman travelled much around Manchester with some little business he had, and was universally respected as a heavenly-minded man. But he, and the others of the Ringley Society, were so quiet that their own children were not attracted to continue to meet, and their grandchildren usually joined some other religious bodies who were more active, and to whose Sunday Schools their playmates and neighbours invited them. The grandchildren of old Thomas Gee, although their grandfather was so lovable and intelligent an old gentleman, had joined a Calvinistic body, and were most active and efficient as teachers in the Sunday School. The old gentleman became ill, of the failing health of very advanced age, and kept his bed in the weakness which terminated in death. This took place in 1831.

His grandson, John Gee, afterwards well-known in the Lancashire New Church as a most zealous and excellent Sunday School superintendent, was then an ardent Calvinist, full of the immense importance of salvation being impossible without a right belief in the atonement—a belief that all your sins, past, present, and future, were PAID FOR to God the Father, by the sufferings and death of God the Son.

The young man was intensely anxious to save his grandfather, by convincing him of this unscriptural modern doctrine of salvation by FAITH ALONE, IN THIS FALSITY. He visited him on the sick bed often. But he soon found that the old gentleman knew the Scriptures very much better than himself, and was shown that God is one and unchangeable, that God is Love, and that God manifest is the Lord Jesus Christ. He saves mankind by conjoining them to Himself, NOT by paying something to another co-equal God, or Divine Person. He showed him that Scripture always speaks of reconciling man to God, never of reconciling God to man.

The result was that the old gentleman converted the young one, and his sister, who afterwards became Mrs. Woodman; and when they saw the Truth, they resolved it should be hidden no longer. They would teach the ATONEMENT, as Paul taught —God in Christ reconciling the world unto HIMSELF (2 Cor. v., 19). They would at least begin a school. This they did in 1831.

I recollect, quite well, John Gee paying me a visit. I was scarcely older than himself, but he explained his plans, and entreated me to help him, so far as to preach for them and at least aid them with charity sermons.

"I'm quite tired," he said, "with these TWO-ARMED CHAIR FOLK, these LOVE AND CHARITY men, that talk and talk, and do nothing."

Of course I encouraged him, and the school was begun in a large upper room, and was quite successful. Many helpers joined in. The Gees, the Monks, the Greenwoods, and others gathered round, right and left, when there was something to do, and I preached their first charity sermons in their garret. The collections amounted to the then, to them, cheering sum of over £6. All were satisfied and delighted. The school prospered so much for several years, and the preaching too was attended in so encouraging a manner, that in 1836 they determined to venture on building a commodious place of worship in a locality most convenient for the largest number of the friends.

The two brothers, James and Roger Crompton, who had large paper works in the valley, and were known to be favourable to New Church principles, though still attending the Old Church, had intimated that they would cheerfully assist and attend if a satisfactory church could be erected.

This was done, and on the 30th of April, 1837, the opening took place. In a record at the time we read: "The chapel was consecrated and opened on the 30th of April last, when the Rev. D. Howarth performed the Consecration Service, after which he delivered a discourse most appropriate to the occasion. In the afternoon, when the place was extremely crowded, the Rev. J. H. Smithson endeavoured to lay the chief corner-stone of the Society, by proving the sole and supreme Divinity of Jesus Christ; and in the evening the Rev. J. Bayley preached an excellent sermon on the 'Descent of the New Jerusalem.' The whole has made a considerable impression on the public mind, and has excited much enquiry. . . . A Sunday School has since been commenced in the Church, which already consists of 100 children, and every Sabbath the number is much increased."

The increase and manifest success of the Society was not pleasant to a curate of the parish church, named Mansfield, and in a short time he felt his sectarian zeal so much annoyed that he gave a violent lecture against Swedenborg and the New Church. It was so bitter that respectable people of the Established Church very much disapproved of it, and of him.

The Society had not then secured the services of a regular minister. A course of lectures was given in reply, and the present writer was requested to give the last, and their next charity sermons. For the first time, I stayed at my friends the Cromptons, and heard through them that the general sentiment was strongly against the assailant. The replies were given with a kindly feeling, which was respectful, yet as convincing as it could be made, and were largely regarded with favour. The Church was much helped by the result. The largest land-owner in the neighbourhood, a generous but somewhat original gentleman, was very loud in his denunciation of the clergyman's attack, though himself ordinarily an attendant at the Establishment.

This gentleman, whose name was Seddon, had "Dictum—Factum" as the armorial phrase painted on his carriage—"Said—Done." Hence, he was commonly called in the neighbourhood Dictum Factum.

Dictum-Factum called at the Cromptons, and was vigorous in his reprobation of Mr. Mansfield, whose scientific and literary attainments were generally regarded as not very profound. "Just think of the two men," he exclaimed, "Swedenborg a man in the very first rank of science, honoured by all the learned societies of Europe, assessor over all the mines of Sweden for years and years, ennobled by his King, made a Baron[*]—Baron Swedenborg. Then," he said, "there's this shallow curate. Who's he? What scientific society does he belong to? Who knows anything of his great

---

[*] Swedenborg, though elevated to the House of Nobles, was not a Baron strictly speaking, though long called so in England.

attainments? What great learning has he shown? Oh, but he is barren too—barren Mansfield. Where's he barren?" And, slapping his hand on his head, added, "He's barren enough—barren there."

The controversy, and the evident capacity of the Society for growth, made the friends eager for a minister; and Mr. Woodman, who had been a teacher at the Woodford School commenced by Wm. Malins, brother of the late Vice-Chancellor Malins, to be a New Church High School for boarders, but was on the cessation of the Woodford establishment made minister at Brightlingsea, and at the request of the people there ordained by the Rev. M. Sibley, on the 7th of January, 1838. In the latter part of the same year he was invited to Kearsley. He commenced an extremely active and useful career. His zeal, his musical ability, his power as an extemporaneous speaker, his industry, and his fearlessness soon produced good fruits at Kearsley. The number of members reported in 1837 was 53, the Sunday Scholars 100, and teachers 30. In 1840 the number of members is reported to be 90, the Sunday Scholars 210, and there has been continued progression at Kearsley from that time to the present.

The Rev. W. Woodman continued in that field of labour thirty-four years, and passed away on the 15th of November, 1872, respected both in the church and out of it, as a sterling Christian and a laborious minister. The church over which our brethren rejoiced in 1837 had long been insufficient for them, and in 1879 they opened a New Church capable of accommodating 750 persons, and costing, with the noble day school, the most commodious possessed by the church, £8,400. The members reported last year were 200, the Sunday scholars 272, and the day scholars 461. The day school was commenced in 1867.

Had the good old friends continued in their quiet way on Ringley Brow, they would simply have died out, and made no sign, and left no mark. By the noble activity of John Gee, and the memory of his grandfather's loving wisdom, the quickening impulse was given which, followed by the effective and continued labours of Mr. Woodman and those who followed him, have enabled us to rejoice over the Society as a "burning and a shining light."

XX.

JOB ABBOTT.

Leicestershire and Nottinghamshire.

MANY friends will recollect the Rev. C. G. Macpherson, B.A., who received the doctrines of the New Church fully in the island of Trinidad, and threw up his position in the Church of England for conscience sake, returning to this country, and after some time entering the ministerial work in the New Church at Liverpool, in 1862. Four years of loving labour endeared him to all who knew him, and at its close by death, in 1866, the expression of the mourning Society was universally felt in the Church to be the simple truth : "The unaffected sympathy and genuine truthfulness of Mr. Macpherson's character, combined with his universally amiable and polished bearing, had endeared him to all, and that between himself and his flock a closer unity had been established than generally marks such a connection."

Mr. Macpherson's reception of the truth was not

hasty and hurried, but thoughtful and steady. I recollect his informing me that his first impressions were obtained from the worthy but very poor man whose name is at the head of this article.

Mr. Macpherson was a curate in the neighbourhood of Loughborough, and when walking out, frequently met Job Abbott, and, speaking to him on religious subjects, was struck with his depth and clearness of thought; and learning he was a reader of Swedenborg, when great perplexity arose later in his own mind, the conversations with this humble friend came up and led him in what he found was the right direction.

Such is the leading of Divine Providence in thousands of instances. We are led by a way we know not. The story of Job Abbott was told later by the Rev. W. Mason, in an admirable work, now out of print I am sorry to learn, but full of instruction and edification. The book was entitled "Job Abbott," and though the subject of it was a poor stocking-maker, of whom Mr. Mason remarks he never earned more than six shillings per week, his career was such as to show

"The rank is but the guinea stamp,
The man's the gow'd for a' that."

In the Midland counties, and especially in Leicestershire and Nottinghamshire, there seem to have been throughout this century remarkable individuals who were known widely in their neighbourhoods as somewhat peculiar, but as profoundly good and wise men.

William Howitt, in one of his early works, mentions such a one in Nottinghamshire who gave him his first leanings towards the appreciation of Swedenborg, and who no doubt assisted him to diffuse

K

the hallowed and beautiful tone which has distinguished the works of that highly gifted family. Many such men there have been in the towns and villages of the Midlands; some I have known and esteemed, and from such men heavenly truths have been given out, and have served to elevate the general atmosphere of thought, and assisted to disperse the old Calvinistic horrors which formerly infested the Midland counties.

No doubt, Mr. Pike, of Derby, must have felt the influence of this change, coming, when he wrote his doleful pamphlet denouncing the blackness of darkness against the readers of Swedenborg, and against all who did not think in the same melancholy way as himself, poor man, one of the most bilious-looking Christians I have ever seen. Job Abbott was born in 1790, in a village in Leicestershire, and the circumstances of his parents were such that he was not taught to write until he had arrived at maturity, and by the kind instruction of a fellow-workman. He was brought up as a stocking-maker, but being of a nervous and weakly constitution he could never earn an average amount of wages, in that ill-paid employment.

In truth, Job Abbott had a soul too active, and a mind too large, for his body. Mr. Mason informs us: "He thirsted for knowledge, and, so far as his scanty means allowed him to do so, he diligently applied himself to the improvement of his mind. Books he had no money to buy, and therefore he was constrained to borrow them whenever he could; and in order to help his memory he used to make copious extracts or copies from them, and that principally during the night, after a hard day's work.

He was particularly attached to the study of astronomy, and having borrowed some books relating to that science, he made copies from them, and by the help of the diagrams they contained he used to pass his nights frequently in the open air, watching the motions of the heavenly bodies. This, after a hard day's sedentary toil, showed his invincible zeal to obtain a practical knowledge in his favourite pursuit; and the result was that persons competent to form a judgment declared that Job Abbott possessed sufficient learning to qualify him for a popular lecturer on astronomy, had he also possessed the necessary language and manner for its public communication. He was possessed of a remarkably retentive memory. Having so much knowledge of music as to be able to read it readily at sight, he was accustomed to copy sacred tunes and pieces, and after copying a book in four parts, all the parts were distinctly impressed upon his memory, as likewise were the hymns or words sung to the music, merely from his joining in the use of them with his friends, or with the religious body with which he was accustomed to worship. Being able also to recollect with facility various anecdotes and statements which he had read (for, considering his contracted circumstances, his reading was remarkably extensive), he was an agreeable and instructive companion, more especially as in conversation he was never forward or intrusive.

It may readily be concluded, from this brief description of his character, taste, and habits, that Job found himself confined, by his poverty, to a sphere of life by no means congenial to him. He lived, however, in a world of his own—a world of clear thought and intelligence, which had nothing in common with the coarseness, sensuality, and ignorance which were often forced upon his notice by those with whom he was constrained by his occupation to mingle. But as their habits were not attractive to him, the evil of their example was not productive of any effect upon him but that of exciting his pity or disgust. No man was more distinguished for purity of life, propriety of discourse, or prudence of behaviour than our humble friend Job Abbott. At early periods of his mature life, the annoyance which low-mindedness in others caused him made him rather irritable; but he learned patiently to endure ills which he could not avoid, and to bear with the fallacies of those around him with an inward feeling of pity and an outward demeanour of dignified calmness which ensured general respect. Hence it was a universal impression with those with whom he associated that he was a remarkably respectable person.

Job Abbott was an attendant upon the Established Church until he arrived at mature age, when he was attracted by the apparent earnestness and zeal of the New Connection of General Baptists, and became a convert to their peculiar doctrine concerning baptism.

He had much edifying intercourse with that body of earnest Christians, until he found them often referring to the covenant and election concerning those who should be saved, which took place among the three Divine Persons in the Tri-personal Trinity before the creation of the world.

The more he thought of this, the more Job was puzzled. He then thought over descriptions he had heard of the council held by the three Persons in God on the subject of human redemption.

"It is commonly believed," said Job, "that a council was held before creation in anticipation of the fall of man; but some suppose that it took place after the fall. The observations of the *First* Person at this council are variously described. Some say that He was greatly enraged at the disobedience of Adam, and therefore condemned all his posterity to hell without exception. Some describe Him as saying, 'I made man perfect, and commanded him not to eat of a certain tree, but he has disobeyed my command; I will therefore wreak all my fury upon him and will torment him for ever and ever, and will not pardon him.' Others describe Him as saying, 'I declared that if man did not obey my command I would punish him eternally; I *must* keep my word, or I should bring contempt on my person and government. I wish I could devise some *scheme* whereby I could, consistently with my honour and dignity, forgive man; but I must punish him either in person or by proxy; nevertheless, I am very sorry for him, and would gladly afford him a way of escape, but I do not see how to reconcile the showing mercy to him with justice to myself and my broken laws, except by the vicarious sacrifice or punishment of some competent substitute. If you, the Second Person, will allow yourself to be punished in man's place, I will cancel my decree against him.' Whichever, then, be the accurate description of the declaration of the First Person at this council, all accounts agree that the Second Person addressed the First, and said, 'You demand a substitute to be punished to satisfy your justice; but neither I nor the Third Person make any such demand; on the contrary, I am willing to forgive man his offence against me without a substitute being punished by me, or at my desire, because I do not see that my dignity requires one. And not only so, but I consent to become a man, and be punished in man's place, in order to satisfy you, provided you revoke your decree of eternal punishment against man and accept me as a sacrifice in his place.' Those who describe the First Person as so exceedingly wrathful describe the Second as using the most urgent and affecting entreaties that He would lay aside His anger against man, and accept Himself to bear all that anger, and to drink the cup of His fury to the dregs, in man's place.

"And then the Third Person is described as saying, 'I neither demand a substitute, nor will I be one myself; but if you two can agree on the matter, I will, for my part, consent to sanctify all those whom you may consent to forgive.' Some say that the First Person would only consent to forgive *a part* of the human race, called 'the elect,' and insisted on punishing the rest, as well as punishing the Son; others say that He forgave the whole; but whether he forgave the whole or only a part, all Trinitarians agree that He declared He would not forgive any at all, unless they should first believe that the Second Person had been punished in their place.

"Whatever ideas other people may entertain of what is becoming to a Divine Being, or to a council of Divine Persons, these descriptions," said Job, "do not agree with my ideas of the 'fitness of things.' To me there is nothing of dignity, or even of decency in them; there is nothing but the grossest contradictions and absurdities!"

Very deeply did these difficulties press upon Job's mind. He did not know how to give up revelation, because he loved its pure precepts of piety, charity, and attentive duty. But he did not know how to retain any confidence in the Bible as a revelation from God until his difficulties should be removed. This state of mental conflict secretly wore down his spirits and irritated his feelings, combined with the recollection of his various experiences of the moral unworthiness of many people professedly religious.

One day, when he was uttering his feelings with some bitterness, the pity of his brother was excited, and he remarked, "There is one sect which you have not yet tried." "What sect is that?" impatiently demanded Job. "The Swedenborgians," was the reply, "they have no chapel at present, but they meet at the house of their preacher."

Thither Job went. He listened to the discourse with astonishment. He went again. Here was a new system of doctrine presented to him, not to be blindly believed, but rationally understood—a system which inculcated the divinity of Jesus Christ without mystery, and which, nevertheless, rejected the supposed vicarious sacrifice, with all its horrors and injustice, and vindicated the Scriptures from the charge of setting it forth; a system which gave a new view of the inspiration of the Scriptures, and which, as Job thought at the time, if it could be established by conclusive evidence, would prove the Scriptures to be indeed the "Word of God," by raising them to that true and real dignity which that magnificent title implies—the dignity of being, in every part of it, the repository of infinite goodness and infinite wisdom. He sought the conversation of the preacher. None of his questions were evaded, but every one was met in the most ingenuous, unassuming, and liberal spirit, and answered in the most consistent, lucid, and satisfactory manner.

He began to read the writings of the illustrious Swedenborg. A new intellectual and moral world opened upon his delighted view. He found he was able to see the Lord Jesus Christ as "God over all, blessed for ever," without qualification or reserve, and in a clear and glorious light, without a single over-shadowing cloud of mystery or contradiction. Without going back to Tri-personalism he could now embrace a new Scripture doctrine of the Divine Trinity, and one perfectly free from every blemish of contradiction, and thus could entertain far more exalted ideas of his Saviour than he was ever able to form while he was a believer in three Persons in the Godhead. He could also now see his God as ONE, because one Divine Person; and in an aspect of love and mercy immensely exceeding his utmost efforts so to behold his Maker, while, as a Unitarian, which he became for a time, he endeavoured to think of God as a benevolent *Somewhat* diffused like an ethereal essence through infinite space.

Indeed he was delighted to find that whatever is good and useful, whatever is lucid and consistent, in other systems of Christianity, is harmoniously brought together in its proper arrangement and connection in the doctrines of the New Church, so that those doctrines may be regarded as embracing all the revealed truth deduced from the Holy Word by all denominations of Christians, purified from all admixture of error and human invention. He found the Divine authority and sanction, the unchangeableness of doctrine, and the infallibility of interpretation, which is the boast of the Roman Catholic, combined with the utmost freedom of investigation, so that the general doctrines of the New Church may be regarded as invisible "bands of love" (Hosea xi., 4) by which the Father of mercies guides and holds His children.

We have now only to remark respecting our friend Job Abbott that he remained in connection with the New Jerusalem Church at Loughborough about seven years, daily increasing in the knowledge of her doctrines, and also growing, as there is good reason to believe, in practical wisdom and goodness, and in the experience of peace, calm serenity, and happiness.

Though a large share of outward trial and bodily affliction fell to his lot, this he piously converted into the means of promoting his spiritual and moral improvement, by the exercise of patience and resignation to the Divine Providence. About six months before he was removed into the spiritual world, his strength gradually decayed, and he felt that he was about to undergo the last and all-important change. This he contemplated with lively hope and silent joy, tempered with humility and heightened by gratitude. This was remarkably evident when he was in the near prospect of death, as was shown by the language which he held to a lady who visited him, and who had long known his worth. After he had settled his worldly affairs, he exclaimed, "Now I have done with the world, and am perfectly happy. My Lord and Saviour found me in my low estate, and raised me up. I am now going to be with Him and live in that state of happiness where I shall be more useful than I can be in this world." Upon being asked whether there was anything in the nature of religious instruction or consolation that he desired, he replied to the enquirer (the New Church preacher in the town), "You have supplied me with this already, and the work is now done." This reply, given as it was with peaceful calmness, testifies that the faith of the New Jerusalem is one which brings peace in death, provided it has previously been allowed to conduct to a humble and pious rectitude of life. Such indeed was the language our friend uniformly held during the short period, only one week, in which his illness became serious. He had a constant and grateful sense of joy and rejoicing, accompanied with a calm and even state of the feelings, and the ground of his joy was this—that his work had been done before his illness. To a question put to him on the day of his departure, whether he held fast to the faith of the New Jerusalem Church, he pleasantly replied, "Do you doubt it?" He departed in peace, at Loughborough, on the 14th day of July, 1839, and in the 49th year of his age.

Our friend left various MS. papers behind him, and an examination of them fully proves that he had made a good progression in the spirit and life of the new doctrines, as well as in the knowledge of them. Previous to his acquaintance with the New Church, he had sometimes manifested a somewhat confident, rash, and condemnatory exercise of the judgment, as appears from some of his papers; but under the blessed influence of the new doctrines he gradually acquired habitual feelings of meekness, kindness, patience, and forbearance. As a proof that such was the frame of his mind, some extracts from his papers are now presented to the reader. The truly Christian reader, of every denomination, will rejoice to perceive, and not without feelings approaching to amazement, how great a deliverance Job Abbott experienced from the woes of doubt, darkness, infidelity, and despair, into which he had fallen; and to what a height of wisdom and peace he had been conducted by means of the principles of the New Jerusalem Church.

We conclude with presenting to the reader some of the overflowings of our friend's pious feelings, expressed in verse. These productions were written about a year before his death:

"Have faith in God."
"Behold, I have set my bow in the cloud."
"Lo! I am with you always, even to the end."

There is a principle within—
Faith in God's love and power;
Upon this moveless Rock I lean
In sorrow's darkest hour.

This oft my drooping heart hath cheered,
With anguish worn, and care;
And all I doubted, all I feared
Have vanished into air!

What though a cloud o'ershade my sight,
Big with affliction's tear;
Yet faith amidst the drops that fall
Discerns a rainbow there.

I need not shrink, I need not fear,
Whate'er the future be;
Since God is love, and God is near
In man's extremity!

ALPHABET OF SOME OF THE DIVINE CHARACTERS OF THE LORD JESUS CHRIST:

My *All* in all, below, above,
My *Benefactor* filled with love;
My *Captain*, all my foes to quell,
My great *Deliverer* from hell;
The *End* of all I have in view,
My *Friend* unchangeable and true.
To realms of heavenly bliss my *Guide*,
My *Haven* when by sorrows tried.
Immanuel, the great I Am,
Jesus the sin removing Lamb.
Keeper of Israel, night and day,
The *Light*, the Life, the Truth, the Way.
The *Mighty God*, the only Lord,
The *Name* by heaven and earth adored,
My *One* thing needful thou shalt be,
The *Prince* of Peace thou art to me.
Quickener art thou of all within,
Refiner from the dregs of sin;
My *Shepherd*, Saviour, Sun and Shield,

> The *Tree* of Life which fruit doth yield;
> The *Vine* from which the branches grow,
> The *Well* whose waters overflow;
> My *Yea*, Amen, both sure and fast,
> In *Zion* thou art First and Last.

Such was the intelligent and estimable character of Job Abbott, of Loughborough; and such was the bounty of the giver of all good to a poor stocking-maker—not a perishable and transient bounty of gold and silver, but an imperishable and ever-enduring bounty of goodness and truth, heavenly love, and heavenly wisdom—a bounty infinitely more valuable than precious stones, because imperishable and eternal!

May the reader of these pages have humility and candour sufficient to discover and correct his errors! May he prove willing to change his opinions when he can do so for the better; and may he be led to sit at the feet of the Lord Jesus Christ as his only Divine Teacher, and account it his one thing needful to learn, and do, His blessed Word! And may his eyes be opened to behold the surpassing glory of the heavenly doctrines of the New Jerusalem!

XXI.

MR. TUTING,

And the Church in Scotland.

THE Conference being held in Edinburgh for the first time in 1852, and Mr. Tuting being the representative of the Edinburgh Society, I was enabled to form an acquaintance with him and his excellent lady. He was one of the eight persons of whom the Society in the beautiful capital of North Britain was formed, in 1816. I visited him in the house at Trinity which he subsequently left as a legacy to the Conference, to be used I presume for the advantage of the Church in Scotland.

Mr. Tuting was a man of a pious, patient, thoughtful character, and on several occasions showed his interest in the Church and the Conference by attending its sittings, and recognising its services for the general good. The property he left is now reported to be at the disposal of Conference, and will it is hoped be so used as to carry out the wishes of its former worthy owner, to aid in the progress among mankind of the Lord's kingdom of Goodness and Truth. Mr. Tuting at one time kept a library of New Church works, that he might circulate them at his own expense and trouble. Amongst the readers was Mrs. Crowe, who wrote the work entitled, "The Night-Side of Nature," and no doubt she received from his library such spiritual views as appear in that remarkable book. Both within and without the Church Mr. Tuting was greatly respected. He left two hundred pounds to the Edinburgh Society, and one hundred to that of Glasgow, and the property now in hand will realise no doubt some hundreds of pounds. Mr. Bruce estimated it at seven or eight. Of Mr. Tuting himself, Mr. Bruce wrote, "I have known him intimately for very many years, and have always entertained a high opinion of him as a New Churchman; and many besides will long remember him as an example of a true Christian."

The New Church made its way very slowly in Scotland, though Mr. Glen, who took so earnest a part in proclaiming the truths of the New Kingdom in America, was a Scotchman. Here and there, however, in the early part of this century, a very few individuals in Edinburgh had obtained a knowledge of the truth, a few in Glasgow, and in Dundee. The chief leader in this respect was no doubt Mr. T. Parker, a retired barrister, who had received the doctrines in London through Mr. Hindmarsh, in 1788. He had been a Wesleyan for twenty years, and a good part of that time a local preacher, and both himself and Mrs. Parker were greatly respected by Mr. Wesley. Meetings of the early members were held at his house in Red Lion Square. His reception of the New Church principles was a great pecuniary loss to him, as his business was principally among his religious friends, and this was entirely withdrawn. While connected with the Methodists he published a Bible with notes, in two large volumes. Having relinquished the bar, he went to Scotland, and it was principally through his instrumentality the church was planted there. He preached the doctrines for some time in Glasgow, and then removed to Edinburgh. He taught the truth privately for a year or two to souls who hungered and thirsted for it; but after the memorable visit of Mr. Hindmarsh, in 1817, he began to preach the doctrines publicly, and a considerable number, among whom was the young man who became the Rev. W. Bruce, looked back to him as the blessed medium of their entry within the gates of the Holy City. He was, however, rather a burning than a shining light. He died in 1829, at 90 years of age. The first public proclamation of the power and great glory in which the Lord is descending to the spiritually-minded, was made by the Rev. Robt. Hindmarsh, who visited Scotland in 1817, and lectured and preached first at Glasgow, and then at Edinburgh.

He lectured every evening for several days at the house of a gentleman named Atwell, to audiences of from 16 to 20 persons. It was the day of small things. On Sunday, however, our friends were enabled by the liberality of the Unitarians to obtain the use of their chapel for morning and afternoon service, and by the equally generous conduct of a Rev. Mr. Douglas, the Andersonian Hall, which that gentleman was in the habit of using and which would contain a large congregation, was obtained for the evening. In consequence, Mr. Hindmarsh states he had a congregation of five hundred persons in the morning, of seven hundred in the afternoon, and in the evening of twelve hundred, many going away who were unable to enter.

In Glasgow there is always great eagerness to hear, and great attention to discuss afterwards what is heard, as I have often experienced; and so Mr. Hindmarsh found it in his time; but as the friends had then no permanent place of worship, what real results followed this season of sowing broadcast the Divine seed is known to the Lord alone. But in 1834, when the Rev. D. G. Goyder went there to labour as regular minister, he stated, "The place of worship was exceedingly small, and I think I may say that forty persons would have rendered it inconveniently crowded. The Society, however, was equally limited in number, I think not exceeding twenty-five." That is after SEVENTEEN years. "They were persons in the middle rank of life, possessed of the ordinary means of subsistence, but their liberality was great, greater than I have ever found in any other society. They subscribed generously towards the support of the Church, as well as of myself. They were very orderly in their general conduct, and punctual and regular in their attendance on the public services of the Church, and I may here say, once for all, that during my FOURTEEN years' residence in Glasgow, I never found the congregation remiss in their religious duties on the Sabbath. At the appointed time, they were found in their places, and neither the minister nor the congregation were annoyed by persons coming in late, except indeed in the case of occasional visits by strangers."

This is very high praise, and still I believe truly deserved by our friends of the Glasgow Society.

Dr. Goyder laboured very arduously during his time, as preacher, lecturer, and publisher of the Glasgow series of tracts, and then returned to England. The present respectable place of worship in Cathedral Street was opened soon after Dr. Goyder's time, and has of course afforded more ample accommodation for the Society's growth, which has been continuous and considerable. Mr. Hindmarsh went to Edinburgh, and found there a state of welcoming excitement even greater than that which he had experienced at Glasgow.

He stayed at the house of Mr. Bruce (I presume the father of the Rev. W. Bruce), and was warmly received by Messrs. Dichmoss, Tuting, and Parker.

"He preached on Thursday evening in the Freemasons' Hall, to about seven hundred persons, and three times on Sunday. The curiosity excited in the town was such that the place was excessively crowded. Above a thousand were present at each service on Sunday, and it was thought as many more had to go away unable to get in. Each time the attention was remarkable, and the effect produced was stated to be very great. One person said his faith was well shaken. Another was heard to declare that now he was in possession of a clue by which he may understand the Scriptures as he reads them by himself. A third, a venerable old lady, said, 'At last, in my old age, I have found the true way of salvation, the sure road to heaven.' A fourth said that at the conclusion of one of the discourses it was with difficulty he could restrain himself from calling upon all present to hold up their hands in approbation of what they had heard.

"Several of our friends have more than once quoted the words of Simeon at the birth of our Lord.

"If a great interest was excited in Glasgow, it appears that a still greater was excited here. Many who attended the first meeting on Thursday evening were determined to be present at each of the three services on the succeeding Sunday, and expecting the place would be crowded BROUGHT THEIR DINNERS with them in the morning, and actually continued in the hall the whole day, that they might suffer no disappointment.

"It would almost appear that the primitive times were returning upon us, for what an Evangelist writes in relation to the Jews of old when they had seen and heard the Lord in person, may not inaptly be repeated in reference to the people of Edinburgh on the occasion of the Lord's second appearance in the spiritual sense of the Holy Word, namely, that they were all amazed, insomuch that they questioned among themselves, saying, What new doctrine is this? (Mark i., 27). Some have come from Glasgow, almost on purpose to hear me again, a distance of forty-two miles."

In a letter written by the friends after the visit, and dated August 9th, 1817, they say, "Mr. Hindmarsh had arrived there from Glasgow, bringing with him a rich supply of heavenly instruction; that he preached to crowded audiences, who seemed amazed yet delighted with the simple yet sublime instruction thus proclaimed in their ears. That all the members of their little Society had felt an uncommon elevation of their affections since his arrival. They have had, as it were, some foretastes of the joys of heaven, and they feel their bosoms heave with gratitude to our Heavenly Father, who hath thus visited and refreshed His infant Church with the Divine truths of His Holy Word.

"The number of true receivers they reckon about twenty-two, and there are about a dozen more who attend pretty constantly: and of these there is reason to think the greater part will now become cordial recipients.

"They think it very probable that the Old Church will *die hard* in Scotland; her people being wedded to her dead formalities, and unwilling to part with their *offended justice*, their *atonement*, their *reconciled God*, and their external sanctity on *sacramental occasions*.

"'The phrase *die hard* in Scotland will be better understood if we take a glimpse of the grim and melancholy effect the Calvinistic Church of John Knox and his followers had produced upon the country. The cruelties of Charles I. and II., and James II., in attempting to force the Church of England upon Scotland, had made the people especially cling to their clergy; and the state of gloom realised by the noble Scotch people from the blight of Calvinism was most withering. It is presented in vivid and terrible colours by Buckle, in his "History of Civilisation," and evidenced by the records of the Church and the sermons of the clergy.

"According to their code, all the natural affections, all social pleasures, all amusements, and all the joyous instincts of the human heart, were sinful, and were to be rooted out. It was sinful for a mother to wish to have sons; and if she had any it was sinful to be anxious about their welfare. It was a sin to please yourself, or to please others; for by adopting either course you were sure to displease God. All pleasures, therefore, however slight in themselves, or however lawful they might appear, must be carefully avoided. When mixing in society, we should edify the company, if the gift of edification had been bestowed upon us, but we should by no means attempt to amuse them. Cheerfulness, especially when it arose to laughter, was to be guarded against; and we should choose for our associates grave and sorrowful men, who were not so likely to indulge in so foolish a practice.

"Smiling, provided it stopped short of laughter, might occasionally be allowed; still, being a carnal pastime, it was a sin to smile on Sunday. Even on week-days, those who were most imbued with religious principles hardly ever smiled, but sighed, groaned, and wept. A true Christian would be careful in his movements, to preserve invariable gravity, never running, but walking soberly, and not treading out in a brisk and lively manner, as unbelievers are wont to do. So, too, if he wrote to a friend, he must beware lest his letter should contain anything like jocoseness, since jesting is incompatible with a holy and serious life.

"The Rev. Mr. Lyon mentions that some of the Scotch clergy, in drawing up regulations for the government of a colony, inserted the following clause: 'No husband shall kiss his wife, and no mother shall kiss her child, on the Sabbath day.'

"It was wrong to take pleasure in beautiful scenery, for a pious man had no concern with such matters, which were beneath him, and the admiration of which would be left to the unconverted. The unregenerate might delight in these vanities; but they who were properly instructed saw Nature as she really was, and knew that as she, for about five thousand years, had been constantly on the move, her vigour was well-nigh spent and her pristine energy departed. To the eye of ignorance, she still seemed fair and fresh; the fact was, however, that she was worn out and decrepit; she was suffering from extreme old age; her frame, no longer elastic, was leaning on one side, and she soon would perish. All the senses were evil, but the eye was incomparably the most wicked. Hence, it was especially marked out for Divine punishment, and, being constantly sinning, it was afflicted with fifty-two different diseases, that is, one disease for each week of the year.

"The world afforded nothing worth looking at, save and except the Scotch Kirk, which was incomparably the most beautiful thing under heaven."

Trained and taught for generations, with fervent zeal and perseverance, and with earnest preaching as contrasted with English sermon-reading, we need not be surprised that a nation saturated with Calvinistic theology would receive slowly the Gospel that God is Love, and Wisdom, and has formed all things in Wisdom and Order, that man should be happy. There was, however, quite as much reception when the truth was lovingly set before them as could have been expected. A Society was begun at Dunfermline, under the leadership of a worthy man, Mr. Paton, the father of the present distinguished artist, Sir Noel Paton.

Another was commenced at Alloa, by a most intelligent and excellent blacksmith, Allan Drysdale.

Dundee had a very curious experience. While the Church was being founded in an orderly way in Glasgow and Edinburgh, by the open proclamation of her doctrines and the acknowledgment of Swedenborg as the Lord's special messenger to the world for their publication, a gentleman named Whitefield, of great attractiveness as a speaker, but not very Christian in his life, had quietly read some of the New Church works in Manchester, where he had resided, but where he does not seem to have been known to the New Church people. He went first to Edinburgh, and remained a short time, and then visited Dundee. He learned there that there was a large chapel without a minister. He preached for them, and was approved. He offered his services, and was told they were willing to accept him if he would be content with such income as came freely in, whatever it might be.

He was willing to commence on those terms, and his eloquence soon attacted great congregations; and though his doctrines were new and strange to the people, they heard him gladly, and admired and esteemed what they heard. After a time, the instability of the man began to appear; he was found to have been intemperate at Edinburgh, and the unhappy weakness in this respect was repeated at Dundee, and his influence declined, so that he could no longer remain in the town. How sad that so promising an effort should have been destroyed by such morbid self-indulgence!

A minister, to lead his people truly, must be felt to be an example, as well as a teacher, and beyond the very suspicion of self-indulgence, as well as guiltless of the reality, or he will lose sooner or later the respect of his people. The minister will not be trusted and esteemed, unless the people believe that when good is to be done self-denial is his law, not self-gratification. It was not so with this poor gentleman, Whitefield. It became known, however, before he left, that he owed what was most valuable in his teaching to Swedenborg's "Heaven and Hell," and quite a number of his hearers began to read some of the works with great profit, and especially one most worthy character, Mr. Peter Smith.

They sent, in 1824, an invitation to young Mr. Bruce, who had been secretary of the Edinburgh Society for seven years, and had deepened his acquaintance with New Church works by thoughtful and diligent study, and shown much aptness to teach.

A distinct Society was thus formed in Dundee, and for three years was constantly increasing, when the labours were found to be too much for Mr. Bruce's delicate health, and he returned to Edinburgh, leaving the worthy Mr. Smith as leader, who was very successful and universally respected, but removed by accidental death on the 27th of December, 1834. Since that time, for want of ministration, the Society has decayed, but latterly, with greater missionary activity in Scotland, Dundee is having renewed attention, and may well become a field for a powerful and abiding New Church Society.

The Scottish Missionary Society, led by our esteemed friends in Glasgow and Paisley, headed by the warm-hearted ministers Potts and Allbutt, has of late years been most enterprising and energetic. Their activity and devotion have been beyond all praise, and increase in their own borders, as well as a great modification of the general tone of thought in Scotland, is the gratifying result.

It almost seems sometimes, at present, that dear old Scotland is going too fast; that the old is dying off before the new can fully take its place; but of course the Lord knows best, and the whole movement is under His most Wise, most Merciful and Providential care.

XXII.

M. RICHER,

And the New Church in France.

FOR forty years or thereabouts I have had the opportunity of knowing and seeing the worthy people who have been the active members of the New Church in the magnificent country at the other side of the Channel, crowded with amiable, intellectual, talented, logical minds. Swedenborg calls them the "noble French nation" (A.R. 725). Every one who really becomes acquainted with the inhabitants of France will learn what grand qualities there are in the characters of the great mass of the nation.

What generous self-devotion there is, anyone will learn who enquires respecting the mode of life of the parish priests in the villages, with the very moderate incomes they receive; the missionaries to other countries, their great abilities, and their self-denying lives; or the faithful supporters of the schools of St. Vincent de Paul. On the other hand, the Protestant portion of the nation, in their heroic sufferings, and patient endurance and faithfulness to conscience for two hundred years of oppression, are the wonder and admiration of all who have read their history.

Their ingenuity and skill have made it doubtful whether the first moves towards the great discoveries of the power of steam, the steam-engine, and the screw-propeller, which they claim, did not *originate* with the French; while the silk trade of Spitalfields, and elsewhere, the crape trade of Norwich, and many industries of the Channel Islands were undoubtedly brought by the fugitives who, to preserve their most sacred convictions, were compelled to give up home and country. Their grace and taste lend a charm to their more solid gifts, and their courtesy has led the way to politeness of manner which when genuine gives a welcome urbanity to the intercourse of civilised society.

Yes, the French are a noble people, and we trust the time will never come again when the two great nations of the Western World will ever meet except in amity, progress, and peace.

The progress of the New Church in France illustrates still further the best qualities of the "noble nation." A faithful few, almost as early as it was done in England, grasped the great principles of the New Jerusalem, and remained faithful to them, notwithstanding the difficulty of diffusing them among a people who know little of the Bible, and who understand religion only as presented in the teachings and ceremonies of the Church.

The first names we meet with are the Marquis de Thomé, in 1785, and the Baron and Baroness Thiebault, the latter of whom I knew well as distinguished as much by their admirable qualities as by their rank, and whose descendants I know and highly esteem at the present day. Some priests of the Roman Catholic Church, and Protestant pastors, from the earliest periods and down to the time at which I write, have dared to avow their convictions of the truth of the principles of the New Jerusalem, and the reality of the seership of Swedenborg.

Pernety, who first translated the work on "Heaven and Hell" from the Latin, was a Benedictine priest; Ægger, the premier vicaire of the Cathedral of Paris, was of course a priest; Ledru, of Chartres, who translated and used the New Church English Liturgy, an excellent man, was a priest; Bayot, whom many of us knew in London for many years, was a priest who became an exile for fear at the beginning of the Empire, after the *coup-d-état*, and who attended Argyle Square Church, and many more, not excepting some among the Bishops. The Archbishop of Rheims wrote a work in two volumes, full of New Church doctrine.

Of Protestant pastors, even so early as 1812, Boniface Laroque, President of the Consistory of the Reformed or Protestant Church of Castres, published two volumes, in which he explained the doctrines of the New Jerusalem with great ability, but without specially acknowledging from whence they were derived. Much later the Protestant pastor at Bayonne, M. Jacquier, who had become a New Churchman when a pastor in Paris, preached there for some years until the *coup-d-état*; when he had to fly to Switzerland, and of whom a few years ago the present worthy pastor said to me, " M. Jacquier was a *tres brave homme* (a most excellent man), though he had some peculiar views."

Besides these excellent men, each of whom (and

they are only specimens of a large number of individuals) must, as one would suppose, influence circles in different portions of the country, there has from the early days been a succession of literary men of unusual ability, and of great and steady zeal, men who have laboured with no popular smile to cheer them, but with persevering love, in obscurity for years, only strengthened by the hope that what they were doing would bless generations unborn. May their memories be for ever blessed. The first of these was Moet, Royal Librarian at Versailles. He undertook in 1786 to translate the whole of the works of Swedenborg, and laboured on to his death in 1807. These remained until John Aug. Tulk, whose memorial tablet is now at the New Church, Kensington, one of the first five who assembled at the London Coffee House on the 5th of November, 1783, went to Paris, when he was 86 years of age, on the overthrow of Napoleon the First, and advanced between one and two thousand pounds to have these French translations published. There were forty volumes obtained from the widow of Moet. This was done, and M. Chevrier writes " It is to these translations that up to 1850 all the disciples of Swedenborg in France owe their knowledge of his doctrines. They are far from being as faithful as those of M. Leboys-des-Guays; however, they are more to the taste of many, because Moet has avoided translations of too literal a kind in certain passages difficult to understand because of the technical terms used."

Judging by the sale, which was considerable, the number of readers must have greatly increased, yet those who presented themselves at the meetings were still very few.

In 1820 there was a company of EIGHT persons,

who met every Sunday at the house of an excellent man, a lawyer named Gobert, who was attached with heart and soul to the cause.

In 1821 there was a Society of about 16 persons at Constance, in Normandy, and small companies at Nantes, Angers, Sisteron, à Cap, and Besançon.

The most active apostles in France about this time were some military men, headed by Captain Bernard, born at Vannes in Brittany. Having received, as was common then, an anti-religious education, he pursued science with especial ardour at Bordeaux, but with that unsatisfied condition of the highest affections of the soul that must ever exist when there is no light nor warmth from heaven. He, however, thirsted for the living God, and a volume of Swedenborg's was placed in his hands—it was just what he needed. He received the sublime principles with avidity, and soon, interested in the same great cause, several officers in his regiment, the 23rd of the line, who received them also.

The Commander De Malherbe, Major Purvis, and the Captains Fraiche, Paillard, and De Foisac, made with Bernard the campaign of 1823, in Spain, and wherever they went the intelligence, the charity, and piety of these remarkable officers made a great impression.

Captain Bernard spread the Writings in Spain. The Bishop of Barcelona, General Palafox, and others, are said to have much delighted in them. A correspondent of the *Evangelical Magazine* of that date, who met with these young officers, wrote thus: "There are among the military of this garrison (Bayonne) some young officers who occupy themselves with serious things. I know two in particular who are separated from the world, and who manifest a conduct worthy in many respects of the children of God; BUT, ALAS! THEY ARE DISCIPLES OF SWEDENBORG. I do not know how to describe to you their zeal for propagating what they think to be truth; the courage with which they brave the reproaches with which they are covered; the benevolence which they show towards the wretched, and the love they witness for the Word! These two young officers have a great affection for me."

On his return home Capt. Bernard converted his father to his views, who was an aged magistrate, and a gentleman of great consideration; and many other notable persons at Orthes and Arles; but above all, Edward Richer, of Nantes, in Brittany, a writer of extraordinary merit, who became afterwards the author of several New Church works, equal to anything produced in proof and illustration of the New Age, either in France or out of it.

Richer was born in 1792, and died in 1834. During his short life he had by his literary labours produced such an impression that one of his friends, M. Piet, has written his biography in a goodly octavo volume.

When Bernard introduced the works of Swedenborg to Richer he was so charmed with their sublime, spiritual and wide-reaching character, that he felt his life would be well consecrated if it was given to advance these glorious principles among men as soon as he was at liberty, by the publication of the manuscripts on literary and scientific subjects which he had accumulated during twelve years. While pondering over this determination some thieves broke into his house, and with strange perversity and malice, perhaps because disappointed at not finding sufficient of their own kind of booty, actually burnt his cherished manuscripts. From that time he determined to devote the remainder of his life, however many years he had to live, to works which would popularise and spread the doctrines of the New Revelation. He wrote the "Religion of Good Sense," as an introduction to his great work. It was translated into English by Mr. Sims, of Belfast, and had a large success both in French and in English. Equally so was the "Key to the Mystery," a general explanation of the book of Revelation. His great work is "The New Jerusalem," in eight vols. octavo. This grand work unfolds at large and systematically the entire system of Divine things as explained by Swedenborg, and is truly remarkable for its clearness, comprehensiveness, and force. And, lastly, Richer composed a work of piety, consisting of prayers and meditations, called "Religious Invocations," which M. Chevrier, an excellent judge, says may without exaggeration rank among the best books of piety which this century has produced.

The style of Richer has all the literary excellencies which are valued in France. He is clear, neat, and eloquent. His erudition is substantial and extensive. He excels in citations which show the agreement which the doctrines of the New Church have with whatever is best in the religious teaching of all ages. Richer is always calm; his style is not controversial, but convincing. The reading of his writings gives repose to the spirit, and leaves the same impression which one has from a conversation with a highly cultivated and most sensible man.

Richer, who was attached to the College at Nantes, had already induced some excellent people in the same city to enjoy the blessings of the New

Church teaching and worship—some ten or twelve. The most fervent of these was M. Tollenare, a wealthy gentleman who had retired from business, in which he had realised a fortune by fitting out privateers with arms. M. Tollenare had devoted himself to works of benevolence, and was treasurer to the hospital of Nantes up to 1848. It was he who supplied the means for printing the works of Richer to the extent of £400.

He was a truly Christian character, but, like Nicodemus, he feared to show himself openly, and timidly sought to appear entirely to conform to the Roman doctrine and worship of which his conscience no longer approved.

The result was that his influence, even in his family, to lead them in the way of truth, was almost nothing, although the clergy were very deferential to him, until he was on his death-bed, when they harassed and worried him to renounce the doctrines of the New Church, and prepared letters to be sent to the New Church friends at St. Amand, London, Tubingen (Dr. E. Tafel), and America, announcing, to their surprise and sorrow, that he had done so.

On a visit that M. Chevrier made to M. Leboys, the latter showed him the letter he had thus received, and Mr. C. took it out with him while he made a short walk, and, reading it again in the warm sunshine of a day in July, some lines written with invisible ink came to view, in which the poor dying gentleman stated he had been compelled to write these letters of abjuration, but hoped that his friends would perceive the other lines, and know that he died in the faith of the New Jerusalem.

Another distinguished French New Churchman of great literary ability was Baron Portal, of a noble family in Languedoc, whose history for centuries had been one of noble deeds, and suffering for righteousness sake, in ages of persecution. There is a history of the family in many volumes; and after Baron Frederic had become a New Churchman he wrote two excellent works full of solid learning, and most interesting as illustrations of the doctrines of the New Church. The first was on "The Symbols of the Egyptians Compared with those of the Hebrews." The second was "On the Symbolic Character of Colours" (Paris, 1840).

The De Portals have been a marvellously clever as well as a wise, virtuous, and noble race.

In the dreadful wars waged by the Inquisition, in the twelfth century, against the Albigenses, they resisted unto death, and headed the persecuted people as long as possible, at Toulouse, and its neighbourhood.

Toulouse was for many generations the home of the Portals, where they were often elected to the highest local authority, a sort of mayoralty, under the name of CAPITOULS. Their manor house still exists in Languedoc.

To escape from persecution, they fled into Provence, and returned to Toulouse, where they were again made CAPITOULS. For them, the Reformation of Luther and Calvin was simply a revival of the former resistance to the slavery of blind obedience to the Pope, and they became Calvinists. John de Portal was beheaded for his religion at Toulouse in 1562. Louis de Portal and his wife were massacred at St. Hippolite in 1683. The governess of Henri IV., when young, was a De Portal. When the reign of terror in the South of France, called the dragonnades, was instituted by the vainglorious and terrified profligate, Louis XIV., in his later years, thinking to atone for his sins by compelling his Protestant subjects to become Catholics by force and cruelty, Louis de Portal was residing at his Château de Portalerie, seventeen miles from Bordeaux. To escape the insults of the brutal soldiers, he fled with his wife and five children to take refuge on his estate in the Cevennes. The dragoons pursued the family to their retreat, overtook them, and cut down the father, mother, and one of the children, and burnt their house. The remaining four children concealed themselves in an oven outside the building, and were thus saved.

The four orphans, three boys and a girl, determined to make for the coast, and escape from France by sea. After a long and perilous journey on foot, they at length reached Montauban, where little Pierre, the youngest, fell down fainting with hunger at the door of a baker's shop.

The humane baker took up the child, carried him into the house, fed and cherished him. The other three, Henry, William, and Mary de Portal, though grieving to leave their little brother behind them, again set out on foot, and pressed on to Bordeaux. They were so fortunate as to obtain a passage by a merchant vessel, on board of which they were shipped in barrels. The youthful refugees reached Holland, where there were relatives and friends who received them, educated them, and enabled them to take the dignified position of their family.

They came over here with the Prince of Orange, and established the family of De Portal in this country. Henry, the elder brother, having learnt the art of paper-making, started a mill of his own near Whitchurch, in Hampshire, on the river

Itchin, and achieved high reputation as a paper manufacturer. He carried on his business with great spirit, gathering round him the best French and Dutch workmen. He shortly brought his work to so high a degree of perfection, that the Bank of England gave him the privilege, which a branch of the family still enjoys, of supplying them with the paper for banknotes.

The youngest brother, who had been taken care of by the humane baker, became a great cloth-manufacturer in France, was faithful to his religion, prospered, and his sons and his sons' sons became Counsellors of State, and at the restoration of the Bourbons the father of our De Portal was made a peer of France. Pierre Paul Frederic De Portal (our De Portal) wrote "Memoires de la Famille de Portal," to which we are mainly indebted for the facts we have recited.

From this Frederic M. Harlé, a kinsman, and associated with the highest Protestant families of France, had his attention directed to the New Church writings, and he became a leader in Paris and a most learned and efficient helper to M. Leboys-des-Guays, of St. Amand, to whom we must now ask the attention of our readers.

A new era for the New Church commenced in France when the New Revelation of Divine Truth was opened to M. Leboys. He was of an ancient family of magistrates, who had held office for ages. He had been a soldier in his youth, in the great wars of Napoleon, and was at Leipsic and Waterloo.

He became later a lawyer; and was made judge in the civil tribunal at St. Amand (Cher), in 1827, and the same year married Mademoiselle Rollet. In November, 1834, he was struck with some marvellous experiences of a somnambulist character with a shepherd boy, and he took the boy to Paris, to ascertain if any learned scientific men in that city could explain the case. A gentleman, named Caudron, informed him that the only work which could give him any light on such subjects was Swedenborg's "Heaven and Hell."

He got the book, and read it with eagerness, wonder, and delight. He bought all the works of Swedenborg he could find, and took them with him to St. Amand. He studied them with profound attention, and as he understood, he loved more and more, and determined he would devote his life to propagate the truths thus made clear to his mind.

For three years the convictions he received became deeper and broader, until he felt he must not only live according to them, but he must worship according to them, and he invited those who by his encouragement thought as he did, to assemble together, and invoke the Lord Jesus as the only God, the Father, Son, and Holy Spirit; and not bewilder himself or sanction in others a worship virtually addressed to three Gods. He respected the conscientious convictions of others, but he claimed that others should respect his; and he commenced public worship at St. Amand on the 18th of November, 1837.

In March, 1838, with the assistance of several friends, he began the periodical, "The New Jerusalem," a review religious and scientific; which was most interesting, and continued many years. The necessity of having a translation of the entire works of Swedenborg in more modern French grew more clearly evident to him; and in 1843, having calculated that at ten pages a day of the Latin 8vo text, he could translate the whole in seven years, he set to work. In 1850 he had finished his sacred labour. A great part was written with the same pen, a gold one, a present from three young Englishmen, who had been residing at St. Amand for some months, and frequently enjoyed his society; two of whose names will be recognised by many friends, and all of whom are very well known to me. They were Messrs. Hughes, E. J. Broadfield, and Green.

The cost of the printing (about £5,000) was borne by subscribing friends, of whom the chief probably were the Count Emmanuel de Lascases, a senator, son of the author of the "Memorial from St. Helena," who contributed largely; and the worthy M. Chazal, of the Island of Mauritius; who between them contributed one half.

This work completed, M. Leboys commenced preparing indexes, which are very valuable, and by his life, his worship, and his labours, was continually increasing in the esteem of all who knew him.

On Sunday, the 18th of December, 1864, he felt rather unwell, and could not perform the service. He retired at five o'clock, and at seven he ceased to breathe, at 70 years of age.

On the evening before his death M. Leboys had corrected the last proof of his last index. His work was done. His labours, however, had not been confined to translation. His "Letters to a Man of the World who Wishes to Believe" have gone through several editions, and have been highly valued both in their French and in their English form.

The various articles, on different subjects, which appeared from his pen in *The New Jerusalem*, between 1840 and 1849, have been printed, and make two volumes 8vo, under the title of "Melanges."

When we survey the French nation as it is in its three great groups, the Roman Catholics, the Reformed, and the Unbelievers, there are features in each encouraging to hopefulness that they will ultimately become a strong nation for the New Jerusalem.

The Gallican Church has always claimed privileges of its own, and a sort of independent character, that has held the Popes in check. The bulls of the latter were not allowed to circulate in France for centuries, unless sanctioned by the French bishops in synod, or by the Government.

Though their kings were allowed by the Popes to be called eldest sons of the Church, however wicked they might be, and some of them were monsters in vice, yet these eldest sons were often very insolent to their fathers, and the bishops often were very zealous in maintaining these privileges of their Church as against the Popes. Bossuet, though violent against Protestants, was a great champion of the Gallican Church. Napolean had a concordat limiting the infallible papal jurisdiction in many ways. Hence, Roman Catholics, and especially Roman Catholics in France, are treated of by Swedenborg as more open to receive the truths of the New Church than some Protestants. This is particularly shown in his explanation of Rev. 17 (A.R. 740), and also in the "Ap. Explained," 1070.

In the former he says : "And the ten horns which thou sawest are ten kings, who have received no kingdom, as yet, signifies, the Word as to its power derived from Divine Truths among those who are in the kingdom of France, and are not so much under the yoke of the papal dominion, with whom, nevertheless, there is not a church, entirely separated from the Roman Catholic religion." In the latter work he observes: "Within Babylon are those in the kingdom of France, and some in Holland, England, Scotland, and Ireland, who have not taken away from the Lord the power of saving men, nor Divine sanctity from the Word, and attributed both the former and the latter to some Vicar; as may appear from the contest which has so long continued, and which still continues, between the Gallican Church and the Roman."

To the same effect, Swedenborg speaks in the "True Christian Religion" (n. 821): "All those of the Catholic Religion who when alive in the world had thought more about God than about the Pope, and had done works of charity in simplicity of heart, when they find themselves alive after death, and are instructed that the Lord Himself, the Saviour of the world, holds the government there, are easily led to renounce the superstitions of that religion. The transition from Popery to Christianity is as easy for such persons as it is to enter into a temple when the doors are thrown open; or into a palace, by passing through the sentinels who keep guard in the outer courts, when the king enjoins admission; or as it is to lift up the countenance, and look towards heaven, when angelic voices are heard therein."

In the "Brief Exposition" (n. 108), there is an interesting passage in which Swedenborg gives three reasons why good Roman Catholics can more readily enter the New Church than others, and he adds: "These are three reasons why the Roman Catholics, if they approach God the Saviour Himself, and not mediately but immediately, and, likewise, administer the holy eucharist in both kinds, may more easily than the Reformed receive a living faith instead of a dead faith, and be conducted by angels from the Lord to the gates of the New Jerusalem or New Church, and be introduced therein with joy and shouting."

If Pere Hyacinthe, with whom I have some slight acquaintance, and such earnest and eloquent priests as sympathise with him, would take these hints, and have their services in the language of the people, set forth the supremacy and general diffusion of the Word, the marriage of the priests, and a good heavenly life for every one, as the indispensable preparation, I cannot but think there would be large accessions to the New Church from the Catholics in France.

There are next the Protestants of France, and these have the great advantage of the diffusion of the Bible amongst them. They have also a history of sublime heroism and endurance under persecution to which the world has few parallels. They are also generally superior and educated people. They have come through much tribulation, and their sufferings have taught them toleration.

The particular doctrines they hold as essential are now very few; the acknowledgment of the Lord, the Word as a guide, and a good life, are now the chief things with them; and the spiritual sense of the Word, the knowledge of the spiritual world, and the life after death, would, I cannot but think, be welcomed if affectionately introduced amongst them.

The greatest desideratum amongst the Protestants, it seems to me, and I have often been at worship with them, is a heartfelt liturgical service in which the people could responsively join; more music, and more warmth. Too often the Protestant service is like an essay delivered in an Athenæum, introduced by speech to the Lord with the eyes shut; instead of an earnest instruction and appeal upon subjects of eternal importance. There is, however, great preparedness among the Protestants of France, and the Calvinism of Fate is almost entirely gone.

Then, there are the unbelievers, and these are a wide class. They embrace, it is to be feared, a great majority of the men. But this is to a large extent only a revolt against superstition and the ignorance of the clergy.

Let views of religion be shown to these which are at once spiritual and rational, illustrated by an upright and charitable life, and a bright hope and heavenly trust in a reasonable hereafter, and I doubt not thousands will hail the boon. The way is already prepared by the faithful preliminary work of our dear brethren in France.

I have known the active people for the past forty years. The first time I ventured to officiate amongst them was in the room of M. Hartel, in the Rue du Mail. There were about twenty persons present, representing, if I recollect rightly, fourteen nationalities. Monsieur and Madame Hartel were full of zeal and devotion. He would go to any distance to spread the truth.

The next time it was at M. Minot's, in the Rue de Monnaie, and Minot was also a most zealous and self-sacrificing man. Then there were the meetings at Dr. Poirson's for a long period. I had an interview with M. Broussais, son of the great physician of that name, a most eloquent man, who preached until necessity compelled him to accept a position at Pondicherry. I have worshipped also with M. Leboys at St. Amand.

And thus a small army of faithful men have led the way in the day of small things. I trust more labourers will be sent in His own time and way by our Heavenly Master and theirs. The fields seem white. Many have gone forth weeping, but bearing precious seed. May they return rejoicing, bringing their sheaves with them.

Such lives as we have sketched are an honour to the Church, and to human nature. They are seeds of a great harvest some day in the "noble French nation." Nor have we exhausted the story. M. E. Chevrier, of Bourges, the author of many excellent works on various subjects, especially on the history of Protestantism in France, is constantly engaged on whatever will tend to advance the New Church in his country. His pen is ever active, his researches are incessant. To his other valuable labours the worthy and learned gentleman has now undertaken to publish the prophetical books in Latin, with the explanations from Swedenborg as far as possible opposite to each verse.

Isaiah and Jeremiah are already issued. The whole will be a great advantage to the Church, and once done can of course readily be translated.

His loving efforts for his Heavenly Master know no stint nor stoppage. To him we are greatly indebted in preparing this article. He and Mademoselle Holmes (now Madame Humann) contributed between them SEVEN HUNDRED POUNDS to free the large stock of New Church books of M. Leboys' translations from the claims of relatives.

Mons. Chevrier is the author of many works of great literary merit, as well as some of local interest in his portion of France, including "The Life of General Joubert," "Protestantism dans Le Maçonnais et La Bresse," "A Life of Swedenborg," and a " Histoire Sommaire de la Nouvelle Eglise." He is from the country of Coligny, the great Protestant victim of the dreadful massacre of the day of St. Bartholomew, in 1672; and, like Coligny, he desires to spread in his native land pure truth from heaven. May his exertions be blessed with a thousand-fold success.

And then there are M. and Madame Humann, who, besides sustaining the worship of the New Church, have erected a pretty church in the Rue Thouin, near the Pantheon, where everything invites to edification and devotion. These and the generous aids to the church in Great Britain and elsewhere from a distinguished friend in Paris, through myself, show how Charity and Wisdom glow in the breasts of our dear brethren in France, and indicate that the day will come, and we pray it may come soon, when godly hearts and eloquent tongues will lead the flocks now so small to become a goodly kingdom, a great nation under Him who is King of kings and Lord of lords.

> A little flock! 'Tis well, 'tis well;
> Such be her lot and name.
> Through ages past it has been so,
> And now 'tis still the same.
>
> Her promised glory comes at length,
> Her feeble days are o'er;
> No more a handful in the earth—
> A little flock no more.

XXIII.

THE NOBLE MOURAVIEFF,

The Chief Promoter of the Freedom of the Serfs,

And the New Church in Russia.

RUSSIA, including in its dominions one-fifth of the globe, must ever be to the reflecting mind an interesting object of contemplation. The Greek Church has furnished Russia with its religion, and it claims with good reason to be MORE ANCIENT than the Roman Catholic; for it includes in its territory, Antioch, where Christians first got their name; Constantinople, the chief city of the first Christian Emperor; Nice, where the first great Council was held; and Greek was undoubtedly the first language used in the Christian service. Hence the New Testament was written in Greek, hence the Greek Church calls itself CATHOLIC AND APOSTOLIC, and looks down upon the Roman Catholic as a restless daughter, always grasping at something new, from the ATHANASIAN CREED NOT ACKNOWLEDGED BY THE GREEK CHURCH to the two new doctrines adopted in our own times, the Immaculate Conception of the Virgin Mary, and the Infallibility of the Pope. In some respects there are fewer obstacles to the reception of divine truths prudently brought before the people of the Greek Church than elsewhere, and they are less opposed to the reading of the Word by the people; but in other respects they are very dull and dead in spiritual things. They are ritualistic and evil, as a rule, priests and people. The priests marry —must be married, but they are often drunkards, and are little respected. The well-to-do people are loose in their ideas and practices in relation to chastity, and the virtues which sanctify and bless a home, in married life.

Hence their religion has but little relation to life; and is an offset they offer before God, to make up for their sins; rather than a struggle against sin, and the practice of a heavenly life. The upper clergy, bishops and archbishops, are monks, and generally stigmatised by the rest as the BLACK CLERGY: every priest is called a pope.

Their religion is very much of a mechanical observance, from top to bottom. On one occasion I was present at a very grand ceremony at St. Isaac's, St. Petersburgh, where about twenty bishops and archbishops, in gorgeous robes of cloth of gold, were engaged, and part of it consisted in combing the aged patriarch's hair. They give the sacrament of the Holy Supper to babies of a few months old, a few crumbs and wine with a spoon.

The result is, that there is a strange, heavy dullness all over the land, and in all things.

Some movements are however being felt in Russia. There are here and there strange yearnings after better things. One religious awakening has taken place in some parts of the empire, and has led to excellent results. There is a body of people who insist on going to the Word itself for the foundation of their faith and life, and they are spoken of as remarkably good people. They call themselves Molokani, which means, if I recollect rightly, the New Born. They are very studious of the Word, and quite familiar with it. There are said to be about six hundred thousand of them. Mr. Wallace, in his work on Russia, in the chapter AMONG THE HERETICS, says of them: "Three or four of them (in one small company with whom he conversed) seemed to know the whole of the New Testament by heart. We agreed to differ on questions of detail, and parted from each other without a trace of that ill-feeling which religious discussion commonly engenders. Never have I met men more honest and courteous in debate, more earnest in the search after truth, than these simple, uneducated peasants. If at one or two points in the discussion a little undue warmth was displayed, I must do my opponents the justice to say, they were not the offending party."

Again, he remarks: "They hold that Holy Writ is the only rule of faith and conduct; but that it must be taken in the SPIRITUAL SENSE."

If a member of the Molokani has been guilty of drunkenness, or any act unbecoming a Christian, he is first admonished by the presbyter in private, and then before the congregation; and if this does not produce the desired effect, he is excluded for a longer or a shorter period from the meetings, and from all intercourse with the members. In extreme cases expulsion is resorted to. On the other hand, if any one of the members happens to be, from no fault of his own, in pecuniary difficulties, the others will assist him. This system of mutual control, and mutual assistance, has no doubt something to do with the fact that the Molokani are always distinguished from the surrounding population by their sobriety, uprightness, and prosperity.

Among the nobles there are several who received the truth of the New Church direct from the worthy gentleman whose name—General Alexander Mouravieff—is at the head of this sketch and who was the eldest of the noble family of that name.

It is now more than fifty years since we first heard in this country of this distinguished Russian and his earnest love of the great principles of the New Dispensation. A clergyman of the Church of England, the Rev. Elijah Smith, then recently from Archangel, informed us that the governor of the city, General Mouravieff, had made his acquaintance for the purpose of learning Hebrew from him, that he might read the Word in the original, and see more clearly its spiritual sense. This clergyman had been previously a stranger to the doctrines, but while he taught the governor Hebrew, the governor taught him the language of heavenly wisdom; explaining to him the divine truths which had dawned on his own mind, and were to him an unspeakable delight.

He learned from their subsequent intercourse that General Mouravieff had met with the "DOCTRINE OF LIFE" in French, in a bookseller's shop in Moscow, had been profoundly interested in its contents, and afterwards read all the works of Swedenborg in French or in Latin, as rapidly as their nature would permit, and felt them an ever increasing blessing.

Not being allowed to print the truths he had

found in Russian, and ardently desiring to see them spread, he maintained two amanuenses or secretaries, constantly writing copies of the smaller works; and these he presented, as he saw opportunity, to his friends, and often with the happiest success. A considerable number of the Russian nobility, as well as a large portion of his own family—one of the most distinguished in the empire—came by this means to delight in the truths of the New Jerusalem.

His life was a constant commentary on his doctrines, and led to his being beloved as well as esteemed in all the distinguished posts he occupied as governor, and these were among the most important in the empire. When he entered upon the high function of governor of Nijni-Novgorod, the ancient capital of Russia, the following extract appeared in the journal of the district, from the pen of Dahl, an eminent literary man :—

"I cannot refrain from addressing you (the people) on the happiness vouchsafed to us in the person of our new governor, the General Alexander Mouravieff. He is a sage such as there are but few. Grant us everywhere such governors, and in ten years we shall have progressed so much that we shall not recognise ourselves. The governor is mild, sensible, independent, experienced: of a HOLY LIFE, accessible at all times, and to everyone; fond of justice and of order, yet merciful. In short, he is native gold and silver; a treasure of goodness and truth without alloy."

Next to his love of the great principles of the New Church, was his love of freedom and right for all men, which is the natural result of those grand teachings which declare "that it is a law of the Divine Providence that man should act from liberty according to reason," and "that a man by these two faculties is reformed and regenerated of the Lord, and that without them he cannot be reformed and regenerated."—D. P. 71. 82.

The serfdom of so many millions of his countrymen—although by many degrees a more tolerable condition than was American slavery—was most repugnant to the noble soul of General Alexander Mouravieff. In his early youth he was banished to Siberia for NINE YEARS, for urging this GREAT REFORM, which later he was enabled to carry out. He laboured constantly to convince the powerful of his land of the sacred claims of man, as man, to entire liberty of person and property, when unstained by crime. He urged the necessity of full freedom to ensure progress and prosperity amongst a people. He held up constantly the divine axiom, "If the truth shall make you free, ye shall be free indeed." He did not hide from himself or from anyone, that the transition from semi-slavery to full social freedom would entail loss upon the landowners, but he felt and he urged upon all the conviction that in due time all would reap a rich reward, in every sense, as the result of doing right.

He was met at first by the contempt and hatred of the powerful classes. They looked upon his innovation as dangerous to their interests. They were not prepared to make such sacrifices as this change for the good of their great country required. Not so Alexander Nicolaievitch; he was ready and willing, if need be, to renounce all he possessed for the cause of humanity and justice. A near relative mourning tenderly his loss writes to me: "The day must and will come when all

men shall acknowledge the service which he rendered to the cause of liberty! Even now the Russian peasantry regard him with heartfelt gratitude and affection. Russian mothers will teach their children to bless the name of that worthy man who aided by his indomitable energy their parents to achieve their freedom and their rights."
Gradually the cause Mouravieff had so much at heart commended itself to a few more earnest and clear-sighted minds, then to more, and finally to the Emperor himself.

In 1858 a committee was appointed to prepare for emancipation, of which Mouravieff was not only a member, but was chosen president. On the 19th of February the committee was opened at Nijni-Novgorod by the following speech of the noble president, which we translate for the benefit of our readers.

"Gentlemen: Having arranged with the grand marshal, the committee, called through the confidence of our sovereign to discuss the measures necessary for the amelioration of the condition of the peasants on the estates of noble proprietors, proceeds this day, the 19th of February, to the opening of its labours. Our monarch has chosen for this purpose the anniversary of his own accession to the throne, as the aurora of the re-birth and the restoration of our country. Could there have been a day more happily chosen for the opening of these debates in an assembly on which reposes the hopes of our sovereign and of the country, as well as the hopes of 25 millions of individuals whose civil existence we are seeking to restore, as well as their dignity as men, of which they have so long been deprived?

"Gentlemen: Enter fully into the spirit of your

exalted mission. Have you not been chosen to be the messengers of Him in whose hands are the hearts of kings, that you may realise those divine words pronounced by Himself: 'Bind up the broken hearted; proclaim deliverance to the captives; and the acceptable year of the Lord.' (Luke iv. 18, 19.)? Since such is your mission, think of the august part you have been called upon to fill among men. Show yourselves not unworthy of it. Do not permit your personal or your material interests to sway you in the work you have to accomplish. Permit not, I say, these interests to weigh with you over the well-being of those who have been confided to your generous cares. Surely material interests ought to yield to moral interests! Ought you not to prove this by your acts? I have said moral interests: yes, gentlemen, the solution of the question which occupies us will raise us assuredly to a higher degree of moral civilization; it will elevate the glory and raise higher the moral dignity of the class called to accomplish this work with self-denial, based upon a consciousness of the rights of man.

"Among the individuals whose material existence we have to secure there are found some who are content with their present condition, and desire no other. Glory and honor to the proprietors of such individuals! But their happiness is merely accidental. You, gentlemen, are called upon to replace hazard by certainty, and remove from the mode of our administration of an entire class of individuals, everything that savours of caprice. But we shall not succeed so long as we regard man as a mere producing animal. We can only succeed by restoring human dignity, so long stifled, and invoking the aid of free labor. It can only be when an intelligent and equitable appeal deprived of all arbitrary command shall call forth the living forces of the nation, and breathe new life into what now appears so dead. Never, then, separate from your calculations, however material, a respect for the rights of man. Render to man what belongs to man, and you will justify the confidence of the sovereign and the hope of the nation. I will say more, you will merit the admiration of the whole world, whose eyes are fixed upon you. Your labours will receive the blessings of the Most High, and those of the entire human race. History will rank you among the promoters of justice, and of the love of the neighbour, while it names you the founders of the prosperity of your country."

This committee happily prepared the way for emancipation, and on the 19th of February, 1861, the most sublime act of modern times—the elevation of 25 millions of serfs to the position of free men—became an accomplished fact.

General Mouravieff and the other branches of his distinguished family, along with the great mass of the Russian nobility, suffered severe losses of fortune by the change, but never lost heart or hope. He was confident that with time all would come right, and he was content to wait. He received from the grateful Emperor when the work was completed, a donation of ten thousand acres of land. How grand is the contrast of Russia freeing her 25 millions of serfs peaceably, bearing the burden and patiently working to make the glorious effort successful, to the frantic efforts of the slave-holders of America, by rebellion, by war, by universal wreck, to hold their infamous human property! See in the gradually returning prosperity of the one, and the awful punishment of the other, how truly nations, like individuals, " eat the fruit of their own doings."

Nothing could surpass the joy of Mouravieff on the glorious morning of the emancipation day, though it took away probably half his property. Many who were in the bloom of youth and vigour regarded the change with fear and dread, he at the close of a glorious life was full of gratitude and hope. He was ready to say with Simeon, " Now, Lord, lettest Thou Thy servant depart in peace, for mine eyes have seen Thy salvation."

When his labors in that great measure were over and his age being nearly 70, he had approaches of weakness and indisposition; but only for two months before his death did he feel seriously and severely unwell. During these two months he was satisfied he would not recover, and to the kind and encouraging remarks of his physicians he would sometimes say—" The physicians do not understand how I am; they say I am better, but I shall not recover." He received the Holy Sacrament three times during his illness. The priest who assisted him found great edification in listening to his pious and enlightened conversation. Some days before his departure he experienced so delightful a state of mind that he said it was just as if he had been conveyed to a brighter region where all within and around him was sweetness and blessedness. It was the foretaste of angelic joy.

He used to hear the Gospel and the Psalms every day, in the translation he himself made 27 years before, and he breathed his last breath as he heard the concluding words of the xiv. chap. of John : " Arise, let us go hence." It was the divine call which gave him strength to draw from those he tenderly loved to the sacred company of the blessed. He departed December 18th, 1863, at two p.m., aged 71.

His loss has been felt to be the loss of his whole nation. His administrative abilities as governor, his fervent and active spirit in every good work, his great share in the emancipation of the serfs, and his counsels as senator, made him one of those noble men whom nations will not forget.

Being strongly urged to visit, and comfort his family after his departure, I arrived at Moscow in July, 1866, and enjoyed the intercourse during my stay with Madame Mouravieff, the Princess Schahoffskoy, the General's sister, and the other ladies of the family, one a maid of honour to the Empress. I learned greatly to esteem the admirable qualities of noble Russian ladies, and their extensive knowledge of languages.

On my leaving Moscow, I was requested to accept, as a memento of my visit, the General's Greek Testament, printed at Mount Athos in Greece, and containing the following words :—

To Rev. Dr. Bayley.

" Keep this Holy text, not only for my sake, but for that of the two beloved and enlightened spirits—your friends in the Lord, to whom, both, it successively belonged, the father and son Mouravieff, who from their heavenly home bless you,

I am sure, for the consolation you have afforded to their lonely friends remaining yet on earth."

All yours in the Lord,
CLEOPATRA PRINCESS SCHAHOFFSKOY.
Moscow, 20th July, 1866.

The only son of General Alexander, John Mouravieff, was unwell when his father died, but seemed to recover; in twelve months after, however, to a day, at 33 years of age, having been only seven days ill, he rejoined his parent whom he dearly loved, and of whom he was worthy, delighting in the same glorious views, and truly heavenly in his life and temper.

XXIV.

CARL DELÉEN,

And the New Church in Sweden.

SWEDENBORG having written his works, especially his theological works, in the Latin language, so that the learned men of all civilized lands would be equally able to read them, and to translate them into the languages of their several nations for the common people, his own country Sweden had no advantage over others in this respect.

Dr. Beyer, the compiler of the first Index in Latin to Swedenborg's works, was Greek professor at Stockholm. Dr. Knös was dean of Swedenborg's father's Cathedral, and Dr. Rosen was an eminent divine; and many other learned clergymen received the doctrines of the New Church by reading Swedenborg's writings in the original; but they did nothing to place the works in the hands of the general population.

Indeed, until the New Age commenced, the idea that every man is a man, and ought to know the truth, was ignored; and the general body of the people were regarded as having little concern with anything but to believe as they were told, and do as they were bid.

In the early part of this century however a noble, soul in the capital of Sweden, CARL DELEEN, read and received the truth. His descendants still kept a book-shop in Stockholm when I was last there.

Carl Deléen saw that the teachings of the truths of the New Jerusalem would be a blessing for all; and he would endeavour that Swedes who were able to read should have the opportunity of learning them.

He was a printer as well as bookseller, and he set to work, with the Latin volume before him, setting the types with his own hands; and this he continued until he had got through his self-imposed task of printing and publishing the greater part of some THIRTY VOLUMES in Swedish. Only think of this heroic work.

He translated, bought paper, printed, advertized and brought the Writings out—thus completing the whole business by himself. He laboured on with few to cheer or encourage him, but believing he was working for the Lord he went on from year to year, making the sacrifice with his whole heart and soul.

His translations continued to be read and to be the great means of diffusing the truth in Sweden, until in 1860, the feeling rose that their style was somewhat old-fashioned and unattractive to modern literary Swedes, and a Society headed by Dr. Seeven at Christianstad was formed to revise and modernize the works, which was encouraged and assisted from England. This work was continued until the lamented death of Dr. Seeven. Several volumes had however been revised and re-published, and when I was at Skara I had the pleasure of seeing the Arcana, vol. 3, in its improved form. The English Swedenborg Society gave I think £15 for each new volume.

The Swedish National Church was Lutheran and did not until 1863 permit separate congregations for worship to be formed, but New Churchmen within its pale had influence enough to cause the public services to be modified in 1809. The Athanasian Creed was removed, and the sentence in the so-called Apostle's Creed " I believe in the resurrection of the body," was changed to " I believe in the resurrection of the dead." The catechism also and book of examination for young clergymen were revised. Ordinarily the clergy had a moderate amount of freedom, but sometimes bitter sectarian souls would spring up and harass those who received the spiritual views of the New Jerusalem.

Dean Knös, Johansen and Tybeck, three able clergymen, wrote much to set forth New Church truth, especially the latter.

Twenty-five different works were published by Tybeck. He seems to have been the Clowes of Sweden. Like Clowes he was summoned before his bishop to answer for his unorthodox sentiments. He was treated more harshly than Clowes, and silenced for a time. But the public papers were so loud in his defence that his enemies were ashamed, and he resumed his duties in peace and passed to his heavenly home in 1837 at the advanced age, like Mr. Clowes, of 86 years.

The last of his works was entitled, "What thoughts does Christian Love inspire with regard to the New Jerusalem ?"

Dr. Kahl, Dean of Lund, formerly Professor of Arabic, though next under the Archbishop of Sweden, for Lund, there, answers to Canterbury in this country, has never, I believe, been much annoyed, though an avowed New Churchman for 60 years.

He has been and is universally respected, and is now upwards of 90 years of age.

Dr. Kahl was present with us in 1857 along with M. Leboys des Guays, M. Harlé from France, and Rev. Mr. Field from America, at the Centenary of the Great Judgment in 1757. All of us felt honored and delighted with the visit of these brethren from abroad. I was President of Conference that year, as of that of the Centenary last year, and saw much of Dr. Kahl.

I have visited Dr. Kahl three times at his home, and always was impressed with the great spirituality of his character, and his broad Christian love.

On my last visit, after giving me a hearty welcome he took up a pamphlet from his table and said with lively pleasure, "See here, I received this yesterday from a town in the centre of Sweden, Wexio, I believe. It is your sermon on the RIBBAND OF BLUE, translated into Swedish. I don't know who sent it."

Whether the clergy who now receive the doctrines are as numerous in proportion as they have been formerly I have no means of ascertaining. Dr. Kahl thought the tendency was rather to sensuality and a neglect of divine things. It was, he feared, the Old Church despising its own absurdities, and not rising to the spirit and life of what is higher and better.

Still, although, like greater part of Europe, Swedes may have to pass through the wilderness of infidelity, yet, eventually, the remnant of good implanted by the Lord, will bring them to yearn after better and holier states of life, and preparation for an everlasting kingdom.

Besides the clergy, to whom we have referred, there have been in Sweden, laymen eminent, and distinguished for excellences of every kind. Count Hopken, the prime minister of Sweden, was a great friend of Swedenborg, and a thorough receiver of his doctrines. Geijer, the national historian, was another.

The first movers for the abolition of the slave trade and slavery, were Wadstrom and Nordenskiold, who formed a small society of the affectionate receivers of the Writings of Swedenborg, at Nordkoping, in Sweden, in the year 1772. In consequence of the favourable account of the African nation, given in the works of that eminent author, the New Churchmen began to think much respecting them. The more this subject came to be considered, the more those gentlemen were convinced that the coasts of Africa could never be peopled by a body of true and faithful Christians unless the Slave Trade, so firmly rooted at that time, and the only object of commerce in those fertile regions, could be abolished.

They formed an Anti-Slave-Trade Society, founded as a result of the teachings of Swedenborg in 1779; and thus began the earliest movement in that great cause, which has continued to spread and intensify until it has overthrown not only the slave trade, but slavery itself among Protestant and many Roman Catholic nations, and made its extinction all over the world certain, at no distant period. It is gratifying to trace this glorious result, not only to the working of the Holy Spirit of our Lord in MAKING ALL THINGS NEW, but also to the instrumentality of those Writings, by which spiritual truth externally was rationally restored to the world. Granville Sharp commenced his labours in 1765, to make it to be declared unlawful to have a slave in England, and Lord Chief Justice Mansfield decided to that effect, in 1777 ; but no society was formed in England for the abolition of the slave trade until 1787, ten years after.

Dr. Kahl, writing in 1862 says : " We find a number of persons of all classes of the people, peasants, tradesmen, noblemen, even princes and kings, who have read and admired Swedenborg's theological works. It is known that Charles 13th as Duke of Ostergöthland was a member of the Philosophical Society whose principal purpose was to publish these precious writings. We know also that Charles 14th, the kings John and Oscar took under their protection Geijer, Landblod, and G. Knös, when some of their writings composed in the spirit of the New Church, had brought upon these distinguished men either the accusation or the suspicion on the part of some ultra orthodox bishops and clergymen of entertaining heteredox doctrines.

"A milder genius has from day to day begun to prevail in our National Church. Even the orthodox so zealous before have been more favourably affected towards the New Jerusalem and its heavenly doctrine, or as our Thorild names it, The Third Testament—that of open truth. They now regard the friends of Swedenborg rather as allies than as antagonists, and suffer them uncensured and unreproached to write and preach according to their conscience. They perceive more and more that no other means of interpretation, but Swedenborg's doctrine of Correspondences is sufficient to explain the Bible, and its spiritual and celestial sense ; and to refute the speculative and hypercritical arguments of pseudo-rationalism which aims at the full denial of the inspiration of the Holy Scriptures and the Divinity of Christ.

"For this alteration in theological sentiment, our thanks are due to the Divine Providence. It is no doubt a very good omen. It proves that a new Religious Age is about to begin even in Sweden, and that our clergy in general are nowadays less fearful of admitting the understanding in any theological subject, than they were in Swedenborg's time."

In 1875, the Rev. Aug. Boyesen, who for several years had been endeavouring to sustain and spread the New Church in Copenhagen with zeal and moderate success, paid a visit to Stockholm, and finding a warm reception, and considerable receptivity, he was induced to go again and again, and in 1877 to settle at Stockholm as New Church Pastor there.

There is a hall used for worship, preaching and lecturing, and sometimes from 3 to 400 it is said attend, and Mr. Boyesen lectures with much acceptance in various parts of Sweden.

The Swedes are naturally a kindly, courteous, good-natured people, and this is the good ground in which to receive the seeds of truth. Having so long been confined to one church and that a church teaching salvation by faith alone, they will not at first be very quick for the reception of spiritual truths, but the Lord has no doubt a remnant there, and "They shall trust in the name of the Lord. The remnant of Israel shall not do iniquity, nor speak lies; neither shall a deceitful tongue be found in their mouth: for they shall feed and lie down, and none shall make them afraid." (Zeph. iii. 13.)

The generous and hospitable character of the Swedes I experienced on my visit to their country in 1866, and on every subsequent journey I made there.

When I landed from lake Venner, at Linkoping on my way to Skara, where Swedenborg's father was bishop, I found at the hotel a company of gentlemen at a festal dinner. They no sooner learned that a stranger, an Englishman, had arrived, than they sent a message requesting my company at their dinner; and when I begged to be excused, desiring quiet after a long day's travel, after dinner a deputation came to request my company for the evening. The next day some of them came to offer all kinds of hospitality and attention. At Upsala, at the castle of Tycho Brahe, on the Malar, in Dalecarlia, I have always met the same friendly and amiable spirit, and therefore I am happy to conclude there will be a receptive spirit for the truth in Sweden.

Having been upwards of seven years in Stockholm, Pastor Boyesen is grateful for the success accomplished, and hopeful for the future, but he considers that it would be a great step in advance if they could have an ecclesiastical structure of their own. They would then be recognised by the state, and many social privileges as to confirmation and marriage would be secured.

The Swedish friends appeal for aid to England and America, from both of which annual assistance has been constantly afforded.

We hope they will proceed prudently in their selection of a site; do what USE really requires, and nothing else; making their zeal visible by generous self-help, so as to encourage friends in other parts of the world to aid those who are making some sacrifice themselves, and all will be well.

It is important that many inadvisable schemes suggested by fanciful persons in days gone by are no more heard of now. To give an extravagant price for a site of a church, on the ground where Swedenborg's house stood, which is in a neighbourhood much altered in its character from what it was in his days; or to preserve his old summer-house as a memorial, and other unwise propositions, are now happily swept away. To promote real use, which is what our friends now wish, and what Swedenborg himself would have approved, is a worthy object, and one which we hope ere long will be accomplished, placing Swedenborg's own nation visibly in the kingdom the God of heaven is now setting up, and which will last for ever. (Dan. ii. 44.)

XXV.

DR. IMMANUEL TAFEL AND
GUSTAV WERNER.

The New Church in Germany and Switzerland.

THE earliest Germans that we know to have become interested in the spiritual experiences of Swedenborg were Heinric Jung Stilling, counsellor of the Grand Duke of Baden, and Oettinger of Murrhard; the latter an inhabitant of the kingdom of Wurtemburg, which also gave to the New Church, Dr. Immanuel Tafel, the uncle of the present Dr. Rudolf S. Tafel, of Camden Road, London.

Dr. Oettinger was really a contemporary of Swedenborg, and received several letters from him.

Both these learned and excellent men fully received the testimony of Swedenborg as to the FACTS OF HIS SEERSHIP, and his relations of what he saw and heard in his intercourse with the inner and eternal world; but they do not seem to have made much progress in the study of the Arcana, and the perception of the SPIRITUAL SENSE OF THE WORD, or the states and progress of the REGE-

NERATE LIFE. Oettinger wrote a book called—
EARTHLY AND HEAVENLY PHILOSOPHY OF SWE-
DENBORG AND OTHERS: and Stilling published
a work in two volumes entitled SPIRITUAL SCENES
IN THE WORLD OF SPIRITS.

The chief use of these distinguished and early
students, was to hand on the knowledge of the
truth they were able to receive, and awaken others.

We have referred to Stilling as the one whose
commendation of Swedenborg induced Oberlin
to read and receive the new information concerning Heaven, and now we have to mention
that in Dr. Immanuel Tafel, whose piety was much
strengthened and directed by reading Stilling, a
much more potent and diligent worker in the
Lord's vineyard was awakened in Germany; one
of those brave and holy souls, true apostolic men,
who affect a nation, or an age.

Having had much to do with Dr. Tafel during
his life, having visited him in the noble old ducal
castle, now used as the library of the University
under his charge, overlooking the plain of the
Neckar, and enjoyed his hospitality in his home,
and then with dear Mr. Watson being charged
to arrange his affairs, dispose of his immense
accumulation of books, and comfort his family
at his death—I necessarily became intimately
aware of his labours and his worth.

From his early youth upwards Dr. Tafel's life
was one the young may profitably follow, and the
mature may esteem and admire, as that of a diligent and faithful servant of the Lord Jesus Christ,
whom Germany has yet to receive as King of
kings, and Lord of lords. By Him their
intellectual strength would then be made gentle
by the softness of love, which forms the yoke

that is easy, the burden that is light, and gives to its possessor REST unto his soul.

Immanuel Tafel was born February 17, 1796, at Sulsbach on the Kocher; he was therefore at his decease sixty-seven years of age. He was the son and grandson of ministers of the Lutheran Church. His father was Christian Frederick Tafel, deacon of Baknang, where he died in 1814; his mother was a daughter also of a Lutheran minister—John Emmanuel Horn, of Tham—a pious, loving partner of her husband, and an inestimable blessing to her children. Both parents strove that their children, four brothers, should have the best information which their limited means afforded. The mother especially, as her son gratefully testifies, made every possible sacrifice in their family arrangements for this desirable end. Immanuel was the eldest son; and his parents arranged for the commencement of his education at Stuttgart, as affording advantages which he could by no means obtain in the small town which constituted the pastoral charge of his father.

Happily at Stuttgart there resided a second-cousin on his mother's side, a mechanical instrument maker, named Baumann, a man of great talent and modesty, who not only received Immanuel but also his three brothers into his house, and watched over their education with the same mild and pious spirit which had blessed them in their paternal home. Mr. Baumann used to read in the evening to his family, and very often from the works of Stilling; and young Tafel became so much interested that he soon began to read these works for himself, and they awakened and strengthened in him, while only a boy, an interest in eternal things. He was confirmed in 1809; and although on his showing considerable talent for engraving, and for scientific study, his relative Baumann wished his father (who intended him for the church) to let him follow a more worldly career—and he did work in his employment for a year—yet an inclination the most decided still determined him to continue a classical and theological career. Stilling, whom he chiefly read, occupied, as many of our readers will know, a sort of advanced position in the Old Church towards the New. Though so young, now fifteen, he was pious and careful to assist his parents, and to take care of his brothers, which we learn from a letter he wrote them at this time, dated December 2nd, 1811:—

"I can write you nothing better, dear brothers, than to pray you to lay the following things to heart; 1st, Give no occasion for anything unpleasant to happen in the house; 2nd, Be ready to render service to each person in the house, of course with difference as to position; never intruding your services, which also might be injurious to yourselves and others; when your uncle or aunt refuses anything, be sure to be obedient; 3rd, Always live in peace with one another, and *never forget your prayers;* 4th, Keep everything in order, do everything at its proper time, and when you have something to do to which you are not accustomed, pay great attention. Look well to your clothes, and remember that your parents are not rich. These are important points, and I hope you will follow them out."

How well would it be if every boy at fifteen was qualified and thoughtful enough to write such a letter! When he was seventeen years of age he first learnt something of the writings of Swedenborg. He had known previously what Stilling said of him, partly favourable, partly unfavourable. Shortly however he met with " The Universal Theology," at the house of George Frederick Hoffacker, of Nierklingen; and he was struck wtth the teaching concerning the Divine Trinity, which appeared to him scriptural, clear, and fully proved. He plainly saw that God was NOT in three persons, but in one only, yet in this one there was a threefold distinction, like that of the soul, the body, and the influence proceeding from both together. The Godhead from eternity he saw was the Father; the Divine Humanity the Son; and the Holy Spirit the overflowing power going forth from both, and operating in angelic human hearts and minds. He desired to read this book through; but when he came to the chapter entitled " The belief that the Passion of the Cross is Redemption itself is a fundamental error," &c., his prejudices were offended. He knew Stilling did not teach this. He consulted his father, whose residence was oniy five miles away, and his father thought Swedenborg in this was wrong. "However," he thought again, " Can God, who is love itself, and who has placed this warm love of truth within the breast, have done so without having determined to satisfy it? Has He not promised help to those who earnestly seek the truth? Has He not said, 'Ask, and it shall be given you; seek, and ye shall find; knock, and it shall be opened unto you?'" He prayed earnestly to the Lord that He would enlighten him, and show him what was truth. Then there came into his mind a strong desire to read more of Swedenborg. He examined the doctrine of Redemption, and closely compared it with the Holy Scripture, and convinced himself that it was thoroughly supported by the Word of Truth, and that he and others had been in great error. He was equally satisfied of the truth of the teaching of Swedenborg respecting Justification, and he saw the sublime lesson that no man had any merit in the sight of God, yet he was not prepared for Heaven by FAITH ONLY, but by willing and doing as well as by believing; and that THE CLAIMS ON THE PART OF MAN OF THE MERITS OF CHRIST WAS AN EXPRESSION ENTIRELY WITHOUT SENSE; that the forgiveness of sins took place only as we in the future course of life abstained from evil in the sight of the Lord. For the doctrine that man cannot keep the commandments of God, and that it is not necessary for salvation to do so, he conceived a great aversion.

On the other hand, the more he read the more the personal characteristics of Swedenborg gained upon him. He could not but admire his great modesty, his calm clearness, and the gentle feeling that filled all he said; and his heart was won.

To some near and dear friends, however, he communicated his new views, especially on the Lord and the Divine Trinity, and explained and sustained them with great clearness and power, considering his youthfulness. At this time also he writes—

"I had many inner experiences which I shall never forget. Once when I was walking in the forest between Merklingen and Flacht, while I was deeply pondering on eternal truths, all around me seemed as if it were glorified, and I was as if Heaven were opened to me. The same thing happened again one morning in Merklingen itself. I was contemplating the spiritual sense of Scripture, and especially the inner meaning of certain passages, and I believe I felt how this sense united us to Heaven and placed us in the very presence of the Lord."

In June, 1814 his worthy father died, and this circumstance led him to change his situation at Merklingen for one near to his mother, that he might live with her and assist her. He was enabled also to take one of his brothers, Guttlob, as assistant to himself; and by the kindness of a friend in Sconberg, to obtain a situation for another brother. He continued to fulfil the duties of his situation, and to rise in the confidence and esteem of all connected with him up to his twenty-first year, when he arranged to go to Tübingen with his mother and brothers, and to work out in full his University course. This he accomplished with great success, having obtained the highest testimonies from all the professors, and during the same time he had greatly extended his acquaintance with Swedenborg, and had enjoyed the happiness of introducing the doctrines of the New Church to several most valuable and most highly esteemed individuals.

He preached with great acceptance on a variety of occasions, and already two ministers had applied for him to become their assistant as soon as he was entirely at liberty.

It is remarkable that he had not yet read either the Arcana Cœlestia or the Apocalypsis Revelata. These works were in the Royal library, most likely as presents from Swedenborg himself;

and now, his University course being fully completed, young Tafel commenced to read them, and he says—

"So soon as I had read the first chapter of the Arcana Cœlestia, the scales completely fell from my eyes. I saw clearly that Swedenborg could never from his own ability have originated so connected, so wonderful, so spiritual, so completely carried out a sense as that here attributed to the Holy Scriptures. The unsealing of the Word appeared to me an ever-increasing miracle, not certainly a miracle to the senses, but to the reason, of man." A similar experience and conviction was related to me, by one of the greatest writers on Natural History of the present day. Young Tafel now felt an inward freedom to speak to others respecting Swedenborg, upon proper occasions, aud a strength which he felt would fit him to become a faithful soldier of the Lord.

Once when he was at an evening party with a great number of students from North Germany and Switzerland, Krummacher, afterwards so celebrated as an author, called out to him—"Eh! Tafel, are not you a Swedenborgian?" He felt at first inclined to say he was neither *ian* nor *ist* of any kind, but only wished to be a true Christian. However he thought that would look like being ashamed of truths he felt were divine, so he replied: "Yes, I am; I have examined the Scriptures, and by the closest logic of a true interpretation the doctrines he teaches are fully proved." He had been known at the University as the "Pious Tafel." There were four Tafels there at the same time, each had his peculiar name, and Immanuel was the "pious." It was a name not unmerited, as a glance we will now give at his private journal will abundantly evince. He was now twenty-three. The following are the entries which we translate from his private journal, beginning with Feb. 16, 1819, that our readers may have the character of this most excellent man fully before them :—

"Ah ! Lord, give me Thyself, and I ask no more either of heaven or earth. Merciful Lord Jesus Christ, lead me ever more and more in thine own way. Impart to me the gift of Thy Holy Spirit. Make me to become a useful instrument in Thy hands. Forward my studies, and so direct them that I may never lose sight of Thee and Thy kingdom as the end of all my efforts. The more I am myself united to Thee, the more can I lead others into this blessed union. O Lord, be ever near to me. Help me rightly to know the secret inclinations of my corrupt heart; and through Thy power ever to walk in Thy goodness, for without Thee I can do nothing. Give me ever a real horror of sin, and a real pleasure in all that is good. Lead, O Lord, all our family to Thee as the Fountain of Life, and let their hearts have no rest until they find it in Thee. O Lord there are a thousand means in Thy hands to touch the hearts of our free spirits and dispose them to faith. O withhold not these from my brothers, also from my friends, relatives and acquaintances, all of whom I desire, O Lord, to include in this my prayer.

" 16 Feb., 1819.—Draw us all evermore to Thee, and fill us evermore with Thy spirit of wisdom and love. Help also our oppressed fatherland, and the whole world. Oh ! let Thy kingdom come !

"17th Feb.—To-day is MY BIRTHDAY, and I wish to renew all my good purposes in Thy sight. But Lord, Thou knowest our weaknesses, do Thou give me strength. Once more will I give myself to Thee. Oh impress upon me the determination to walk holily in Thy presence. O beloved Saviour fill me with Thy power, that I may win others to Thee. Afford me, O Lord, that love of which I am so needy. Grant me also courage that I may not sink. Regulate also my outward lot, according to Thy good pleasure, and grant that it may ever lead me to Thee.

"18th Feb.—O Lord Jesus Christ, grant that my yesterday's resolutions may spread throughout my life. Impress them upon my heart and enable me every moment to see what is Thy gracious will. Yesterday, O Lord, I was not entirely in Thy presence; but, O Lord, to-day be the light unto my feet and my salvation.

"19th Feb., half-past five in the morning.— O Lord, how far is my heart from Thee? O Lord, what is the cause that so often not Thy will but mine comes ever forward?—that Thy voice is not followed, but I take counsel of flesh and blood? What a phlegmatic being I am, especially when Thy commandments require obedience. Too much am I swayed by humour, by circumstances, by times. Strengthen me and give me courage, O Lord. Let my pleasure be ever more and more in Thee, and give, Lord, full success in my studies.

"20th Feb.—O, Heavenly Father, again yesterday I continued not in Thy presence. Have patience with Thy disobedient child. Draw me mightily to Thee, for in Thee alone I find that rest which the world cannot give. I fell into an outburst of ill-feeling with my brother, and gave way to external passion. Oh, how can such failings be well pleasing in Thy sight! O, lead me back to Thee and Thy divine order. Give me, O Lord, a deeper love of Thee, and lead me again to Thy commandments, and regulate all my inclinations. If it is Thy will, grant me my wish of to-day, and let me have a dwelling in the town. Help me in my studies. Be with me, my kinsmen, my acquaintances, my fatherland, and the whole human race.

"21st Feb.—O Lord, my heart is often far from Thee, yet raise me to Thyself. Return, O dear Lord Jesus, to me, and drive out every inclination which is opposed to Thee. Grant me love and delight in my duty. Give me, O gracious Father, that wisdom which I so much lack. Give me an insight into Thy Holy Word and a true love for it. Give me a sound body, that I may have in it a healthy soul. O God, I am guilty in Thy sight of extravagance. I have spent too much. How much better it would have been if I had spent the same sum upon my mental improvement, or for the Missionary or Bible Society, or any other benevolent work! Forgive me, O Lord, for my unrighteous stewardship.

"22nd Feb., quarter to five, morning.—O Lord! I mourn once more over yesterday. My tongue is not yet well ordered in Thy sight. The impure scenes around me were allowed to rise up in my mind, and I was too little resolved to defend Thine honour where it was necessary. In the Church, too, I allowed my thoughts to wander, and I was not true to my promise to meet my friend in time. Alas! what will become of me? But Lord, have patience with Thy disobedient child. Fill me with Thy Spirit of love and faith. Help me by Thy goodness to withstand what is wicked. Help me especially to withstand that wicked one.

"23rd Feb.—Lord God, while I thank Thee for the rest Thou hast given me this night to enjoy, I beseech Thee also to forgive me for my many sins of yesterday. Ungovernable, I am prone to self. I am careless in my college duties. O help me to draw near to Thee. Let me not lie down in my sinfulness. Grant me power to resist evil and do good. Help also my brothers, Lord. Give them a direction to what is good, and my friends, and my kinsmen, and my fatherland, and the human race. And if, Lord, it is agreeable to Thy will, give our cloister a better government—give us our freedom. Thou willest that we should serve Thee from freedom, not from constraint. Unite also our college government and that of the King, to see that true goodness can only be attained upon the ground of freedom. I give Thee thanks, O Lord, for the light Thou gavest me yesterday in my studies, in which I sought the law by which the highest conceptions are attained. Bring me still further in my studies. Without especial hindrance I will refrain from supper and go early to bed, that I may rise at least at three.

"24th Feb.—I thank Thee for this night's rest. Last evening, O Lord, I was not as I ought to be. I was ill-tempered. O help me Lord yet to find the right way. The path is so narrow and the door so strait that leads to life, yet give me power to stand on the former and to enter the latter. I give Thee thanks, O Lord, for the gift of light over my studies with which Thou hast still blessed me.

"25th Feb., half- past three, morning.—I thank Thee, O Lord, for my preservation during the night and the day that are passed. Oh, make me freer from self. Enable me to be constantly good in Thy sight. Lead my brothers back into Thine own way. Give them no peace until they are restored. Be with my friends, acquaintances, and my family, my fatherland, and the whole world. O Lord, grant me wisdom, active love, and peace."

The report had spread that Dr Tafel was a Swedenborgian. His position became then (1821) the subject of discussion both publicly and privately. Some maintained he could hold office in the Lutheran Church, some that he could not. There were three clergymen who offered to take him as vicar (curate) if he signed the regular forms. There were eight clergymen known to him who were receivers of the writings and preached the doctrines. He gave his own views respecting his position in relation to the Church in a letter which we translate:—

"As soon as I came here I found a permission from the Government giving me the year I sought to travel, and requiring me on my return to appear for my examination preparatory to taking holy orders, when it would be seen whether my views are indeed an obstacle to my entering the Church of my country. At present it is required that a candidate should sign the articles of religion as contained in the authorised doctrinal works (chiefly the Augsburg Confession of Faith drawn up by Melancthon), and if this is to be insisted upon unconditionally I can never enter the ministry, for I am satisfied that these books have falsified the Word, and undermined all true religion. I am a Protestant, and I protest against every kind of Pope, and all human interference in matters of faith; and I will not sear my conscience for gain of any kind. I can labour without any church office, the Lord can make me useful without any human appointment, and I can make my necessities very small. People shall never say that my proceedings are matter of reproach. I know whom I serve, and He will never leave me. The New Church needs for her acknowledgment nothing underhand—no subterfuge, but real truth and uprightness. When our requirements are few in eating, drinking, and clothes, and when we spend anything we have superfluous to further the Lord's divine will, what a blessed reward we have! As my prospect of entering the Church is so slight, I am not so anxious about my journey immediately; and I wish to give myself to a thorough study of religious history. However, I will not go my own way, but look to the Lord for direction. He shall dispose of me, and my only care shall be to make myself as far as possible a fitting instrument in His hands to forward His kingdom."

Ultimately it ended in Dr. Tafel refusing to sign, and he was not allowed to enter the Church without. He proceeded with his work of publishing, and first he issued the "Doctrine of the Lord."

In each successive issue for some time Dr. Tafel was attacked in the newspapers and reviews, and in various ways, but he well maintained his ground, and was the means of introducing the truth to a considerable number of receivers ; and his great learning was generally acknowledged. His position too was improved by an offer from the Government of the office of Librarian of the University, but accompanied by the condition, that while he held that appointment he must cease directly or indirectly to publish Swedenborg's or other similar works. This offer was made September 4th, 1825, and the appointment at first was for a given time—a year only. At the end of the year it was confirmed, but still with the condition affixed. It was hard for Dr. Tafel to brook this condition ; but it was smoothed by the assurance that the Government by no means wished to interfere with his personal convictions, and besides, he must remember that Rome was not built in a day. He accepted the appointment. This condition remained until the 25th March, 1829. Dr. Tafel had become so uneasy under it, that he had petitioned the King, for conscience sake, and stated that if the condition of not publishing the works of Swedenborg were persisted in, he must resign, as he felt it was a duty the Lord required of him. In reply, he had the happiness of receiving a renewal of the appointment without any conditions. The obstacle had continued THREE YEARS AND A-HALF.

From that time on he continued indefatigably to labour, republishing the Latin works, and thus reducing their price from £52 for a copy of the Arcana to about £5, and others in proportion, and at the same time translating into German every New Church work he thought calculated to benefit the Church in his country—the Catechism, the Liturgy, tracts, &c. The catalogue of publications which he has thus brought out included SEVENTY-FOUR distinct works; many of them, it is true, tracts, but many containing several volumes each. It is indeed a wonderful monument of the labour of one man, patiently continuing for forty years—little praised, often assailed—using all his available means to forward the Lord's kingdom for conscience sake.

Dr. Tafel married, August 22, 1832, a lady the daughter of Herr Müllensiefen, one of the earliest receivers of the principles of the New Church in Germany. Herr Müllensiefen was a Prussian, of Westphalia, and heartily embraced the doctrines in 1782. Dr. Tafel's marriage at my first visit had been a happy one, and blessed with nine children, five daughters and four sons. The youngest was a young lady of thirteen, the next older a youth of sixteen still at school. Two sons were in America.

The length of this sketch will preclude our dwelling upon the incidents connected with his several publications, and the circumstances of his visits to us in 1851, and also his visits to Switzerland for the encouragement of the friends of the New Church in that country. He had a quarterly meeting of the brethren in Stuttgart, which he called a Conference, and at which I have been present, when about 100 attended.

We will conclude this article by the description from Fraulein Cönring, a German lady, (but for several years resident in Sweden, on a visit to Switzerland and to him,) of the whole period of his leaving home to his decease, drawn up at our request, and only adapted by us to English readers. This deeply interesting document, we are assured, will be read with eagerness by all our friends, as the last sketch of one whom we have long known, loved, respected and revered; one of the Church's best members on earth, and one best prepared to be a pillar of the New Jerusalem in Heaven.

THE LAST DAYS OF DR. TAFEL, BY FRAULEIN CÖNRING:

I had been kindly invited to the assembly at Zurich, and it had been arranged that I should join Dr. Tafel there, and visit with him the members of the New Church in Switzerland. I was however agreeably surprised to meet him at the station at Stuttgart, and we were then enabled to travel together to Friedrichshafen. This was on the 14th August. On the steamer we had a long conversation about religion, and the blessings of the doctrines of the New Church, which, he said, ought to be accepted by every reasonable and reflecting person.

On this and on the following day, though poorly, he was cheerful. As we dined, looking at the strangers around us, he observed in English, "The Church of the Lord is an invisible one. He only knows who are His." Another time he said, "The uniform is no matter; many a person in the Old Church may be BETTER THAN I AM. Neither is the quantity of work we do the thing we have to care for; the one needful thing is to abstain every day from all that is wrong, and thus purify ourselves. So even our Divine Saviour purified the human He derived from His mother."

He returned several times to the subject of his projects concerning the New Church in Germany, the Printing Society, &c.; yet leaving the whole with entire confidence to the Lord. We reached

Ragatz on Saturday the 15th, about three in the afternoon. On Sunday morning, before he was obliged to seek his bed, he remarked, " I don't say with Paul, I have a desire to depart and be with Christ." I replied, " Why not ? " He then said, " In early life I had always an ARDENT DESIRE TO DIE, and thus to leave this world of darkness and of sin ; but it is so no more. Eternity is sure to come ; but while we live here we can be active to spread divine truth, and be useful to the kingdom of the Lord ; and I have still much that ought to be done." Then he spoke about the Concordance of the Spiritual Sense of the Bible, at which work he particularly wanted assistance. He was compelled to retire early in the day to bed, and a physician was sent for. Though the symptoms appeared grave, the physician declared there was no danger. The same assurance was strangely enough repeated every day, though violent pains, and a total absence of appetite, seemed to indicate inflammation of the bowels. After his sudden death, the medical man stated that such was the fact.

Though he suffered much, and was hardly one moment free from pain, he NEVER UTTERED A MURMUR, but showed the most pious and enduring patience—that of a true Christian. Until the last night, his thoughts were perfectly clear, yet he spoke but little, from weakness. Still his soul was evidently occupied by the highest objects, and lifted up in prayer to the Lord. He did not think death so near, neither did we. He hoped to recover. He wished to go on and meet his dear friends at Zurich.

Even in the delirium, which took place the last night, there was no horror at all ; on the contrary, even the vague utterances of his imagination only manifested a good and holy soul, in which no room was left for anything evil. At the last there was no visible combat, no agony; only twice in the last night did he lift his hands to be raised. About nine o'clock in the morning he became extremely pale, his hands and feet became cold, and about an hour afterwards his eyes shone for a moment with inexpressible splendour; then the eyelids sank half down, and without a sigh or a movement he passed away. His soul had ceased to communicate with his body.

This was August the 29th, at about ten in the morning. Two days after and the body—the organ of his dear and active soul—was interred in the Roman Catholic burial-ground at Ragatz, near the tomb of Schelling.

His brother, and son Theodore, and many New Church friends, who had hastened thither hoping to find the dear one still alive, only arrived in time to take part in the funeral, at which also were present a great number of the inhabitants of Ragatz, as well as strangers. I look back at the last days of our lamented friend, and brother in the Lord, with unmingled veneration, and am grateful that I had such an opportunity of intercourse with one of the Lord's servants—one of the truest and the best.

On learning the news of the departure of Dr. Tafel, and being aware from our knowledge of his life's long devotion to the re-publication of the Works in Latin, necessary to make them accessible to students, that no time had been left him to make even a modest provision for his widow and family, (before his time a copy of the Original Arcana required £50 for its purchase,

Dr. Tafel and Gustav Werner. 239

he had also his German Translations and numerous defensive works,) the friends of the Swedenborg Society felt a vivid desire to render help where it was so much needed and so well deserved.

They requested therefore the treasurer Mr. Watson, and myself, as known to the family, to go with an address of condolence, and to advise and aid on the part of the Society whatever kind feeling and wise discretion might suggest.

We left London in September, 1863, and passed rapidly through France and Switzerland, going from Zurich over Lake Constance to Friedrickshafen, to Stuttgart, and so to Tubingen, which is situated on the river Neckar, about twenty miles from Stuttgart, the capital of the kingdom of Wurtemburg. We can reach Tubingen now, however, by rail. As we approached the fine old castle, on the heights overlooking the beautiful valley and the town where Professor Tafel had so many years lived and worked for the New Church, our hearts were deeply moved. We knew his widow and family were now in mourning and perplexity. As I was known to them, the introduction was soon over, and a conversation explaining their sorrows preceded on the one side, the kindest consolations from the New Church in England being offered on the other; the sympathies of the Church being gratefully accepted and acknowledged. The difficulties of Madame Tafel's position were freely laid before us, and our best advice and assistance requested.

There were five daughters at home, and one son still at school Dr. Tafel's entire efforts had been given to the New Church for forty years, and the results were (besides the number of persons to whom his labours and writings had imparted the truth) thousands of books, which remained on hand from the editions he had printed, and which could not be sold in any way to relieve sensibly their necessities. The family were compelled also to remove to modest apartments, instead of their now spacious dwelling, so that it would be totally impossible to store the mass of books. We desired to see them, and were shown FIVE ROOMS FILLED, and subsequently an EIGHT-STALLED STABLE ALSO CROWDED WITH BALES OF VOLUMES AND SHEETS. The great bulk was of Latin works, the new editions of all Swedenborg's publications, of which Dr. Tafel had generally published 1,000 of each volume, and sold probably about 100. He felt sure they would have value some day; and, though the burden was great, in the meantime, he yet worked bravely on.

There were also the German works, but of these a much larger number had been sold, as they were published, and there was a greater likelihood also of a sale in a reasonable time for what remained. Besides Dr. Tafel had only translated four volumes of the Arcana, and not all of the other printed works of Swedenborg. The number of German books on hand was comparatively manageable.

We were at first astonished at the magnitude of the affair with which we had to deal. We went to our hotel, and for a time felt the difficulty so great, that all we could resolve to do was, on the next and following days, to apply ourselves with the assistance of the family to take account of what there was, and to continue until we could make an inventory. This we did, and day after day toiled at it until a complete account could be made out and sent to London. The result was that we felt we might assure the family that the Church in England and America would give £500 certainly, perhaps more, but not less, and take and manage all the books.

This proposition was evidently a flash of sunshine in the gloom. In carrying it out we offered half the Latin Works to our American friends, and invited them to raise and present to Madame Tafel and the family half the proposed amount. This was most liberally done, so that more than THREE TIMES what had been promised was given. These efforts of the Church, as I have said, were gladly and gratefully accepted by Madame Tafel and her family; and ere we left for Stuttgart we took occasion to present in a kind and solemn manner the address of condolence from the New Church in England, which was printed in the October number of the Intellectual Repository.

Madame Tafel replied to the address with deep emotion, and acknowledged the kindness which had dictated all that had been done, in terms of the most touching character, assuring the deputation that the fraternal regards and attention of the New Church in this trying period of her hour of mourning would ever be remembered with esteem and affection.

We took our leave grateful that the Lord had enabled us to be of use in a cause so really deserving of our best help, and trusting that our brethren at home would enable us to make good all that we had ventured to propose to be undertaken. Having accomplished what required our joint judgment, although much of a detailed character remained to be done, we parted at

Stuttgart, Mr. Watson to join some friends who awaited him at Heidelberg, and I to return to Tubingen, and finish the work that remained, which took several additional days ; and what is added relates only to myself.

On Sunday, September 27th, 1863, I went to Reutlingen, where I had long known Gustav Werner resided, a college friend of Dr. Tafel, and like himself unable to sign those formularies which contain the erroneous systems of the Old dispensation. I had also known that this excellent New Churchman had for many years been fostering institutions for educating and employing the poor and helpless, especially poor orphan children ; and I resolved to see for myself all he was doing. I passed a most interesting day. Werner is a man probably fifty-seven years of age ; his wife about the same, an admirable help-meet for him.

On reaching the small town of Reutlingen by rail, I inquired for the Institution, and soon found it. Werner was known and universally respected. He commenced more than twenty years ago, having no children of his own, to take in and sustain some orphan children. He had more and more who applied, and he took them in, and preached in the churches, and had collections for their support. This continued, and grew, until he found it necessary to strike out some employment for the young people, and he took some land and sold the produce. He believed that he ought not to turn any suffering applicants away, if they would learn to work, and be obedient to the rules. He preaches the principles of the New Church, and the spirit of those principles reigns in all the arrangements of his Institution. This

Institution has grown, until at Reutlingen there are 644 poor persons—131 children under 14 years of age. There are twenty-four branch institutions including in the whole 1,746 persons. These are clothed, fed, lodged, and cared for bodily and spiritually. They pursue trades of different kinds. At Reutlingen there are mechanics' shops, moulding shops, furniture shops, agriculture, and agricultural machine making, cloth weaving, stocking weaving, ribbon weaving, engraving jewellery, bookbinding, the grinding of corn, and some other businesses, besides school-teaching. Over all is the spirit of love.

I heard Mr. Werner address his congregation, consisting of part of his Institution, and people from the town who joined them. He was earnest. clear. and eloquent. He preached the necessity of regeneration, and I felt delighted with what I heard and saw.

After the sermon we had a long conversation. He had long known me by name, and welcomed me gladly. He took me over the Institution, and then asked me if I would dine with his large family, and on their humble fare. He stripped some of his clothes, to make himself like a waiter, while he served out the meat. They sung a grace; four hundred sat down together, and I sat and ate with them, and rejoiced that the Lord had filled this good man with His Spirit to accomplish so great a work. I took my leave in the evening, accompanied by Mr. Hahn, one of the committee, whom I found to be an intelligent New Churchman, and returned delighted to Tubingen on foot, the distance being only seven miles.

Conclusion.

It is interesting to consider that in these two excellent men the New Church was presented to Germany in its two chief aspects; its intellectual greatness and culture; its charity, stooping to raise and comfort the lowest, in Werner; and both in the central kingdom of Wurtemburg; for Wurtemburg and Bavaria form geographically and I think morally and intellectually a pivotal part of the great German Fatherland. For many years, now, direct and earnest efforts have been made in various parts with great missionary zeal to spread the truth in Germany and in German Switzerland.

Mr. Mittnacht, formerly in America, but now of Frankfort, has been of late years the mainspring of continual efforts to publish abroad the glad tidings that the Lord has come again in Higher Wisdom and in Grander Love, to restore the golden age. His zeal and untiring energy have stimulated others both in Switzerland and Germany.

Mr. Bauman, whom I knew at St. Gallen, the friends at Vienna, and the Rev. Mr. Gorlitz, in Wurtemburg, have been labouring in their Master's vineyard during the burden and heat of the day.

I cannot but hope and trust, and pray, that in the great German people the seed thus happily and plenteously sown may, in the Lord's good time, be blessed with rich and heavenly increase, some thirty, some sixty, and some a hundred fold.

XXVI.

THE TWO SENIORS,

FATHER AND SON.

The New Church in Yorkshire.

THE great and important county of York, teeming with vast numbers of a population distinguished for strength of character, shrewdness of mind, and clear common sense, has not made a progress equal to some other parts of the kingdom in the reception of New Church principles.

It may be that Methodism, which spread greatly in that county before the commencement of the New Church, and with its fiery zeal, instantaneous salvation, and undoubted increase of external piety, had moved the Yorkshire people as far as they could go for a time, and therefore only a few here and a few there could accept higher and more far-reaching principles. These things are mysteries to us, the Lord knows all about it, and overrules the progress of His Church with unerring wisdom. In Yorkshire, exciting and powerful preachers, and chiefly earnest energetic local preachers, stirred the people and drew them from sinfulness and deadness in sin, to life much nearer to God and goodness, than that they had formerly led.

Unlike Calvinism, the Methodists contended strongly for good works, though often in their excitement meetings, making so much of instantaneous conversion as to seem to make it the whole of religion instead of its being regarded only as the commencement, the enlistment of the recruit who has afterwards to be drilled to do the work of the army, and to be a good soldier of the Lord Jesus Christ. The theme very largely dwelt upon in their addresses was the conversion of the thief upon the cross; and the effect was that a sudden spasm of conversion, leading them to believe that the crucifixion had paid all that God required from such as believe it to be so, spread a superficial surface of religion, satisfactory to the believers for a time, but in some cases short-lived, in others, leading to sanctimoniousness, with little improvement in temper or uprightness; but in others, and indeed in a great number of others, we rejoice to say, the formation of a truly conscientious, devout, and Christian life; which under the name of sanctification, is also an important part of Methodist doctrine. The improvement in practical life from the energetic sermons of such earnest devoted men as Hicks, the village blacksmith, and Mr. William Dawson, of Barnbow, commonly called Billy Dawson, will be illustrated by the circumstance mentioned in Everett's life of the latter eloquent preacher, who was dwelling as he often did on the exposures of the Day of Judgment, when fraudulent dealers would have to give an account of their wicked use of short measures. I give it from memory.

A pedlar, whose yard was two or three inches too short, and whose conscience had been troubled at former sermons, as the preacher proceeded in his vigorous appeals, cried out in the congregation, " Here it is, Billy, here it is ; I'll break it up and never use it any more ! " suiting the action to the word.

Largely, however, in other cases, there was, I fear, too much reason to conclude with an old gentleman, whose reply to a Methodist friend inviting him to go and hear a sermon on the thief upon the cross, was repeated to me on my first visit to preach in Leeds about fifty years ago, " Na, na. Ye've been preaching about Thief on't cross until ye have made one half o'th' nation thieves. I must go where I can learn never to be a thief."

Whether this previous success of Methodism in Yorkshire has really been a hindrance to the diffusion of New Church truth, at least as extensively as it prevails in Lancashire, we cannot positively say, yet there have been bodies of faithful receivers, and individuals of great excellence from very early times. If the Lord should raise up real energetic preachers, real sturdy Yorkshiremen, we cannot but think the fields are white for the harvest. Let us pray that the Lord may send forth more true labourers into His harvest. The first society in Yorkshire was Keighley, and representatives from Keighley appeared at the earliest conferences. The first preacher was Wright, then Enoch, and afterwards Michael Pickles.

Probably the very first who became interested

in Keighley was Mr. William Illingworth, who had married a sister of Mr. Hindmarsh, and was an earnest New Churchman in 1789.

There was an interesting account of him in the "Intellectual Repository," by Mr. Hindmarsh, on his death, in 1814.

He had been a Methodist, but became a New Churchman, and continued a steady reader of the writings, especially the Arcana, and a devout Christian in life for twenty-five years.

Mr. Illingworth was the first man in Yorkshire to introduce Sunday Schools, and while his health permitted, he was a most active and zealous supporter of that noble institution.

From his diary, amongst many other excellent things, Mr. Hindmarsh quotes the following:—

"I hereby solemnly declare, that notwithstanding I had been among the people called Methodists for upwards of twenty years, and then loved the Word of the Lord, yet I knew little of its heavenly virtue and saving power, until after impartially reading the writings of that illuminated author Emanuel Swedenborg, wherein the Lord and His Word are set forth in such light, as is vastly superior to anything I have ever seen, and I now begin to think far beyond what the world hath ever before known.

"Written by me, W. I. Keighley, Feb. 1, 1798, after about ten years perusal of said writings."

Again, in 1811, he observes, "I have now for upwards of twenty years had delight in reading the writings of E. S., particularly the Arcana Celestia, most of which I have read three times over, and some parts three times three in private or alone, besides reading them on many occasions in public.

"In all my reading of these heavenly works I have found nothing to find fault with; but the more I read, the more I admired; and I am fully convinced, that besides the revelation of the internal opening of the Word, they must all be written under the Divine auspices. I consider them the next in use to the Holy Word itself, they being the only true correspondent explanation of the Word, given by revelation from the Lord, and the only key given to open, unlock, and enter into its inmost contents; while at the same time I consider the Holy Word the grand connecter of heaven and earth, the Divine within the Church, and the Lord Himself dwelling with men. To interrogate the Lord is to interrogate His Word; and to live as it directs, is the same as to attend to His speaking to us. Hence He says 'I in you and you in Me. He that keepeth My commandments, he it is that loveth Me.'"

From this excellent man, estimable and spiritually-minded in his life and in his death, others were drawn to the truth, and the Keighley Society commenced, and has continued to the present day.

Not much later, however, there was a sprinkling of New Church receivers in various parts of the country: Mr. Dean, of Addingham; Mr. Storry, the father of the Rev. R. Storry, at Pickering; a few at Hull; one or two at Barnsley, and a few other places; and Mr. Senior the elder, George Senior, of Dalton, near Huddersfield, who at the age of 23, soon after his marriage in 1793, made the acquaintance of a Mr. Hinchcliffe, who had been warmly interested for two or three years in the Writings of Swedenborg, and with four others met for reading and worship at Cooper's Bridge, a place five miles from Dalton, in the house of a friend named James Hammerton.

After many earnest conversations, Mr. Senior —who had long been religious, and become one of the Independents, then very Calvinistic—saw in the New Church Doctrines something far beyond what he knew before, and began to attend the little meeting, making the congregation six, with sometimes two or three visitors from a distance.

The little company had some very happy times together. Mr. Senior being a very energetic young man, both in business, as a cropper or finisher of woollen cloth, and also in spiritual things, made great progress in heavenly knowledge, and after a short time was requested to read for the congregation, and, being gifted with ready utterance, he was encouraged to preach, and to become the leader of their little flock.

Their meetings now became more numerously attended. In a short time a room was engaged at a place called Colne Bridge, which would accommodate fifty persons, the owner being Francis Drake, who was one of the most zealous promoters of the heavenly doctrines in that part of the country.

Here Mr. Senior commenced preaching regularly every alternate Sabbath afternoon: the distance to walk being between two and three miles.

Besides preaching at Colne Bridge, he had frequent invitations to take services at other places, at distances of eight or nine miles.

Being full of energy, he commenced business on his own account, and with a fair amount of success; not, however, without severe trials and difficulties in the vicissitudes of trade, but ultimately with decided prosperity.

The demands of business made it necessary to devote his evening hours to reading the Word and the writings of Swedenborg, and he often said that so great a light would sometimes enter his mind from the spiritual explanations, as to be almost overpowering. His mind was so delighted with the discernment and acquisition of truth that he scarcely allowed himself sufficient time to recruit his bodily powers. He was a fine example of a noble nature acquiring knowledge under difficulties, for few men had a more accurate acquaintance with Scripture; and the happy, homely, yet earnest way in which he would communicate this knowledge to others, rendered his ministry peculiarly edifying and delightful to those who regularly heard him.

In 1796 Mr. Senior became acquainted with the Rev. John Clowes, whom he always regarded with the greatest veneration. Mr. Clowes was in the habit of visiting Yorkshire once a year: when on his journey, he spent a day or two at the house of a gentleman at Halifax named Hayle, and Mr. Hayle's was a house at which Mr. Senior occasionally preached, he was therefore extremely delighted to meet Mr. Clowes on his visits.

The conversations were exceedingly edifying to all present, and charming to Mr. Senior, who always found his mind much instructed, strengthened and animated with new zeal to proceed in the good cause he had so affectionately espoused. He also met Mr. Clowes at the homes of other gentlemen in Yorkshire, and his venerable, pious and intelligent character greatly tended to confirm the receivers of the heavenly doctrines in the truth, and to lead them to that life of usefulness to which the truth invariably points.

At Mr. Hayle's it was that Mr. Senior became acquainted with the Rev. W. Hill, who afterwards went to America. He was the translator of the "Apocalypse Explained," a gentleman distinguished for his piety and intelligence, and greatly beloved by all who knew him.

On one special occasion he and other friends had Mr. Hill in company, and he received such delightful impressions from his enlightened and pious conversation that he often alluded to them; they were never forgotten. Mr. Senior entertained very great esteem for Mr. Hill, and was in the habit of calling him "a second Clowes."

In the year 1818 the Sabbath services were removed to Upper Heaton, a small village about the same distance from the Seniors' home as Colne Bridge had been, but where his partner in business, on building some cottages, had arranged for a large room which would contain one hundred persons, and which should be used by Mr. S. rent free. Mr. S then preached morning and evening, and besides his daily avocation in what had become a very prosperous business, he did all the work of a minister until the year 1825.

In that year, having been blest in his admirable wife, his children, and his business, as well as in his inestimable spiritual privileges, and having the means to accomplish the desires of his heart, he resolved to erect a commodious chapel, and house for a minister, which was accomplished, and the place of worship was opened in August, 1825.

The time had come in which his strength required relief, and he arranged for a minister, and provided that whatever was needed to furnish a comfortable support he would make up.

A few years later he erected a commodious Sunday School, capable of accommodating 250 scholars. This school he placed under the especial charge of his son, Mr. Joseph Senior, who had early shewn his heartfelt interest in the truths deemed so sacred by his father, and his love for Sunday Schools. With this provision for the well-being of the Society he had raised and loved, and occasional assistance in the pulpit, with cheer and encouragement to every one coming within his sphere, often expressed in language like this reported by Mr. Smithson— " The doctrines of the New Church must sooner or later prevail; because," said he, with peculiar emphasis, " they are essential to the welfare and peace of mankind, and I verily believe they are of God, and cannot be overthrown "—he reached his 71st year, and passed to his eternal home on April 24th, at Dalton, in 1841.

The principles he had so long known and preached gave strength, comfort and consolation during the changing states of his sickness, which for a few months were very trying, but his end was entire peace. His constant and only regret was that he had come far short of that heavenly life to which the doctrines lead.

His son, Mr. Joseph Senior, had long shown that he was actuated by the same affection for the New Church which had so distinguished his excellent father, for he had not only taken constant interest in the Sunday School, but when an unusually violent attack was made on the doctrines by the Rev. Mr. James, curate of the adjoining parish of Almondbury, in 1834 he wrote and published an admirable reply, in a work of 139 pages.

The success of the New Church at Dalton appears to have excited a feeling of opposition in the minds of the clergy of the neighbourhood, and they resolved that they would give a course of lectures against the doctrines, in the two nearest parish churches, those of Kirkheaton and Almondbury.

Mr. James' style of lecturing was especially rude, personal and unbecoming. Mr. George Senior, the father, replied in a course of lectures most satisfactorily, removing the prejudices excited in the neighbourhood; and then his son, Mr. Joseph Senior, replied in the work we have named.

He had called upon Mr. James to publish his first sermon. The Rev. gentlemen replied by announcing another, which turned out to be still more violent, and which Mr. Senior had caused to be taken down by a professional reporter.

We are not disposed to trouble our readers with many of this gentleman's unruly utterances. One or two paragraphs will be quite enough to exhibit their quality. In his first letter he classed the Swedenborgians with infidels. In his last he delivered himself thus—

"The Swedenborgians believe that Jehovah the Father was manifest in the Person and the Character of Jesus Christ: but this" he said, "was impossible; it could not be: for the Father and the Son are two ENTIRELY DISTINCT

PERSONS, as much so as any two men are distinct one from another; and if the Swedenborgians possessed the least particle of sense, they could not believe such a doctrine as that the Father was manifest in the Son." He also denounced the Swedenborgians as heretics and deceivers, asserting that their conduct as well as their doctrines, were damnable.

When he had finished a discourse in this style he felt so delighted with his performance, that he gave utterance to his charmed condition at his success as follows :—

"Now I have demolished the Swedenborgian opinion on the doctrine of the Trinity completely. I have brought that pitcher of earth, which was made by man, to the Rock of Ages, and have dashed it into a thousand pieces. Let the Swedenborgians go home and gather up the broken fragments, and make it whole again if they can. This is their work for them. The truth has these distinct marks which prove it to be the truth, in defiance of hell itself. It is impossible for the truth to be mistaken, if you only take time to examine it. I have brought the doctrine of Swedenborg, and examined it with the texts which they quote, and have shown that the Father and the Son cannot be one Person, else all the Apostles were lumped together in one person, and I am sure they will not admit that."

Mr. Joseph Senior's reply was all that a reply ought to be, calm, careful, and convincing. He shows from the Divine Word that Jesus was Jehovah, the Saviour in the flesh, and considers the texts upon which the assailant dwells, showing their entire harmony with New Church teaching. He called it THE BROKEN PITCHER.

He concludes with the following address to Mr. James:—

"I may now venture to say that the very texts you here bring forward to confound our doctrines are as clear and conclusive in support of them as any you could have chosen; and instead of any opinions entertained by us, on the doctrine of the Trinity being completely demolished, they remain as firm and secure as ever—if anything more steadfastly established in our own minds. And with respect to your boast, that you have brought that pitcher of earth, which was made by man, to the Rock of Ages, and have dashed it into a thousand pieces, it proves nothing except your own vanity. For who is the Rock of Ages? We believe the Lord Jesus Christ to be that Rock; for the term "Rock" is always applied to the Lord in respect to Divine Truth, and Jesus is the Word made flesh, or the Divine Truth personified before men. And it would be strange indeed if those doctrines which exalt Jesus as the Highest in the thoughts and affections of our minds—which teach that He reigns supreme in Heaven and earth, which lead the devout mind to HIM as the fountain of living waters, and the source of all life and blessing—should be dashed in pieces by being thrown against Himself. No; we feel strength and consolation in the promise, 'No weapon that is formed against thee shall prosper, and every tongue that shall rise against thee in judgment thou shalt condemn. This is the heritage of the servants of the Lord; and their righteousness is of me, saith the Lord.' (Is. liv. 17.)"

It is perfectly clear that Mr. Joseph Senior was well able to take care of the Church his father had founded, and for which he had so long laboured; and so it turned out. By his own active usefulness in the Sunday School, and his support of the ministers who were successively engaged to carry on the good work at Dalton, the Church continued to prosper. First, there was that excellent man, Mr. Margetson, who ministered in his own loving way for many years, and who lived until lately with his eldest son in London, a perfect specimen of the innocence of wisdom—a good New Churchman, over the age of ninety, ripe for Heaven.

Then the Rev. Mr. Storry took charge of Dalton; afterwards Rev. Mr. Marsden; and ultimately the worthy Secretary of Conference, the Rev. Eli Whitehead.

Besides sustaining the Church in his own vicinity, Mr. Joseph Senior aided whatever he believed would promote its usefulness everywhere. He rendered great assistance to the work of Dr. E. Tafel in Germany, and to all the active efforts of Dr. D. G. Goyder in Scotland and in England alike. The Manchester Tract Society was largely aided by his liberality, and when he thought the Leeds Society would be benefited by a commodious chapel in a central situation, he bought the chapel of the celebrated Dr. Hamilton, and gave it to the Society, placing it in the charge of Conference. We cannot therefore doubt that our readers will be satisfied that we have rightly chosen to place in our list of New Church Worthies, the two good Yorkshire Worthies—the Seniors, father and son.

It has been mentioned that early in the diffusion of New Church Truth, there were a few here and there in varied parts of the great county, between 1790 and 1800; but they were chiefly quiet, meditative men, good modest Christians, who said little of the New Light, though they loved it and walked in it.

Such are known to have been at Skipton, Holme, Barnsley, Sheffield, York, and several other places, and particularly at Hull and Leeds.

Hull had an unhappy experience : when in my early youth, sixty years ago, attending one of the coffee meetings in Manchester, I heard read a letter from the secretary of the Society at Hull, complaining of the bitter attacks upon them, by Pharaoh and his hosts.

The doctrines had in some way got among the congregation of a chapel with an unfortunate name—the DAGGER LANE CHAPEL.

Some received the New Church views, others did not; hence disputings arose, which continued a long time ; and ultimately there was a law-suit which confirmed the possession of the place by our friends, but it was of no service to the Church. I once preached there in 1836, but was not very favourably impressed with the persons I met there.

There seemed also bitter feelings spread about it. It never prospered for any length of time. I have described its short bright days during Mr. Hodson's stay in Hull, when it was famous and crowded, but this was a limited period, and evanescent. Mr. Hill, editor of the Northern Star, became its minister, a gentleman who had been an unbeliever, but brought back to Christianity by the New Church. He had some general knowledge of the doctrines, but was very weak in the spirit and the life which alone can testify their worth.

He ultimately sold the place, as I understood, simply for his own advantage ; and no doubt it was well lost. There are many losses which are really great gains. Our friends in Hull now are in a legitimate position, and I trust will be truly prosperous and happy.

In 1823, the Hull Society, writing to Conference, state in relation to the labours of Mr. F. M. Hodson, to whom we have referred elsewhere : " Since Mr. Hodson has taken the ministerial labours the congregations increased to about 200 in the morning of the Sabbath day, and from 500 to 700 in the evening ; this has been the case for nearly three months, and they see no reason to doubt its continuance. A Thursday evening lecture, which at first was attended by fewer than 20 persons, is now attended by 80. The highest encomiums are given to the preacher through whose medium these improvements have been effected."

Leeds had a more satisfactory New Church experience. Our friends had a comfortable chapel in Byron Street, and a very capable minister in the Rev. Mr. Gilbert, whom I heard deliver, at the Conference at which his ordination was sanctioned, a very edifying discourse on the rings and poles by which the ark was to be carried about. But Mr. Gilbert died early, and the flock for a considerable time was without a shepherd.

At length, on acquiring the chapel, bought and presented by Mr. Joseph Senior, Mr. Edleston was invited to become the minister ; and his youthful devotion, energy, and ability, rapidly increased the congregation, and yielded a promise of Leeds taking the position in the Yorkshire

New Church, corresponding to its importance as the most important of Yorkshire towns.

Circumstances however led to the period of his ministry being shortened before the fair beginnings were carried to full fruition; but no doubt the exertions of the Rev. Mr. Edleston were of permanent value to that portion of the great county of York.

Bradford, Sheffield, and York, are centres of population and power, and each of them contained a considerable number of most estimable New Church people, but not sufficiently numerous to sustain the regular services of ministers of their own, until comparatively recent times, when Bradford first, and Sheffield since, have been able in this respect to do what is needful—and have an efficient ministry. Barnsley, by the zeal and loving care of the excellent Capt. and Mrs. Bufham, has had courses of lectures and services, which have brought the sacred truths of the New Church before great numbers of the people, and doubtless so much seed will some day ripen into fruit.

We have noticed previously that very early in the growth of the New Church, there were in many parts of Yorkshire sprinklings of quiet, thoughtful, worthy Christian souls, who in some way, towards the latter part of the last century, had got hold of the New Light, probably through Mr. Clowes and his friends from Lancashire; however, so it was. There were one or two at the fine old market town of Skipton, notable also for its striking castle; and there was one such good old Christian at Embsay, who had received the doctrines between 1793 and 1800. His name was

Wigglesworth; he was respected by every one, as a truly good man, but quite wrong, they thought, about the Atonement, and the scheme of Salvation. His own wife was a zealous class-leader among the Methodists, who were the leading religious people in Eastby, where the Methodist chapel was. This one chapel was deemed sufficient for both villages: there was no place for Church of England service nearer than Skipton. The district of Craven, in which these villages are, is comparatively little known, except to its own inhabitants; but in bold, romantic, picturesque country from Bolton Abbey and grounds in Wharfdale, on one side, to Settle, including Pennigent, Ingleborough, and Whernside, on the other, is really unrivalled in England.

It contains Clapham Cave, nearly a mile into the interior of Ingleborough; Gordale Scar, with its striking natural arch; and Malham Tarn, with its old Swedish name for a small lake; all well worthy of a visit, and to everyone who loves nature there will be great delight in the contemplation of these magnificent scenes. The first time I beheld this country was in 1834. A messenger came to visit me in Manchester, and related to me the following account of Embsay.

The people were chiefly Methodists, attending Eastby chapel, but the chief religious people had erected a substantial building for a Sunday-school in Embsay to be taught by good teachers of any denomination, and with a pulpit that might be used by any preacher who would come and preach to them if not otherwise engaged. It had a tablet in front declaring it to be a HOUSE OF PRAYER FOR ALL PEOPLE.

One of the leading teachers was a young man named John Mason: he was very pious and very thoughtful. It had been reported that good old Wigglesworth was likely to die, and as he did not believe that Christ had paid all the debt of his sins to God the Father, and so pacified the vengeance of God, he would be tormented in hell for ever and ever if they did not set him right in this respect.

John Mason was deputed on this errand, as he was conceived to be the cleverest among the teachers. He visited the sick and aged Wigglesworth, and found him a most spiritually-minded man. He delighted to visit and talk with him again and again; and before his departure the old man had fully converted John Mason to his views, and through him many of his fellow-teachers. Shortly after, they resolved to have a New Church minister to preach for them, which could easily be done, as they had a " house of prayer for all people."

They applied to the Rev. Thomas Pilkington, of Haslingden, the father of the late Dr. Pilkington, and he consented to go.

This was talked about and arranged, but some narrow sectarian minds were sorely tried at the idea of the New Light people coming into Embsay; and bigotry is seldom nice in its means to carry out its vicious ends; they forged a letter and sent it to Mr. Pilkington, signed as if from one of the New Churchmen, stating that there would probably be ill-will and disturbance, and he had better defer coming to some other time.

So the matter remained; but on the Saturday afternoon the clever concocter of this mean trick mentioned how he had contrived and completed the scheme.

No sooner did the New Church young men hear of this, than they sent one of their company with a gig, thirty miles, to bring Mr. Pilkington during the night—which he did. The bigots, however, fastened the school doors, and kept possession of the pulpit. These proceedings nevertheless roused the neighbourhood, and a great crowd came, and at service time Mr. Pilkington addressed them from a horse-bench, in a most forcible and convincing manner, and thus was the first New Church sermon preached in Embsay.

The opposition party held possession of the schoolroom, six of them standing in the pulpit, if I remember rightly, morning and afternoon, that no entry should be effected there; and the preaching in the street being concluded, they supposed the danger was over, and retired to their homes.

After tea, however, the friendly ones got possession of the key of the schoolroom, soon passed the word round the neighbourhood that Mr. Pilkington would preach in the evening, in the schoolroom, which was done with great acceptance, and so the *second New Church sermon was preached in Embsay.*

My informant who related the account of these proceedings came to desire me to come and spend a week with them, and stated that the opposers, by their unworthy conduct, had brought so great a blame upon themselves, that if a good effort could now be made, they were quite sure the fields were white for the harvest. The time was fixed upon to be at Midsummer, when their barns would be at liberty, and with something raised to stand upon, a cart or a barrel for a pulpit, there would be no difficulty in addressing the people. And so it was. We had services on Sunday twice in a barn, with most attentive and appreciative hearers. On the following days up to Thursday, I think, services were held in the large kitchens of the people, in various parts of the village, and most remarkable confessions of conversion and good will took place every day. Some are worthy of special record.

One was the old lady, the widow of good old Wigglesworth. She exclaimed one evening: "Blessed be the Lord, here is a wonderful thing. I lived thirty years with my husband, bless him, and he was one of the best men that ever lived, but I couldn't understand him, and now the Lord has sent this young man, and he has opened my eyes at eighty years of age, and I see it all as clear as daylight."

Another was the case of the leading class-leader of the place, and I think an occasional local preacher; at whose house the Methodist preachers were wont to stay on their visits to Embsay. He invited me also to stay with him; part of his family, including his thoughtful and excellent wife, having already taken hold of the doctrines of the New Church. Indeed, before the father gave way (for he was a sturdy Yorkshireman) all his grown-up family had come over.

I accepted his hospitable invitation, and was glad to find that this did not in the least prevent him from supporting his idea of the THREE DIVINE PERSONS IN THE GODHEAD like a man; though he admitted he did not feel very strong respecting the personality of the third. Of the Father and the Son being two distinct persons he was quite certain. Kindly conversation led to no breach of good temper, and, after a few visits, he entirely gave up the Holy Ghost as a separate divine person; and, at the end of about twelve months, he told me he saw clearly that the Father was in the Son, as the soul was in the body, and they formed ONLY ONE DIVINE PERSON, God over all, blessed for ever; and, he added, "I see and feel that this one real divine person is far more blessed to me *than all the three I had before.*"

At my first visit I became familiar with John Mason, and his brother Stephen, both unmarried, and a considerable number of warm-hearted Yorkshiremen named Mason, for that name was very common in the neighbourhood. John was tall—very tall, pious, thoughtful, solid, and devout, the make of a good preacher in him, which he afterwards became. Stephen, burly, broad-shouldered, full of kindness, intelligence, and good-humour; both admirably calculated to give their neighbours specimens of what the New Church would make her members to be.

Subsequently it was determined to build a chapel, which I opened, and of which Mr. John Mason became the clear, cogent, and much-valued preacher until his death.

The Rev. Mr. Woodman and others visited and aided them from time to time, and I visited them almost yearly until I removed from North Lancashire to London.

The growth of the Society has been steady, with constant progress. They subsequently built a separate school, to serve as Sunday-school and also for day-school.

The Wigglesworths have continued to be a worthy family in many branches; and one who resided at Barnoldswick, a few miles away—Mr. John Wigglesworth—was not only a genuine and most intelligent New Churchman, during his life, always supporting and visiting Embsay, but at his death left some property to the New Church, on the condition that one New Church sermon yearly at least should be delivered by a New Church minister in Barnoldswick.

The Society has now for some years had an excellent minister in the Rev. Mr. Jones, admirably suited to advance the New Church in that part of Yorkshire, and with whom they all work in perfect harmony, making the Church a real blessing in the midst of the land.

The Yorkshire Colportage Association is also, and has for a long time been, one of the most useful agencies of the Church; and its active colporteur, Mr. Stephenson, is indefatigable, and worthy of universal esteem.

Such have been the various channels through which the rivers of living water have commenced their flow into the great county of York; and now that many of the Societies are led by earnest, capable, vigorous, young ministers, we may confidently hope that the Lord, blessing their labours, will make them a thousand more than they are, and a blessing to all around them.

XXVII.

MR. WATSON,

The Model Deacon, and Friend of his Society at Argyle Square, and of the Church in general.

IN the very early days of the Apostolic ministry it was manifest that there were many duties for the comfort and charities of the Christian church which could be efficiently performed by faithful men who, though not endowed with great gifts in preaching, could yet be intermediate between the ministers and the people, relieving the former of many labours impairing their studies and devotion to the Word, and encouraging the others by gracious little attentions and acts of kindness. Hence SEVEN DEACONS were appointed, and the first, Stephen, had also the distinction of being the FIRST MARTYR.

St. Stephen's Gate, at Jerusalem, leads down to an open space as one goes to the garden of Gethsemane, which is still known as the place of the martyrdom of Stephen.

Hence deaconship became a recognized arrangement in the Christian church, and the character becoming for deacons is spoken of in language but a little less elevated than that used for ministers of the Word—then called BISHOPS OR OVERSEERS OF THE CHURCH : " Let the deacons be grave," said the apostle; and again, " Let the deacons rule their children and their own houses well. For they that have used the office of deacon well, purchase for themselves a good degree, and great boldness in the faith which is in Christ Jesus." (I Tim. iii. 12, 13.)

The usefulness of kind, courteous, and intelligent deacons, cannot be too highly estimated. They relieve the minister of small cares, they make known to him the circumstances and wishes of the congregation with which he might not so readily be acquainted. They suggest ideas of great usefulness and value, which, when carried out, contribute to the success of the grand cause —the diffusion of the Gospel of Jesus Christ, the general aim, and blessing of them all.

Mr. Watson was in all these respects a model deacon. He was also an earnest New Churchman, always punctual in his attendance when not out of town, and seldom from home.

During all my time of nearly twenty years at Argyle Square, and for several years before and after, until his last illness, he was the ever-ready helper in the vestry, ready with any kindly attention to a stranger, or ready with any little act of courtesy in the congregation; never flurried or disagreeable, always at hand with the gentleness of a Christian gentleman.

His family had been amongst the few who were very early attached to the visible organization of the Church. The name of Gerardin occurs nearly from the first in the modest meetings which they called Conferences, and Mr. Watson's father married a sister of Mrs. Gerardin, and the husbands of the two sisters became partners in a business under the name of Gerardin and Watson in Poland Street, which remains to the present day. They were partners in business and partners in religion.

Hence, Mr. Watson had inherited the blessing of a New Church home; both parents having themselves been educated in New Church principles from early childhood, and greatly esteemed as members of the Cross Street Society.

They died within a few months of each other, leaving Thomas (Mr. Watson of our present sketch) at twenty-three years of age, in the winter of 1834-5, the head of a family of five, three of them comparatively young.

He attended well to the family and the business and probably the early responsibilities of which he acquitted himself so well, combined with his evident devotion to the New Dispensation, marked him out for the respect of the Church.

It may be safely declared, that few have laboured more assiduously in the offices of the Church, few have filled so many important positions, or exerted themselves for so long a period for her real and lasting welfare.

In 1839 he became secretary to the Society then recently formed in Burton Street, and in a small memorandum book of that time he entered a representation of the place, and a drawing of the interior, giving a plan of every pew and sitting, and the name of each occupant, in his inimitably neat handwriting.

When the friends of Burton Street united with the Society of Friars Street, Doctors Commons, under the Rev. Manoah Sibly, who died in 1840, he was made secretary of the united body, and when they removed to the newly-erected church at Argyle Square he continued in the office of secretary for twenty-eight years, until he resigned it to be taken up by his excellent eldest son.

As a secretary he was all that a secretary should be, and it has been well said that a good secretary is ONE-HALF towards the success of any office or business with which he has to do.

Mr. Watson was always punctual to time, entered all business in a clear and orderly manner and in a most neat and beautiful hand; while his ever cheerful and affectionate temper diffused a sunny atmosphere about him, and kept everyone in good working harmony together. He was a model secretary as well as a model deacon.

He had a habit of keeping small diaries, in which the entries were made in small writing, but in characters so clear, perfect and exquisitely written, that they would be taken for excellent printing; and in one of these every incident in the history of almost every society, and of every individual of any mark in the Church, was noted down.

He was so esteemed in his own Society, that he was invariably sent as one of the representatives to the Annual Meetings of the Conference during twenty-eight years, and he was so valued by that body that he was soon elected a Trustee of Conference, and the general confidence in his good feeling and good sense was such, that his presence was usually sought on as many important committees as possible.

For more than twenty years he withdrew, like Mr. Broadfield of Manchester, from business, that he might devote himself to the welfare of the Church.

He was a zealons member of the Swedenborg Society, which he entered in 1833, was soon elected on its committee, and was made its treasurer, which office he continued to hold with one short interruption as long as his health would permit.

He was governor of the New Church College, and seconded the efforts of his friend, Mr. Bateman, in his many endeavours for the good of the New Dispensation.

In fact there was no effort for the good of the Church which did not find in Mr. Watson a friend and helper.

He had a very gentle heart for the poor and needy of every kind; hence he assisted in founding the Argyle Square Benevolent Fund, in 1842, for the relief of its poor and aged members, and was its secretary and treasurer until his death. His presence was the life of its monthly meetings, and his delight was to aid the old friends with a kind word and a liberal hand. His cheerful way of bestowing assistance made it doubly valuable. Whether at home, amidst his amiable family of five, two sons and three daughters, where piety, order and elegance reigned—at church, as deacon superintending the communion or other arrangements, or extending to visitors or strangers a courteous and kindly welcome—he was just what a New Churchman should be.

He was a devoted husband; and probably the engrossing character, night and day, of the long illness of Mrs. Watson, brought on the heart disease which seriously impaired his naturally excellent health, and ended his earthly career on

Tuesday, September 22nd, 1879, at the not very extended period of sixty-seven years.

The influence in a congregation of a man so pious, so orderly, so clever, possessed of so much good taste, and so genial as a friend, is invaluable. The minister enjoys it, the people feel it, and it diffuses over the whole congregation an atmosphere of peace and goodwill, the surest prelude and presage of success. I have had the aid of such-like deacons as the one dear Mr. Watson, of whom I now speak so tenderly and so warmly, I have such assistants still, and I regard them as the very salt of the earth.

Mr. Watson's illness was not a protracted one. His habits and spirits were so excellent, that his health was usually almost uniformly good. When sickness however came, he endured it patiently. On the departure of Mrs. Watson, it was evident to his friends that much watching and concern had worn him very seriously, and rest and change were essential.

With these, and a sojourn at Hastings, his impaired health did appear to improve, and he attended the annual meetings of the Swedenborg Society, and his own—the Argyle Square Society, on the 16th of July.

The Conference being held at Kensington that year, 1879, he attended once, and enjoyed the greetings of the many old friends there on the Thursday of Conference week.

On the very day following he was reported to be again seriously unwell, with heart difficulty and other serious complications. With great care he continued for about three weeks, not getting seriously worse; but then came an aggravation of the disease until the close, borne with Christian patience and fortitude. I was with him very nearly to the last; and after a short season of prayer he clasped my hand fervently, and kissed it, saying, "Oh, my second father!"

Such was Mr. Watson, the Model Deacon. "Let me die the death of the righteous, and let my last end be like His."

MR. FRANCIS OLIVER FINCH,

OF ARGYLE SQUARE, LONDON.

The Artist, and Friend of the Mutual Improvement Society.

BORN as young people now are in the improved condition of society—the result of the New Dispensation of the Second Coming of the Lord, though yet in its early infancy in the world—they are apt to suppose that Sunday-schools, and kindred institutions, for the healthy and elevating progress of the young, have always existed pretty much as they now do. Thus they do not fully value the already patent blessings of the New Age in the world.

Before THIS CENTURY, however, there were no Mechanics' Institutions, no Athenæums, no Mutual Improvement Societies, connected with religious bodies, in the world.

These latter commenced, I believe, with New Church congregations first, and have been of great value, both with them and with religious bodies generally, throughout this country and America.

The idea used to be taken for granted, that young men were wild and foolish, and must not be expected to be sensible, rational, and virtuous, until they had got into many troubles and disgraces, and suffered much from bitter experience. Health and fortune were often seriously impaired —sometimes fatally ruined, before mature age was reached.

Whereas, if the acquisition of knowledge, the cultivation of the intellect and literary taste, with agreeable society and religious principle, were provided, the young would have orderly, healthy, and elevating pleasures, without descending into any unworthy path, or coarse and unbecoming company of any kind.

Indeed, young people with spiritual pursuits, and literary tastes, would feel repugnance at any contact with those so-called dashing blades, young men without any religious principle or reasonable conception of things, manifestly without common-sense.

Every religious body ought therefore to encourage and assist the young people to have a good Mutual Improvement Society among themselves.

There was a very excellent one, commenced at Argyle Square in its early days; and two of the senior members, who felt pleasure in the company and pursuits of young people, were appointed to meet with them, advise, and aid them in every way. These were, Mr. Sandy, a most excellent and genial spirit, and Mr. Finch, whose name heads this sketch, who as an artist had admirable classical taste, combined with literary and poetic feeling; and such a genial and amiable character, that he formed a charming companion for young men, one they would respect and esteem, as well as admire and love.

Mr. Finch was a water-colour artist, and his works were greatly admired by those who were familiar with them. They combined great beauty and truth to nature with a certain classical grace which imparted a continual charm.

The Mutual Improvement Society had readings sometimes from Swedenborg, sometimes from Shakespere, doctrinal and occasionally literary discussions, and sometimes political debates. There was the greatest freedom, yet always courtesy and decorum, avoiding anything involving disrespect for the feelings and views of others. But I remember, occasionally some of the old gentlemen thought they made too free with Lord Palmerston.

They had their weekly meetings, with Mr. Finch in the chair, or some other respected senior member, or one of themselves.

At these meetings I may say all were greatly assisted in the formation of their characters and abilities, as well as in their friendships, and capacities for future use in the Church; among these the Rev. John Presland, and Mr. Jobson, long the able secretary of the Missionary Society, and the worthy author of several admirable New Church pamphlets, and many others, who have distinguished themselves.

The feeling of the young men and young ladies as a body towards Mr. Finch will be evident from the letter addressed by them to his excellent widow, Mrs. Finch, on his departure into the eternal world in 1862:—

Argyle Square Junior Members' Society,
September 6th, 1862.

Dear Madam,—The committee and members of the above society desire to record their sense of the valuable services rendered by Mr. Finch to their society as a body, and to its particular members as individuals. They thankfully acknowledge that the present welfare of their society is to a great extent attributable to his kind assistance and counsel, to the high character which his presence conferred upon their meetings and to the wisdom of his numerous addresses, which they believe and hope lives, and ever will live in their memories.

While most sincerely and respectfully expressing their sympathy with yourself in your present bereavement, they trust that you will remember, among the sources of consolation left to you, their affectionate memory of Mr. Finch, and their hope that his Christian conversation and demeanour will prove an example for them to follow, as well as a recollection to love.

In behalf of the committee and the entire society

I am, dear Madam,
Yours very respectfully,
JOHN PRESLAND, Hon. Secretary.

Mr. Finch's eminence as an artist of course gave him weight and prestige among the young people, while his genial and amiable manners endeared him to them all.

More than two hundred specimens of his artistic power, chiefly landscapes and views and scenes of earth and sky, remain as illustrations of his genius; they are valued by those who possess them as gems of beauty, and as recollections of a mind they would not willingly forget.

He was said " To be the last representative of the old school of landscape-painting in water-colours; a school which had given pleasure to the public for half-a-century, and contributed to obtain for Englishmen in that department of art an European reputation."

Mr. Finch was extremely clear and cogent in his rational perceptions, and therefore well calculated to assist his young friends of the Mutual Improvemeut Society on their argumentative evenings. This is very evident from his tract on "The Existence of God." From the two self-evident propositions, which the ancients declared and unbelievers admit, he obtains all the leverage he wants to demonstrate the conclusion he seeks.

He says: "You cannot get something out of nothing."

"You cannot get out of anything that which it does not contain."

From the first of these propositions it follows there must have been an Eternal First, from which all things have been, which was not nothing, for something cannot come out of nothing.

But this Eternal something must have been adequate to produce all things which exist, for according to the second axiom, "You cannot get out of anything that which it does not contain." You cannot get a sovereign from a pocket which does not contain one.

Human beings have life, affections, and faculties. The cause, whatever it was, which gave the first human beings their faculties, must have had such things to give. What it gave it must first have possessed.

Man is a living-being, and therefore the cause which produced life must have had life. Man thinks and reasons. The cause which imparted these powers must, by previously possessing them, have been intelligent. Man has love or affection. This must have come from a cause possessing it, and so of every other faculty.

All life, all love, all wisdom or intelligence that ever existed in subsequent existences, together with all power, from this cause must have been derived, and in it must have had their eternal residence.

And if, of such qualities, the first, the eternal cause is possessed, must it not be a person; for if living, loving, thinking, and acting do not constitute personality, what does?

Altogether, then we think no rational man can doubt the soundness of the positions we have taken, or fail to draw from them with us the inevitable conclusion to which they lead, namely that the first cause must be God, and can be nothing else, and consequently that thereby is proved the existence of God.

To this most satisfactory demonstration by our friend Mr. Finch, some philosophical opponents started the objection,—if all things come from God, then matter came from God, and if so God must Himself be material, according to Mr. Finch's second proposition, " Nothing can be obtained out of anything, which that thing does not contain." To this Mr. Finch replied " The mistake these gentlemen run into in jumping to the conclusion that because God produced matter, He must be Himself material, appears to me to be this: they assume that every CAUSE must have the same mode of existence as its EFFECT, whereas it can easily be shown that no such necessity exists." Mr. Finch explained that the origination of the material universe from the Lord was according to the LAW OF CAUSE AND EFFECT, in which the effect differs from the cause by a discreet degree. The substance being the same, but the *mode of existence* different. Matter is the name we give to the collection of properties which we perceive by their action upon ourselves. What the force is which makes itself manifest in so many forms, no one knows. But, in the Divine Being, it is not matter.

He illustrated his views very perfectly by THOUGHT, and the RESULTS of thought; thus: "The *words* I am now writing come out of my *thoughts*, and it is a proof of my axiom, 'You cannot get out of anything that which it does not contain,' that these words must exist in my thoughts before I can write them. Well, when I have written them, they are material; I can measure their length, can scratch them out with my penknife, but that does not oblige my thoughts and intentions to be material also. I cannot touch or measure *them*, nor have they *any property* of materiality belonging to them."

Mr. Finch's affectionate and refined tone of mind loved to express itself in poetry, as well as in painting, and he has left many very sweet sonnets, as well as one poem of considerable length called "The Artist's Dream." We will conclude this sketch with a short extract, expressive of the author's devout hopes and firm faith for the future of the Church he loved and

honoured so highly, and which will long cherish
his memory:—

> "Long hast thou trod the thorny ways of earth,
> Divinest Charity; thy royal seat
> One called Religion fills, whose alien birth
> Darkness and cold attest, and all the dearth
> Of Christian brotherhood, and hence the cheat
> That gold outvalues love, has still to meet
> Its doom in aching hearts; but now the worth
> Of all things must abide that look Divine
> That fills the world with light; already shine
> The morning splendours of thy coming reign.
> Great Charity! thy twelve-starr'd crown again
> God will restore and evermore sustain,
> And Earth, through thee, her Golden Age regain."

MR. BATEMAN,

(Fellow of the Royal College of Surgeons),

AND

MR. CROMPTON,

The Founders of the New Church College in Devonshire Street, Islington.

IN my earliest visits to London, the first of which was in June, 1840, when I witnessed the procession of Her Majesty on her way to coronation, I became personally acquainted with my late dear friend Mr. Bateman.

Argyle Square church was not then erected, the friends who subsequently in conjunction with the Society from Doctors' Commons built that beautiful place of worship in 1844, occupied the small chapel in Burton Street, and Mr. Bateman, then a comparatively young medical man, was one of the most active amongst them.

I had learned much, even at that time, of the devoted and excellent spirit of Mr. Bateman from Mr. Moss, the first New Church day schoolmaster in Manchester, who, like himself, was from Burton-upon-Trent. Both of them had received the doctrines from Mr. Knight, a solicitor, subsequently very well known in the Church.

Personal acquaintance rapidly increased my esteem for Mr. Bateman, and in my later visits to London, which became tolerably frequent after the church in Argyle Square was opened, I stayed usually with Mr. Bateman, and for many years his loving family circle, even when he removed to Compton Terrace, was my London home.

His life was one of truly Christian piety, order, and benevolence. He was attached, as surgeon, soon after he came to London, in addition to his private practice, to the Islington Dispensary; and, when that fearfully desolating plague, the cholera, visited this country for the first time, in 1832, he was made surgeon to the Cholera Hospital, and by his skill, assiduity, and urbanity, obtained universal goodwill and admiration.

When, after a few years, he devoted himself mainly to private practice, his success was great and rapid. He was the Christian gentleman as well as the medical adviser, and his presence would soothe and comfort his patients as much as his undoubted efficiency in surgery and medicine, imparted confidence, while he ameliorated and removed their diseases.

Many who became highly estimable New Church people were attracted to enquire into his principles of religion, from the admiration they acquired for his character in the sick room.

His experience at the Dispensary and the Hospital, and his feeling for the sorrows of the poor, induced him, in addition to his extensive body of regular patients, to give aid gratuitously to needy sufferers, from six to nine in the morning.

This generous care was so much valued, and

the necessity was so great, that on occasions when I have been staying at the house, his kindly and efficient help was given, before sitting down to breakfast, to as many as SEVENTY persons, including often surgical cases, at which he was remarkably cool, firm, and skilful.

This admirable work was so well known, affected such large numbers, and continued through so many years, FORTY-FOUR I believe, with some little variation of detail, that it came to be commonly reported in Islington, though without any true foundation, and is still believed by many, that a legacy had been left to him by some wealthy person to perform this labour of mercy and love. His own treasure of goodwill was the only wealthy person to whom this heavenly work was due.

The New Church, however, was his chief delight. He was punctual and constant in her services, diligent at her meetings, and generous in his support. He was the leading spirit in the erection of the church in Argyle Square. He loved the Gothic style for ecclesiastical structures, and though when first opened the church had a stunted look, when completed as it subsequently became it formed a cathedral-like building which is always admired. The merit of this form is chiefly due to Mr. Bateman. He also presented, I am informed, the handsome font.

The blessings of New Church principles were so great, and so soul-satisfying to him, that they pervaded his whole life, and while he burned to impart them to others, he was convinced that if they were presented under the same favourable circumstances under which other forms of religion exist, New Church societies might far more rapidly be spread around in every direction.

Hence he was more pressing than some New Church friends have been to come rather nearer in externals to the forms of the Church of England, always however preserving Divine Truth inviolable.

No sooner, therefore, had he satisfied himself that Argyle Square Church was solidly established, and could safely be left to carry on its spiritual work, than he determined to commence another, nearer to his own residence, and combine with it a College and School, which would mutually aid and support each other.

The College would help the Church, and the School would prepare students for the College. The whole should have a beautiful ecclesiastical structure.

Many of the other friends were not so sanguine of the society at Argyle Square being strong enough to spare the energetic help of Mr. Bateman, and feared it was too early to attempt to carry out to completion the plan of a School and a College, and therefore hesitated for a time to assist much in this new enterprize. Mr. Bateman's hope and trust were robust enough to begin, however humbly, and by perseverance he was convinced the little one would become a thousand, and the small one a strong nation.

The commencement of the new effort was indeed very humble. A very few people, a very few children, and a very poor little room over a carpenter's shop. In 1850 the children for a short time were brought down to Argyle Square.

About this period Mr. Crompton, of Prestolee, near Kersley, Lancashire, a warm-hearted and sympathetic New Churchman, came to London from time to time, and regarded with esteem and affection Mr. Bateman's zeal and energy.

Mr. Crompton's friendship was, no doubt, increased by an attachment he formed for a lady friend of Mr. Bateman's, an aunt of the present Rev. John Presland, a lady who in time became Mrs. Roger Crompton. Mr. Crompton and his brother had borne a handsome part in raising and strengthening the New Church at Kersley, and rejoiced at every well-meant effort to extend the kingdom of the Lord Jesus upon earth, as we have elsewhere brought under the attention of our readers.

Mr. Crompton was a very old friend of my own, and never have I known a man of warmer heart, of more affectionate character, or one with more loving reverence for the truth, than the excellent Roger Crompton. I stayed at his house on my not unfrequent visits to Kersley, and when he recognized some growth the Church was making anywhere, or when he was bringing under my observation and explaining to me some fresh improvement in paper-making in his extensive manufactory, his eyes would sparkle with a delight which was charming.

I remember on one occasion his showing me a new machine for making paper, by which twelve miles of paper could be turned out per day.

Mr. Crompton became interested, as I have said, in the earnest efforts of Mr. Bateman, and seeing a certain amount of progress in Islington, felt himself drawn to aid his excellent friend, and when a convenient site for a place of worship was selected, and he learned the other worthy objects Mr. Bateman had in view, he intimated his desire to assist.

Towards the purchase of the freehold land in Devonshire Street, on which it was proposed to build on one side a Mission-room, and School-room with living apartments over, and which cost some £550, Mr. Crompton contributed £300, Rev. Augustus Clissold £100, and no doubt Mr. Bateman the remainder. This was in 1852.

When the buildings we have described were erected and completed in 1854, Mr. Bateman thus writes in the August number of the I. R.: " I would now advert briefly to another subject, that of the New Church College, to which it is intended to devote as soon as possible our freehold in Devonshire Street, with the church, &c., upon it. The whole of the purchase money has been paid, and the entire cost of the erection defrayed, so that Mr. Crompton and I hope to have the delight, almost contemporaneously with the meeting of Conference, of handing over this property to the Church, entirely free from debt, and a few pounds over, which we shall then have in hand towards the legal expenses."

Thus did these two worthy men pay between them, I always understood in equal portions, the cost of the buildings, about £2,000, and present them freely to the uses of the Church. Mr. Crompton's sympathies with Mr. Bateman's efforts would probably be strengthened because in his early days he attended with his good father and brother New Church worship with a few in a room at Ringley Brow.

From that time did Mr. Bateman labour with indefatigable zeal to maintain the service, gather a congregation, and perform all the uses of a society for many years, always sustaining and proclaiming the idea of eventually having there a New Church School and College. He never lost heart or hope, but worked on cheerfully, urging the Conference and the Church generally to aid him in carrying out his idea to completion.

His efforts to a moderate extent were successful, but though Islington was large enough to furnish people for very many congregations, yet Argyle Square and Cross Street were near enough to attract those who preferred to worship with congregations having regular pastors, and whose conditions were more complete than they could be with a small company in a moderate sized room.

Nothing, however, could daunt Mr. Bateman's energies or loving earnestness. Islington was never forgotten at the Conference or in the Magazines. A quiet growth and happy meetings went on, with the co-operation and encouragement from time to time of the other societies.

Then came 1859, when Mr. Crompton, after a short residence in London, was called to his better home, and it became known that he had bequeathed to the Conference £10,000, to mature and carry out the views of Mr. Bateman and himself, in founding the New Church College at Islington, to promote the instruction of candidates for the ministry.

This was a great joy to Mr. Bateman, and a great satisfaction to the Church generally; though there were some who doubted whether it was judicious to spend a large portion of this sum in buildings, while the students would probably be few.

Many discussions took place, especially in the

annual meetings of the Conference. Mr. Bateman was eager that no time should be lost in carrying out what he believed would be most useful to the Church—completing the College buildings; others being of opinion that for some years it would be better to use the interest of the whole money in assisting students to have theological instruction and oversight while they resided in the homes of New Church friends, and the classical and scientific education in the public Colleges or Universities. In these discussions the admirable qualities of Mr. Bateman were signalized for years, and won him the esteem of those who most firmly differed from him.

He never lost his temper, or departed from genuine courtesy. He was invariably the Christian gentleman. Every one who differed from him (sometimes, I fear, myself included), did so with regret. He listened to speeches and arguments against his views with the most perfect patience and equanimity.

At last a compromise was effected, and ultimately £5,400 of Mr. Crompton's bequest was spent in completing the buildings for College and Church, and Mr. Bateman's design and style of the whole were completely carried out.

The bequests of other friends furnished what was needful to meet the expenses of the entire erection in Devonshire Street, comprising £2,000 from Mr. Finnie, £1,000 from Mrs. Becconsall, and £600 for a magnificent window by Mr. and Mrs. Crompton Roberts, the latter being Mr. Crompton's only child.

After the design was completed, Mr. Bateman sought with the same energy to realize all his hopes in relation to it, and to some extent succeeded.

There was, then, a noble ecclesiastical structure, a beautiful church; elegant though rather small, a home for the principal, and six rooms for resident students; with commodious school-room, and an additional suitable room for meetings and library; a play-room below, and a variety of other conveniences for the future uses of the establishment.

There can be no doubt that all Mr. Bateman's desires and aims were excellent, and I trust will be, with time, more and more carried out.

The excellent school-room is well adapted for boys of the middle class, on moderate terms, and real New Church schoolmasters are invaluable.

For many years the school was admirably carried on by Mr. Beilby, and Mr. Woodford, and it seems a pity that no really competent New Churchman should offer himself from some part of the country inspired by the Lord to carry forward that really inestimable use.

It is to be hoped, also, that promising men in greater numbers will stand forth as candidates for the ministry; not too young; men who have already manifested a ministerial character, pious, thoughtful, studious, and devout, with power to attract others to listen to the great truths they teach—not merely doctrinal men, but men of sympathy, and power to excite the sympathy of others, for all that concerns the good and happiness of mankind.

Such young men in increasing numbers would claim the aid of the College to its full extent, making the labours of the estimable professors Presland and Omant more delightful to themselves, and more valuable for the Church.

Such as it is, the College has done good work,

and I pray that its value in the estimation of the Church, and its real sacred use, may rapidly increase, and each stage of its success will heighten the regard of all concerned for the memory of its worthy founders, Mr. Bateman and Mr. Crompton.

Coeval with his efforts to afford more efficient training to the candidates for the ministry, he was led to set a high value on the necessity for having the letter of the Word revised, so as to be free from the imperfections well known to exist, and which often obscure the spiritual sense to the spiritually-minded New Church reader.

He therefore commenced very early a handsome subscription for himself, and induced other friends to unite with him in providing for the accomplishment of that important object. At the close of his valuable life, in 1880, the sum for this purpose had amounted to £726 0s. 2d., and it was placed in the possession of the General Conference, to be used under its direction in due time to defray expenses that may arise in the work of procuring and publishing an accurate translation of the Divine Word into English.

Thus in labours of benevolence, piety and usefulness, passed the life of our worthy New Church brother, Mr. Bateman.

In his large family, among his large circle of friends, and in his public life as a citizen, he was loved, esteemed, and respected.

His last illness was borne with saint-like patience and trust in the Lord who had been his constant Guide and Director, until he slept in peace on earth, to awake among angelic friends, leaving behind a memory amongst all who knew him well, of every virtue, associated with the name of Henry Bateman.

HIRAM POWERS,

The Great American Sculptor.

AT the magnificent display of the arts of Peace in the Great Exhibition of 1851, the fruit of the noble aspirations of Prince Albert, it was the wide-spread conviction that the gem of the department of Sculpture was the touching and wonderful figure of the Greek Slave, now in the possession of the Duke of Cleveland, in the drawing-room of Raby Castle. Everyone spoke of the Greek Slave, everyone praised it; everywhere there was astonishment expressed that America had produced an artist of such transcendent ability, as was manifested in that statue; but everyone did not know that the artist was an earnest and faithful New Churchman.

It is in this sense only that we can speak of Hiram Powers and several others as little known in diffusing the truths of the New Church. He was one who raised the fame of his native land for art; and zealously desired to increase the happiness of his country by spreading the truths of the New Dispensation.

Mr. Powers was born at Woodstock, a town in the State of Vermont, on the 29th of June, 1805. His father was a physician. He was the eighth of a family of nine children, and very early manifested strong indications of a bright fancy, and of great mechanical ingenuity.

While Hiram was but fourteen years of age, his father migrated from New England with his family to a farm in the West, and settled six miles from Cincinnati. His early death led to a separation of the family, and Hiram went to live with an elder brother, a lawyer in Cincinnati, until he finished his school days.

He went through two or three occupations as a young man, but ultimately became employed by a Mr. Lieman Watson, who was an organ-builder and clock-maker, and here found good scope for his mechanical ingenuity. There are said to be organs still in Cincinnati whose melody his genius had greatly enriched. He made an improvement in the reed-stop, which he tuned by merely turning a screw. He gained great credit also in the management of clocks, so as to be treated by his employer more as a friend than as a servant.

This employer, Watson, was a zealous New Churchman, and from him Hiram learned, and quickly appreciated the great truths of the New Jerusalem, in which he continued to grow and to live as life and work went on.

When he was about twenty-one years of age, he became acquainted with a Prussian artist, a sculptor named EKSTEIN, and spent what time he had to spare in the studio of that gentleman: here his own deep affections were brought out, encouraged, and directed. From Ekstein also he took lessons in French and Drawing, and soon began to show good progress in modelling in wax and clay at his own rooms. Shortly after this he took the position of assistant and artist to the Western Museum at Cincinnati; and among the objects exhibited were many wax figures, and Hiram did a considerable work in mending and making them. He showed his ever bright humour in these, by presenting popular characters of the day in droll attitudes, but wonderfully life-like. Many a good story is told by the old folks of jokes played off by him in those merry days.

He continued, however, to keep on modelling, and discarded entirely the practice then common of taking masks from living persons lying down and having their faces covered with plaster, half smothering them; and took his likenesses by studying the features as if he were painting a portrait.

His genius came out more and more brightly, and calls for his work increased, so that he determined to devote himself to the art of sculpture alone; and in 1834 he removed to Washington, soon after his marriage to Miss Gibson, an amiable young lady who continued to be his help and comfort during life, and remains his widow.

At the capital of the United States he quickly made many friends, and obtained as sitters—President Jackson, Senator Calhoun, Chief Justice Marshall, and other eminent persons.

His works were appreciated there, and he was greatly encouraged by the kindly criticism of the press.

Mr. Powers spent over two years in Washington, and in 1837 determined to take up his abode in Italy, at Florence, where he could compare his work with that of the great masters of the art, for at that time there was nothing in America which he had not already greatly exceeded.

He arrived in Florence, bringing with him a number of casts he had executed in the United States. He had entered a country where the arts had been flourishing for ages, to compete with those who from their youth had studied their profession with the aid of masters, academies, and the finest examples of the art ; yet what was the result ?

When the American artist exhibited his busts, the very sculptors themselves were obliged to confess themselves surpassed by the stranger, and he gave an impulse in Florence to that important branch of sculpture—the execution of portrait busts.

He took up his abode in an old convent in the city, and soon afterwards commenced the series of ideal statues—commencing with Eve, which really raised him into the very first class of his art. His fame led to a visit from the world-renowned Thorwaldsen, the noble Dane who had himself reflected the highest glory on his country and the Museum containing his works—now one of the greatest attractions of Copenhagen. When the old artist, the beloved of kings and princes, stood before Power's statue of Eve, the young American modestly observed, " It is my first full-length statue, sir." "And any sculptor," replied Thorwaldsen, "might be proud to have it for his last." And then the grand old Dane left the studio, declaring that in these modern times a MICHAEL ANGELO had again arisen among men in the person of the young American.

Thorwaldsen on another occasion, when examining Power's busts, declared that the art of portraiture could go no farther. To this branch of his talents our artist applied himself with his accustomed persevering energy, and he executed more than one hundred and fifty busts, including presidents, statesmen, generals, poets (Longfellow, Bryant, Taylor and others,) and distinguished people of all kinds.

While employed on that of President John Quincy Adams, the president himself addressed and presented to him the following feeling lines, which we have extracted from Abbot's Monthly for November, 1883, a work to which in this article we are much indebted.

To Hiram Powers.

Sculptor, thy hand has moulded into form
   The haggard features of a toil-worn face,
   And whosoever views thy work, shall trace
An age of sorrow, and a life of storm.
And can'st thou mould the heart ? for that is warm ;
   Glowing with tenderness for all its race:
   Instinct, with all the sympathies that grace
The pure and artless bosoms, where they swarm.
Artist, may fortune smile upon thy hand !
   Go forth, and rival Greece's art sublime ;
   Return, and bid the statesmen of thy land
   Live in thy marble through all after time.
Oh ! snatch the fire from heaven, Prometheus stole,
And give the lifeless block a breathing soul.
                —*John Quincy Adams.*

Washington, 25th March, 1837.

In the latter part of the struggle between Turkey and Greece, in which so many noble minds viewed with grief and indignation the barbarous and cruel deeds of the Turks, to crush out the efforts of the Greeks to secure self-government, Mr. Powers expressed his sympathy in the production of the Greek Slave. In this exquisite figure of delicate beauty, modesty, and suffering, he moved at once admiration and hearty approval from all who hated oppression, as well as patriotic delight in his own countrymen, who rejoiced in this fresh manifestation of his talent. The people of America clamoured to see it. It was sent over and publicly exhibited in all the great cities. Thousands visited it, and it became not only the gem of the Great Exhibition, but probably what it has been said still to be, "the widest known statue in the world."

Eight reproductions of this statue have been required and executed.

The statues with which it has most frequently been compared are—the Venus de Milo in Paris, the Venus de Medici, the Venus of Canova, and the Niobe in Florence, the Venus of the Capitol in Rome, and the Psyche in Naples. Beyond them all it expresses womanliness and purity, and has been known and loved above them all.

Mrs. Browning, like Powers himself a receiver of New Church principles, writes thus of the impressive figure :—

They say Ideal beauty cannot enter
The house of anguish. On the threshold stands
An alien Image with her shackled hands,
Called the Greek Slave: as if the artist meant her
That passionless perfection, which he lent her,
Shadowed not darkened when the sill expands,
To so confound man's crimes in different lands
With man's ideal sense. Pierce to the centre
Art's fiery finger, and break up ere long
The serfdom of the world ! Appeal, fair stone
From God's pure heights of beauty, 'gainst man's wrong.
Catch up in thy divine face, not alone
East griefs but west—and strike and shame the strong
By thunders of white silence overthrown.

The Fisher Boy, the statue of America, and the portrait statues of the greatest men of the

United States—Washington, Franklin, Jefferson, Daniel Webster, and others, kept Powers employed, and increased his fame unto the last: and he left to his sons the continuation of his studio, and his work, especially to Preston Powers whose name recalls the memory of his father's staunch friend in his early manhood, Mr. Preston of South Carolina.

Soon after my settlement in London, I received a call from Hiram Powers, and had thus the opportunity of making his personal acquaintance. There was a charming frankness in his manner, a brilliancy in his dark eyes, and a hearty geniality in his language, that made you at home with him at once.

His deep affection for the New Church was manifest in all he said, and in his whole bearing. He spoke of his great wish to do a statue of Swedenborg, which he wanted to make somewhat worthy of its subject. At different times of his life he returned to this idea, but something occurred again and again causing it to be deferred.

Fully aware of his father's wishes and ideas, at last this wish was carried out by Mr. Preston Powers, so far as the beautiful and noble bust is concerned, which now stands in the Swedenborg Society's large room.

On visiting Italy I stayed at Hiram Powers' request at his house, the Villa Powers, outside the Porta Romana, and learned there to esteem his dear lady, and the family. On more than one occasion since have I been welcomed to their hospitality.

When the Swedenborg Society was troubled with some temporary misrepresentation, and somewhat under a cloud, he wrote a cheering letter, expressing his hearty sympathy, and requesting (if it was thought to be of any use) that we should publish it, that everyone might know that he deemed it to be a glory to belong to the Church of the New Jerusalem.

At Florence he was universally respected as a man and a Christian. He was the steady attendant at the small Society's Sabbath worship, and the works of Swedenborg and the principles of the New Jerusalem were the themes of his happiest conversation with all to whom they were objects of interest.

At his entrance into the eternal world he had been a New Churchman close upon fifty years.

He was a sincere patriot, always regarding his country with filial love, and Woodstock the place of his birth and boyhood with undying admiration as the prettiest little town he knew.

He had hoped, ere weakness and illness came on from age, to be able to revisit the United States, at least once, for a short time: but it was not so to be. After a life of almost unfailing health, in his sixty-eighth year, there came on a general weakness and break-up for several months, probably the various symptoms and results of heart disease, concluding at last in apoplexy, on Thursday, June 27th, 1873. Up to a few days before his departure he was able to be wheeled around the beautiful garden surrounding his villa.

"The respect and love he had won for himself," said a newspaper correspondent, "was evinced by tender enquiries on all sides for news of his daily condition, and by the universal feeling shown when his death was reported, that a man of singular purity of character, and of a large-hearted nature, had passed from the scenes of earth."

Rev. Mr. Ford, the New Church minister at Florence, wrote: "A husband and father loved almost to adoration has been thus withdrawn from his family; a man of high gifts from Art, a great name from American Sculpture, and from the small Society at Florence its chief stay and ornament."

Of him it could be truly said, He lived in the Lord, and he died in the Lord. Blessed are the dead that die in the Lord.

MR. BECCONSALL, OF PRESTON,

The Meek and Benevolent Christian.

ABOUT 1839, in carrying out a devout desire I had that every town within a few miles around Accrington should have a New Church Society, I had delivered lectures at Haslingden, and Blackburn, Burnley, and Clithero, with good results; but Preston, quite a large, intellectual, and important town, stood invitingly near, and no effort had been made there.

Two or three persons had been heard of who were favourable to the New Church, but nothing more. There was only the theatre to be had for my lectures, which was but little used for histrionic displays, but was coming into service for temperance objects, so the first New Church discourses in Preston were delivered on the stage.

Mr. Becconsall was heard of, Mr. Parkinson (the father of Mr. John Parkinson of Preston) came to the front, but Mr. Stones, afterwards well known, and Mr. Edleston (a young man in Mr. Stone's employ—afterwards the Rev. Richd. Edleston), were the chief helpers on the occasion of these lectures. Mr. Edleston was full of life, zeal, and helpfulness.

The result of these and succeeding efforts was

that a number of those interested resolved to have New Church worship in Preston. Some half-dozen earnest young men in Accrington had been reading the Works of Swedenborg diligently and practising at the weekly public meetings of the Society until they could address an audience with effect; (they have almost all gone now); these undertook to supply the young Societies for a time, including that of Preston.

A modest room up a passage was taken, not very commodious or attractive, but one where many a delightful meeting was held during two or three years.

Then I heard of old Mr. Nuttall, who had for many years had worship by himself on a Sunday in Longridge Fells, reading the service and the sermon, and singing the hymns accompanied by himself on the violoncello, with as much exactitude as if he had been accompanied by a congregation of a thousand people. Also of Mr. Becconsall, who heads this article, who had been long in Preston as a grocer on a large scale, but retired to Ashton several years before. Both these gentlemen intimated that if there were a proper place of worship erected, and a congregation formed with a suitable pastor, they would come and join. The Becconsalls had frequently attended at the room, but felt that something more was wanted.

Finding the other friends delighted at the prospect, Mr. Becconsall further intimated that he would build the church, and the house for the minister, if agreeable to the other brethren.

There were only entire satisfaction and gratitude expressed by the friends generally, that the Lord had raised up such a helper; so the work was soon begun, and went briskly on. The foundation stone of the church was laid on May the 18th, 1843, and on March the 7th, 1844, it was opened for divine service by the Rev. E. D. Rendell.

I had now become acquainted with Mr. and Mrs. Becconsall, and learned their previous history. Mr. Becconsall was a man of very composed and upright character, extremely meek and staid in his manner, but very decisive also.

His reception of the doctrines shows what great results may come from apparently insignificant beginnings. A person with tracts to sell called at his shop about the year 1807, and he was struck with the title of one—" The Greatest Truth ever published, Jesus Christ the Only God." It was a Birmingham tract, price 6d. Mr. Becconsall read it, and was much impressed by it. He showed it to his brother Edward, who was also led to approve. They then lent it to a young lawyer, whom they expected to be equally pleased, but he returned it with the endorsement, " THE GREATEST LIE EVER PUBLISHED: "—so much depends upon the previous state of the mind to which the Truth is presented. The greatest truth to one is the greatest lie to another. " Open mine eyes, O Lord, that I may see," should be the prayer of every one to Him who has promised, " I will bring the blind by a way that they know not; I will lead them in paths they have not known. I will make darkness light before them, and crooked things straight. These things will I do unto them, and not forsake them." (Isa. xlii. 16.)

Not at all dismayed by his young lawyer friend's decisive and unfavourable judgment, Mr.

Becconsall had noticed in the tract that there was a minister named Proud with a New Church place of worship in London; and his youngest brother then residing in London, he desired him to visit the place and report. The brother did so, and sent a very favourable account, with a list of the works then published, including "The Apocalypse Revealed, two volumes."

Mr. Becconsall had long conceived a desire to understand more perfectly the Book of Revelation, and on reading this work he was fully convinced as he said that the truths it contained were the real truths of the Word of God, and the most pure and unadulterated that were ever published by man. From time to time he obtained the Arcana Celestia, the True Christian Religion, and others, which he partly enjoyed, but after awhile somewhat flagged in his spiritual appetite and suffered himself to be greatly absorbed in business, and then fell into many severe trials, temptations, and troubles.

These he regarded afterwards as divine means of spiritualising his character, and needed for his highest good. "By their results," he says, "I was at length brought out of the land of Egypt."

When the New Church truths had been publicly opened in Preston, Mr. Becconsall had long been weary of hearing preaching that taught the sacrifice of one God called God the Son, to make atonement to and satisfy the justice of another God called God the Father, but "I now saw," he says, "that this was one of the mysteries of Babylon; and so I came out of the house of bondage."

He was joined in his spiritual progress by his

wife, and they both considered it a desirable thing to concur in the new movement, and promote it by the means Divine Providence had placed in their power.

They removed to Preston again from Ashton, and not only resolved to build the church, but TO SUPPORT A SUITABLE MINISTER ALSO, as long as it might be needed. He writes, as we read in a brief sketch handed to the Rev. E. D. Rendell, "As we had thought of doing something for the establishment of the church at some future time, we determined to begin at once, so that we might have an opportunity of seeing something of its progress, and hearing some of the hidden things of the Word. We set about the work, and built the church in Avenham Road at our own expense, the foundation stone of which was laid on the 18th of May, 1843, and it was opened for divine service on the 7th of March following, by the Rev. E. D. Rendell preaching on the descent of the New Jerusalem."

The orderly, upright, patient and benevolent life of Mr. Becconsall was a constant and impressive illustration and recommendation of the principles of his religion, through the twenty years from the erection of the church in Preston to the time of his removal into the eternal world in the 90th year of his age. His end was gentle and peaceful, like that of the old men of the Most Ancient Church. "No man," says Mr. Rendell, "could have a stronger conviction of the goodness and mercy of the Lord, in Whose hands he was, nor of the reality of the world to which he was being removed. He passed away in peace, to which I was witness."

It was on Tuesday, February 2nd, 1864, when

Mr. Becconsall passed from the natural into the spiritual world.

On the WILL of Mr. Becconsall becoming known, it was found that in his own quiet way he had left a number of bequests, of £500 each, to many of the younger preachers of the Church, including some who had recently joined from other religious bodies. No doubt he had concluded that such a welcome would encourage these comparatively young men to labour heartily for the spread of the great truth he devotedly loved.

The pleasure excited by this little shower of legacies was somewhat moderated, on its being learned that the payment would only take place on the death of Mrs. Becconsall.

Besides these he left very considerable aids to some of the Societies in which he felt special interest. To his own Society—Preston—he left nearly £1,000, to Blackburn £800, and to Accrington £1,200, in round numbers.

To Southport, the sea-side resort in Lancashire which has been called the Montpellier of England and where New Church visitants are very often found, he left, under the safeguard and direction of Conference, Water Works Stock to the amount of £1,733 6s. 8d., to be used for the support of a minister for the Southport Society, when one should be formed with a minister, which has happily been accomplished now for many years.

In 1873, a few earnest and generous New Church friends, who had for some time met as a small congregation in a room, determined to take steps to obtain a more suitable position and a minister, no doubt encouraged by the knowledge of Mr. Becconsall's bequest.

In December of that year, the year of Mrs. Becconsall's departure, the foundation was laid, on a suitable site in Duke-street, and on July the 11th, 1875, the beautiful and comfortable chapel the friends now enjoy was opened by myself. Under the affectionate and earnest ministry of the Rev. Mr. Ashby, that Society is now a comfort and a blessing, both to the inhabitants and to the frequent New Church visitors.

Mrs. Becconsall survived her worthy husband nine years, in which she carried out the same help to the Preston Society which he had afforded during his life, and an equally kindly disposition to aid the Church in general. By her Will she bequeathed £1,000 to the Preston Infirmary, £100 to the Preston Blind Asylum, and to the New Church Society in Preston she added to what her husband had done £1,000, for the support of the minister.

She left for the New Church College £1,000, and to various other charitable uses in the Church £1,800, making in tha whole from her bequests the handsome sum of £3,800.

Such were the worthy friends who mainly contributed to the establishment of two New Church Societies, and a great number of pious and excellent uses, and who deserve to be lastingly held in remembrance as at once meek and truly benevolent Christians.

JOHN FINNIE, ESQ., OF BOWDON,
NEAR MANCHESTER,

The Successful Merchant, the Munificent Helper of Charitable Uses, Founder of the Society of Kensington, London

MR. FINNIE was one of those orderly, clear-headed, persevering young Scotchmen, that have made their countrymen admired and esteemed, and their country respected all over the world.

He was born in Kilmarnock, in 1790, and arrived in London when he was only seventeen years of age, a religious, thoughtful young man.

This was at the time the Rev. Joseph Proud, formerly a Baptist minister at Norwich, but subsequently an earnest and eloquent expounder of the truths of the New Church, was drawing large congregations at the chapel in York-street, St. James's Square, formerly the Chapel of the Spanish Embassy. He preached there from 1799 to 1812.

Young Finnie listened thoughtfully, hailed the clear and heavenly doctrines he heard set forth with such scriptural power and fervour, and resolved, if he succeeded in business, he would do his best to support those grand truths, and spread them in the world.

How different is such a reflective, thinking young man, from the heedless youth who runs about after silly or profligate pleasure, keeping late hours, spending his spare money with loose people—those earnings above expenses which if taken care of are the beginnings of thrift and of fortune. With random young men Sunday is the day of wild excitement, jauntings with senseless people, excess in eating and drinking, laying the foundations of disease, and discordant uproar; returning the young man to business on Monday weakened and dissipated, instead of rejoicing in health from the refreshment, peace, and strength, which come from a Sabbath well spent.

In the meditations and sound principles of the thoughtful young man are all the seeds of his future prosperity and happiness.

While giddy young fellows were flying about here and there in a brainless way, young Finnie was enquiring where the most valuable preacher could be found, and he was informed of Mr. Proud. He went and heard, and was convinced the truth was there. It came as new light from heaven. It said to him, "Arise, shine, for thy light is come, and the glory of the Lord has arisen upon thee." He determined that he would regulate his life by these new truths, and both directly and indirectly they had no doubt much to do with his great success.

The credit of steady behaviour, and uprightness in word and deed, create confidence; and confidence doubles and quadruples a man's means of prosperity.

An elder brother of Mr. Finnie was already established in Rio Janeiro, and when John was twenty years of age he was invited to join him there.

He went, and showed so much ability and

trustworthiness, that year after year he was more and more valued, and by his shrewdness, his competency, and his perseverance, he realized a large fortune ; never forgetting to increase his spiritual riches at the same time, or the purpose he had formed some day to aid the spread of New Church truth amongst young and old.

He returned to England to enjoy what he had realized in a calm and useful old age.

Having been engaged in business in connection with the goods of Manchester, he chose to settle near that city, and fixed his home in a beautiful neighbourhood called Bowdon, about eight or nine miles out, well known to Manchester people.

In his quiet way he visited the New Church service at Peter-street, Manchester, then under the ministry of the Rev. John Henry Smithson, but Mr. Finnie was some time, during these occasional visits, before he made himself known to any one, or the interest he felt in the New Church.

The very respectable-looking aged gentleman coming at intervals was noticed ; but the friends feared to intrude, and as he did not seem to invite attention, went without further notice away.

He had however rather handsome rich-looking gold spectacles ; and it was noticed by some of the more observant, that when there was a collection, and the gold spectacles were there, the amount of the collection was always very respectable. At length he made himself known to Mr. Smithson, and an affectionate intercourse came to exist between them. After awhile, conversation arose respecting the uses in the Church that could be aided, and through Mr. Smithson, much for a time, was anonymously done.

Mr. Finnie had a strong wish that his native town, Kilmarnock, should hear the principles of the New Church, and he desired Mr. Smithson to go and deliver a course of lectures there, which was done by that respected gentleman, at Mr. Finnie's request.

During the delivery, Mr. Smithson was taken ill with a severe attack of carbuncle. He finished the lectures on March 22nd, 1864, and feeling severely ill, he hastened home to Manchester. Four days after, on the 26th of March, he breathed his last, to the great regret of Mr. Finnie, and a wide circle of friends.

At his funeral I was introduced to Mr. Finnie for the first time, and was gratified to notice his unassuming manner, although even then he had begun to do some of those striking acts of generosity which ultimately arose to such a gratifying extent.

He sent his first cheque to Mr. Gunton, the treasurer of the Conference, in 1862. It was for £2,000, and to aid the National Missionary Society. The name of the donor was not disclosed, I believe at his special request; it was not mentioned in the minute recording it. The year following he sent another cheque for £2,000 also. This was for the Pension Fund. He reflected that for a very considerable time the early labourers in the ministry would be scantily paid, and would be able to lay up little for old age or the comfort of their widows. The Pension Fund was to supply the necessity in this class of cases. In 1866, desiring to encourage pious young men to prepare for the ministry, he sent a cheque of £4,000, of which £2,000 was for the College, and £2,000 for the Students' and Ministers' Aid

Fund; thus endeavouring to add to the number of those who spread abroad the tidings of the God of Love. In 1870 he gave another £1,000 to the National Missionary Institution.

In the early days of the Church not many of those interested in the writings of Swedenborg resided at the West end of London. Mr. Hindmarsh lived in Clerkenwell, near where Swedenborg had resided; and the friends generally in the City; hence the places of worship were erected in the North and central portions of the Metropolis.

Need therefore had at length been experienced for places of worship convenient for the inhabitants at the West End, and Mr. Finnie entered into this feeling and authorized three gentlemen, Mr. Pickstone, Mr. Gunton, and myself, to select a suitable site to build a church upon, or to purchase a church already erected, if one likely for the purpose could be found for sale. In either case HE WOULD PROVIDE THE FUNDS.

The latter was the course deemed advisable, and the eligible church in Palace Gardens Terrace being advertised, was authorized by him to be purchased, and everything to be done to make it elegant and comfortable, as is usual for New Church worship, not forgetting a goodly organ.

A beautiful wood was provided for the pulpit and reading desk, the communion rail and book boards by Mr. Pickstone; but with that exception the entire expense of the whole purchase was defrayed by Mr. Finnie.

The cost of the building was somewhat over £5,000; the internal changes, organ, &c., came to £1,696; and the endowment, £5,000. The entire outlay amounted to £12,050, as will be seen from the circular tablet now placed in the church to commemorate this munificent act of charity and liberality.

The inscription in the church reads thus:—

THIS TABLET
IS ERECTED TO THE MEMORY
OF
JOHN FINNIE, ESQ.,
OF
BOWDON LODGE, CHESHIRE,
WHO
DEPARTED THIS LIFE
1875
AND WHO HAD
PURCHASED, RENOVATED AND ENDOWED
THIS CHURCH IN
1872
BY THE MUNIFICENT GIFT OF
£12,050
TO PROMOTE THE WORSHIP OF
THE LORD JESUS CHRIST,
THE ONLY GOD OF HEAVEN AND EARTH,
AND THE EXTENSION OF HIS
KINGDOM AMONGST MANKIND.

When we bear in mind, that he never saw this church, and never appeared ostentatiously in any proceedings in relation to it, we must be impressed by the extreme modesty of his character.

He trusted those who he believed were earnest that good might be done, and he found the means. The one great love of his Lord and Master animated him, and he sought no inferior motive. He let not his left hand know what his right hand was doing. Had he seen the result of his noble generosity at the present time he would no doubt have experienced internal delight, and gratitude to his Heavenly Father who had prospered the work of his hands. There is a cheering attendance in the commodious church at the morning and evening services.

Members to the number of 418 have been entered in the twelve years. There is a crowded Sunday-school, with a large singing-class admirably attended to; classes for working men and for studious young men; a mutual improvement society; with various works of benevolence for doing good in the neighbourhood. Indeed this Society is what every New Church Society ought to be, and will be, if it is truly genuine, praying and working for all around—A BLESSING IN THE MIDST OF THE LAND.

About the same period Mr. Finnie assisted several other Societies who were obtaining new places of worship. He gave £100 each to Nottingham, South London, Deptford, and Brightlingsea; while to the Cross Street Society (to enable them to finish their beautiful new church in Camden Road without debt) he sent two cheques of £1,000 each.

The sum total of these noble instances of modest benevolence amounted to £23,346. There was no ostentation, no self-righteousness, no claim of merit in this. It was Christian love doing its holy work.

He had a truly New Church feeling in relation to the good work which was being done by other religious bodies. He regarded their conscientious convictions with respect and deference, and, when they needed it, liberally helped them. This was especially the case as to the Church of

England, in rebuilding the parish church of his district. His feeling was that the New Church was the church to unite the good Christian people of every name ; and, by evincing charity, to strengthen and bring out charity as much as possible.

The generosity of Mr. Finnie was not confined to religious instances, his kindness in fostering a good object, or a good person to whom a little assistance would be valuable, was continually experienced, and the large number of kind remembrances of servants, old friends, and others, in his Will, was quite unusual, all attesting his affectionate, though not demonstrative, nature.

He did good in secret, and blushed to find it fame. He took great interest in the work of making our coasts more secure for our hardy seamen in stormy weather; and himself contributed a life-boat for the protection of his native Ayrshire. He longed to see the time when safe harbours would everywhere be in reach of our brave and toiling mariners when tempests threatened serious danger.

We have taken a survey of Mr. Finnie's outward life, and seen his calm and quiet diligence in doing good. We must, however, always remember that a man's doings are really the outbirth of his character, and that is chiefly built up and shown at home. Have you lived with him ? is an important inquiry to be made, when anyone undertakes to give a genuine account of another.

Happily a very dear friend of my own, a relative of the family, who once resided three years with his uncle in his home, has given me a description, from which I am happy in being permitted to quote.

"He was remarkable for his punctuality. His home was regulated with the precision of a working chronometer. The day was divided into sections for work, constitutional walk, and enjoyment, which are now beautiful to recollect.

"He read prayers morning and evening, for the household and the servants. His reading was with a rich, sonorous voice, which impressed one with profound veneration, and showed how deeply conscious he was of the majesty, the sublime dignity and grandeur of the heavens and the earth, and of the Almighty and Adorable Maker. His self-command was admirable, and when he had read anything in Swedenborg which had much impressed him, or any collateral work with which he was greatly pleased (and he was a diligent reader), he would not expatiate much himself, but would hand the book and remark, 'Read that, you will find good in it.'"

Such was John Finnie, the steady, thoughtful Scotch laddie, who set out to do his duty and to make his fortune, the fine old Scottish gentleman, whom we delight to own as a New Church Worthy.

His parents were poor. When he was a boy he ran about bare-footed; but, no doubt, the mental faculties of the family were excellent, as is the case with a very large proportion of the Scotch working classes. One of his nephews became Member of Parliament for a division of Ayrshire; and another, the largest colliery proprietor in the county. Such men can help themselves, and help others also.

How glorious a thing it would be for themselves and for the world, would young men generally cultivate their intellectual faculties diligently as young John Finnie did; embrace for their affections the sacred principles of modesty, uprightness, diligence, order, goodness, and perseverance, of which a true New Church life consists, and then character would follow, that would sanctify and bless the home, and faith would fortify them in temptations, and enable them cheerfully to adopt the sacred words, "I shall dwell in the house of the Lord for ever."

Mr. Finnie passed peacefully from earth, at Bowdon, where he had long resided, at the ripe age of 85, on the 20th of July, 1875.

JOHN FLAXMAN,

The world-renowned Sculptor.

WHOEVER contemplates the magnificent memorial raised by the Queen and her people to manifest their admiration for the character of Albert the Good, may observe the group of distinguished sculptors on the west side of the white-marbled base, and at the head of these stands the figure of Flaxman.

All who are moderately acquainted with the history of art will know how great was his eminence in sculpture, in some respects unrivalled, how universally he was esteemed and beloved for his amiable and gentle spirit by his great contemporaries in art and literature, for these have been described by Allan Cunningham in his history of great painters and sculptors, by Dr. Smiles in his excellent Self-Help, by Harriet Martineau in her History of the Thirty Years Peace, and many others, but few are aware that he was one of the very earliest readers and receivers of the Writings of Swedenborg; and formed his character and conduct by the truths they contained, from his early manhood to his life's end.

In the list of those who attended the meeting

with Mr. Hindmarsh and others in the New Court, Middle Temple, in 1784, when as yet they had no place of worship of their own, given in page 23 of the History of the Rise and Progress of the New Church will be found Mr. John Flaxman, the celebrated sculptor, Wardour Street. This was only two years after his marriage which, as we shall see later, took place in 1782. In 1797, the friends who desired to worship in strict harmony with their convictions, took possession of Cross Street, then recently erected, and they enjoyed the ministry of Mr. Proud. Flaxman was one of the committee for two years, at the end of which time the Society found the expenses too heavy for their early condition, and accepted an offer of the eligible chapel, at a very moderate rent, in York Street, Hanover Square, better suited to their circumstances, and in which they continued to worship for fourteen years.

Flaxman constantly supported the Society for printing and publishing the Writings of Swedenborg, now called the Swedenborg Society, from ITS COMMENCEMENT IN 1810 TO HIS DEATH, attended its meetings, and advocated its objects. At the annual meeting in June, 1817, he is reported to have been present, as a distinguished member of the Royal Academy, and to have made a very eloquent and appropriate speech, to weaken the prejudices entertained by many against Swedenborg and his writings.

He was a bosom friend of Charles Augustus Tulk, then chairman of the Society, who, on the death of Flaxman, in 1826, wrote to *The Times* of December 15th, assuring the readers from his personal knowledge, that Flaxman's " religious sentiments had for many years been formed entirely on the doctrines of Swedenborg."

Members of Mr. Tulk's family have mentioned to me from time to time how devoutly Flaxman was in the habit of expressing his indebtedness to New Church principles, not only in his life, but in his art. And, from one of that family, a very dear friend of my own, one of the members of the Kensington Society, we have three tablets done by Flaxman, now erected in our church in Palace Gardens Terrace, which had remained with them from Flaxman's time.

Two are in the church itself, illustrating the two sections of the Lord's Prayer, "Lead us not into temptation," and "Deliver us from evil," and there is one in the schoolroom, which represents "Mercury bearing Pandora to earth," all three exquisite specimens of his spiritual and refined genius.

Having shown how thoroughly Flaxman's mind and character belonged to the New Church I will now request my reader to accompany me in a survey of his life and works.

He was born at York on the 6th of July, 1755, and was brought to London, where his father brought his family when John was a very little, weakly boy, and settled as a seller of plaster casts. His shop was in New Street, Covent Garden.

He was five years old, and could only hobble about on crutches at the time of the coronation of George III., but he was for all that a bright, intelligent little fellow, and entreated his father to bring him one of the coronation medals back, that he might take an impression of it.

He usually sat behind his father's counter,

propped up by pillows, for there was a curvature in his back, and would amuse himself by drawing, and getting help while he strove to learn to read.

He got on rapidly, and was so studious and intelligent that a kind clergyman in the neighbourhood named, Matthews, took an interest in the boy, brought him books, and encouraged him in every way.

In the meantime he got stronger and at length could lay his crutches aside, and then he was invited to visit his friend at home, and Mrs. Matthews made him also a favourite, praising his youthful efforts, which, for a boy almost self-taught, were extremely good.

He began to imitate the figures in his father's shop, in modelling with plaster of Paris, wax, and clay. His kind friends told him much about history, and the Greeks and Romans, and interested him in Ajax, Achilles, and Homer. They gave him lessons in Latin and Greek, which he prosecuted with ardour at home.

Don Quixote, and Paradise Lost, also, they introduced to him, and found that these writings were a constant delight to the earnest boy.

His chalk drawings, poor enough at first, gradually improved, and Mrs. Matthews was at length so pleased with them, that she got a commission from a lady friend, for him to draw six original sketches, in black chalk, of subjects in Homer.

His first commission! The boy duly executed the order, and was both well praised, and well paid.

At fifteen Flaxman entered as a student at the Royal Academy, and in the same year he won the prize of the silver medal. The next year he competed for the gold one, but did not succeed, though his fellow students generally believed he deserved it.

A young man named Engleheart, however, obtained the prize, of whom nothing, or next to nothing, was afterwards ever heard.

The failure did Flaxman no harm. When a youth is made of the true stuff, he feels he will succeed in the end, and he continues to bring out his ever-improving powers. "Give me time," said young Flaxman to his father, "and I will yet produce works that the Academy will recognize." He redoubled his exertions, spared no pains, and consequently made steady progress.

Having now grown to be a young man, and becoming better acquainted with life, he observed the bare living which his father was able to obtain for the family, and he resolved to lay Homer aside for a while, and heartily assist his father in plaster-cast making. He was willing to work for years at this humble business, and he did so, and kept the wolf from the door, and made the family circle more comfortable.

We observe in this the excellent disposition of young Flaxman. He drudged with his father a long apprenticeship at very humble work, but this was ultimately for his good. It accustomed him to steady work, and to self-sacrifice; at the same time he communicated a grace to what he did, which came to the ears of Mr. Wedgwood, then greatly desirous to improve the style of English pottery.

Anyone, who has gone to observe the beautiful wares at the Japanese Palace, at Dresden, where the Saxon elegant manufacture is set forth to great advantage, and compared it as is pretended to be done with the artistic work of other nations, will have seen the dowdy articles, the blue old teapots, and the crude cups and saucers, which are set forth to exhibit English skill and taste. They were what could be seen in full use before Wedgwood's time, but are the veriest caricature of what has since been produced in the elegant work of Copeland, Spode, Elers, Minton, and others, leaving the Saxons and their finest past work far behind. From Wedgwood's time undoubtedly England in porcelain has stood first, France second, and Germany third.

During my own residence in Dresden, thirty years ago, I was often greatly annoyed at seeing the old fashioned wares of England, a century ago, set forth as specimens of what the England of 1855 could do. The English authorities resident there ought to have taken care to have the country properly represented in such things, but they were overlooked.

Wedgwood, as has been remarked, having heard of young Flaxman's taste and skill, paid him a visit, and addressed him in an openhearted cheery way, "Well, my lad," he broke out, "I have heard you are a good draughtsman and clever designer, I am a manufacturer of pots, named Wedgwood. Now I want you to design some models for me; nothing fantastic, but simple, tasteful, and correct in drawing. I'll pay you well. You don't think the work beneath you?" "By no means, sir," replied Flaxman; "indeed the work is quite to my taste. Give me a few days, and call again, and you will see what I can do."

"That's right, work away. Mind, I am in want of them now. They are for pots of all kinds;—teapots, jugs, teacups, and saucers. But especially I want designs for a table service. Begin with that. I mean to supply one for the Royal table. Now, think of that, young man. What you design is for the eyes of royalty!"

"I will do my best, I assure you." And the kind and generous Wedgwood went smartly out of the shop, as he had come in.

Young Flaxman did his best. By the time Mr. Wedgwood called again, he had a numerous series of models, prepared for various pieces of earthenware. They consisted chiefly of small groups in low relief, the subjects taken from ancient history and poetry. Many of them are still in existence, and are equal in beauty and simplicity to his after designs in marble. He visited the museums, where the celebrated Etruscan vases were to be seen, and these suggested to him the most graceful forms, to which he added his own elegant devices. Stuart's Athens, then recently published, also furnished him with specimens of the purest shapes of Greek utensils, and he was not slow to adopt the best of them, and work them up into new and wondrous shapes of elegance and beauty.

For several years he worked on at the employment chiefly provided by Mr. Wedgwood, executing but few works of art of any other kind, and at rare intervals. He lived a quiet, secluded life, working during the day and sketching and reading during the evenings. He was too poor to find much marble for his works ; so generally confined himself to plaster of Paris.

He had however met with an amiable young lady, Miss Denman, a bright-souled, cheery, well informed, intellectual, noble young woman, with whom he felt he could be entirely happy, so he resolved to marry, and he left home and rented a small house and studio in Wardour-street, Soho. He was confident that with such a helper he should be able to work with greater devotion, for she too had a taste for poetry and art, and besides was an enthusiastic admirer of the genius of her lover. They married in 1782, and made their little home a paradise. He was then 27 years of age. Sir Joshua Reynolds, himself a bachelor, met Flaxman shortly after, and broke out upon him in sharp reproach, " So, Flaxman, I am told you are married; if so, sir, I tell you, you are ruined for an artist." Flaxman continued his journey home, and soon seated himself beside his wife, and taking her hand in his said with a look of great concern, " Ann, I am ruined for an artist." " How so, John ?" she replied, "Who has done it, and how has it happened ?" " It happened," he rejoined, " at church, and Ann Denman has done it."

He then told her what Sir Joshua had said, whose opinions on that subject were well known and had often been expressed. He maintained the absurd proposition, that students who would succeed must suspend all other pursuits, however proper and natural, and bring the whole powers of their minds to bear upon art from the moment they rose in the morning until they went to bed, as if proper leisure and change did not strengthen the mind, and prolonged monotony did not weary and weaken it.

He added, "Sir Joshua said no man can be a great artist unless he studies the grand works of Raffaelle, Michael Angelo, and others, at Florence and Rome: and I (said Flaxman) wish to become a great artist." "And a great artist you shall be, John," said his wife, "and visit Rome too, if that be really necessary to make you great." "But how?" asked Flaxman. "Work and economize," rejoined the gallant wife: "I will never have it said—'Ann Denman ruined John Flaxman for an artist.'" And so it was determined by the pair that the journey to Rome was to be made when their means would permit. "I will go to Rome," said Flaxman, "and show the president that wedlock is for a man's good, rather than for his harm; and you, Ann, shall accompany me."

For five years he worked patiently on in their humble home in Wardour-street. The affectionate couple, cheerful and happy, never lost sight of the journey to Rome, he working mainly for the Wedgwoods, who were good paymasters, and she taking care that not a penny should be wasted on useless expenses, but, after necessary home comforts were provided, the surplus should be hoarded for the journey to Italy and the sojourn at Rome. They solicited no help from others, no aid from the Academy, but trusted to their own patient labour and love to achieve their object.

During this period Flaxman exhibited very few works, but obtained many commissions for monuments, by the profits of which he added to his store; and he was thriving, hopeful, and progressive. He was universally respected by his neighbours, and his artistic circle of friends, amongst whom were Blake, also an earnest reader of Swedenborg, and Stothard, both great artists, and in many respects of kindred spirit.

All who knew Flaxman greatly esteemed his sincerity, his honesty, and his unostentatious piety.

It was at this period (1784) that is about three years before leaving England for Rome, that he became interested in the Works of Swedenborg, then being translated into English, and met with other friends similarly affected, to cultivate their spiritual knowledge.

When Flaxman, with the aid of his true helpmeet, his invaluable wife, (to whom on all suitable occasions he refers by her pet name Nancy), had saved enough to undertake their journey to Italy, they left England in 1787. He was then 32 years of age, and had already achieved a high reputation.

Arrived there, he applied himself diligently to study, making copies from the antique. English visitors soon found out his studio, and gave him commissions, and it was then that he composed his beautiful designs in illustration of Homer, Æschylus, and Dante. Flaxman worked for Art as well as money, and the beauty of his designs brought him new friends and patrons.

In 1781 his beautiful memorial to Mrs. Morley and her child had been placed in Gloucester Cathedral; and his Chatterton for St. Mary Redcliffe Church, Bristol, was finished in 1784. There was a quiet spiritual beauty, and a refined imagination about his productions thus early, which had made him known to the judges of high Art beyond the precincts of England.

On arriving at Rome, and in the early months of general observation, he became acquainted with Canova, whose own glorious talents enabled him to appreciate a kindred nature, and who encouraged and befriended Flaxman on every occasion.

Canova was in the full zenith of his popularity and his studio often filled with visitors from the British nobility. He often intimated to those who were pressing more commissions upon him than he could possibly accomplish, that they would do well to go and look at Flaxman. He was astonished that they so little noticed their own countryman. "You Englishmen," he said on one occasion, "I believe, see with your ears." This friendly appreciation by Canova (great in his own beautiful talent and without envy) continued after Flaxman's return, and was warmly appreciated by him.

Some years later, when Cambridge wanted a fine statue of some great man to adorn one of the buildings of the University, and formed a Committee of Public Taste to decide what should be done, Sir Charles ——, the chairman, being asked who should do the work, oracularly declared that there was only one man fit for its accomplishment, and that was Canova in Italy.

Canova was consulted, and declined, saying he was too busy, and besides they had the right man in England. They wrote again to ask who it was, and Canova replied he was sorry they had a Flaxman in England, and did not know it. One English nobleman, Lord Egremont, the most intelligent Art patron of the time, was a warm adherent of Flaxman, both when he was in Italy and all his life afterwards. For him, his great work of Michael Conquering Satan, very late in life was executed, and it remains at his seat at Petworth. On the base his Lordship affixed the following appreciation of the sculptor :—

"This group was executed by John Flaxman, R.A.P.S., a man who presented the most striking example of the pre-eminence of the mental over the corporeal faculties of human nature, in the union of the most tender frame with the strongest energy of character, with the most exalted sentiments of honour, with a heart actuated by benevolence, and with a sublimity of genius of which this work remains a splendid monument, hardly surpassed by the most celebrated productions of ancient times, and certainly by none in his own."

During all his time in Italy he continued to supply Wedgwood with designs and patterns, and, considering the rate of payment for Art at that time, was generously supported.

He also executed his drawings of the Illustrations of Homer, Æschylus, and Dante, which were sought after, and were a source of income.

At the end of four years of residence in Rome, and travelling to the south to see Naples, Paestum, and Virgil's country, as well as Herculaneum and Pompeii, he was preparing to return home, when his friend Canova introduced the Earl of Bristol, who was also Bishop of Derry, and who prevailed upon him to execute for him a large work, The Fury of Athamas, which kept him two years and a-half longer at Rome.

In December, 1794, he returned to London, and settled in Buckingham-street, Fitzroy Square, to the great joy of his old friends, and with increased public estimation.

He was appointed to execute the monument to Lord Mansfield for Westminster Abbey, which greatly increased his fame, and is the object of public admiration still. The great judge is seated in a curule chair, supported by Wisdom and Justice, with Truth represented sustaining the background. This was followed soon by the memorial to Mr. Bosanquet, in Leyton Church, with the representation of The Good Samaritan.

Thenceforward his work was called for in the great cathedrals, and distinguished churches far and wide in England, so as to keep himself and his pupils incessantly employed.

Besides St. Paul's and Westminster Abbey, Winchester contains several of his works; Chichester, I think eight; Gloucester, Christchurch, Harrow, Oxford, Cambridge, and many others.

Each work is an historic picture, as well as a specimen of the highest art and beauty.

Take the one to Sir William Jones—the great Indian scholar, said to be master of twenty-eight languages—which was set up in the Chapel of University College, Oxford: you see Sir William himself, the picture of kindness and intelligence, with open book, and Hindoo pundits and pupils before and about him.

See the one on Charity in Campsull Church, near Doncaster, Yorkshire; and the tablet set up in St. John's Church, Manchester, to celebrate the fiftieth anniversary of the ministry of the Rev. John Clowes, which was done in 1818. Flaxman, we are informed in the biography, was a particular and esteemed friend of Mr. Clowes.

This beautiful tablet will have been seen and admired, no doubt, by many of my readers, and represents the reverend subject of it addressing three generations—the children, their parents, and grandparents—an angel standing behind, with palm branch, the emblem of victory. The intelligent observer of the works of Flaxman will have noticed the influence of his religious views on his art in many ways, but especially in his so often representing both angels and evil spirits without wings. It is not only the conclusion of thoughtful minds like that of Dr. Young that—

> Angels are men in lighter bodies clad,
> And men are angels, loaded for an hour:

But the direct and distinct teaching of the New Church is, that all angels and devils are from the human race. Indeed, without this, it would be very difficult to give a reason for the creation of this world at all.

The human body, with its glorious arms, hands, and fingers, the embodiment of human power, and its adaptation, is the perfection of form.

Wings are not something higher than arms, but, indeed, are far less perfect. They are the imperfect substitutes for arms in a far less noble creature. Fins are the same things for fish, and, though the indications are there, serpents drop them off altogether.

Wings are the emblems of the elevating and protecting power of truths, and so may be allegorically used, as they are in Scripture. The good man is said to mount up with wings like eagles; the Almighty to protect us with His wings; but neither one nor the other have these appendages literally.

In representing his angels and evil spirits, as he frequently does, without wings—as in the illustrations, "Lead us not into temptation" and "Deliver us from evil" in our New Church, at Kensington, in Mr. Clowes' tablet, and many others—Flaxman was presenting the real forms of angels; while in other instances, as in "The Guardian Angel," where a lovely baby is guarded by a motherly angel with very large wings, he is indicating the great protection needed by helpless infancy and innocence.

In 1800 he was made an Associate of the Royal Academy; in 1803 he became Fellow; and in 1810 the Academy instituted a Professorship of Sculpture, and requested him to accept it, which he did.

He delivered several courses of lectures, some of which were printed, and were so saturated with the exalted spirituality which pervaded, as religion ought to do, everything of the Professor, that Fuseli, who was a great artist and a devoted friend of Flaxman's, too, but with little religion, used waggishly say, he was going to hear the Reverend Professor Flaxman.

In 1818 he completed that splendid work of art, the "Shield of Achilles." It was the labour of many years, done for Rundel and Bridge, goldsmiths, and the history of the world, in the flow of time, is depicted upon it. During its progress the Duke of York would occasionally come in and admire it.

The practical wisdom of Flaxman was evinced in his evenness of temper; if he experienced from anyone the irritability which they had not yet been happy enough to subdue.

Mr. ——— called about a work which had taken longer than expected, and the purse-proud gentleman was noisy and insolent. Flaxman quietly explained the fact, and took no notice of the ungentlemanly manner or expressions. After a little time, his assistant mentioned his astonishment at his gentleness, when Flaxman replied, "I always think it the best way to treat such persons; they are much to be pitied. They lay themselves open to their own unhappy reflections. For they cannot but feel as the victims of their own ignorance and bad temper; and in such reflections find the bitterest self-reproof."

G. F. Teniswood, F.S.A., to whose admirable papers in the *Art Journal* for 1867 and 1868 I am greatly indebted in this sketch, says, of Flaxman, "Among his brother artists no man enjoyed a higher share of sincere regard. Beloved by Lawrence, the bosom friend of the gentle Stothard, the intimate companion of the mystic Blake, and the admiration of the philosophic Fuseli, his position with those among whom he worked and walked is more than explained. So thoroughly unselfish was he by nature, and so touchingly alive to the thought of human misery, that the ministrations of private charity were his frequent office. To the suffering he had ever a word of consolation; to the striving he brought encouragement; while his power of winning the esteem of all lay in the sincerity of motive regulating his actions."

In 1821 a change took place, which very sadly affected Flaxman. After nearly forty years of the happiest married life, the dear partner of his toils and triumphs ended her career on earth. She had been his true helpmeet, his other half, his better half; and he could not exhibit at the Royal Academy that year. Her sister, Miss Maria Denman, a lady of kindred spirit, filled her place in the household as well as it could be done by another; his own sister also resided with him; but the remaining years of his life were somewhat as those of a dove that had lost its mate.

He was sixty-six years of age, and his pupils and assistants were friends, full of admiration and affection; but it was evident that a certain charm of his life was at least dimmed for a time.

There is an interesting story told of one of his pupils, Mr. L. Watson—the same who executed the marble statue of Flaxman, now at the entrance of the Hall of University College, London. After his afternoon labours, Flaxman usually had a moderate quiet walk through the fields towards Hampstead, now covered with houses, and took a little refreshment at the end of his journey, for a short rest, and then returned.

Young Watson would follow at a distance, wait until his master came out, notice his kindly acts to the poor, and go happily home. This habit continued for a long time. Such are the deep attachments which arise from genuine goodness.

In 1826, on the 7th of December, his health having been long declining, a severe cold in three days brought his beautiful life on earth to a close, in his 72nd year. His remains were followed to the grave by the President and Council of the Royal Academy. Part of the burial ground where his body was laid was taken by the Midland Railway but the portion including the grave of Flaxman has lately been put into good order, and his monument is kept in a position of honour, and near which children now can rest and play.

On the 11th of December, before the funeral had taken place, Sir Thomas Lawrence, at the annual meeting of the Academicians, pronounced on Flaxman a high and solemn encomium pointing to his genius, his abilities, and his virtues, which will fully warrant our placing him among the most estimable and beloved of our New Church Worthies.

We extract from the Morning Herald of Dec. 19th, 1826. After the delivery of the premiums, the President in his address to the students introduced the following tribute, which we have somewhat abridged to the memory of Mr. Flaxman:—

"I know that the regulated proceedings of this night might justify or impose my silence: but why, when the form of that estimable being, whose death we are lamenting, is not consigned to earth—why should we not speak to you, gentlemen, who may be considered as part of the family of this mansion, of the loss we have mutually sustained? Why should we hesitate to offer to you sympathy and condolence, and to claim them from you? It is just that you should admire and revere him—it is just on every principle of taste and virtue that you should venerate his memory! And is it not equally so that you should mourn for him who toiled to do you service? You remember the feebleness of his frame and its evident though gradual decay. Yet it was but lately that you saw him with you, sedulous and active as the youngest member, directing your studies with the affection of a parent, addressing you with the courtesy of an equal, and conferring the benefit of his knowledge and his genius as though he himself were receiving obligation.

"If on the last meeting of this Academy, any member had been justified in declining to quit the happy seclusion of his studies, it surely was this admirable man; whose solitude was made an enjoyment to him, by a fancy teeming with images of tenderness, purity, and grandeur, and whose imagination, at the close of his life, was severely intent upon subjects which called for his greatest energy; and which, had he lived to execute or direct them, would have left permanent records of his genius on the palace of his King. But nothing of present distinction, or future fame, made him forgetful of a duty.

"On the Friday, when the premiums were to be voted, he was punctual in his attendance in these rooms, patiently going round to the performances of the candidates—intently observing each, and if a doubt existed in his mind, with that modest candour which never left him seeking to guide his own opinion by the impressions of his friends. To you, gentlemen, this was benefit and honour. Yet it was but one example of the tenor of his conduct in this Academy.

. . . .

"Mr. Flaxman's genius, in the strictest sense of the words, was original and inventive. His purity of taste led him in early life to the study of the noblest relics of antiquity, and a mind, though not then of classical education, of classic bias, urged him to the perusal of the best translations of the Greek philosophers and poets, till it became deeply imbued with those simple and grand sentiments which distinguished the productions of that favored people.

. . . .

"He was still more the sculptor of sentiment than of form, and whilst the philosopher, the statesman, and the hero, were treated by him with appropriate dignity, not even in Raffaelle have the gentler feelings and sorrows of human nature been traced with more touching pathos than in the various designs and models of this estimable man. The rest of Europe knows only the productions of the early periods of his fame; but these, which form the highest efforts of his genius, had their origin in nature only, and the sensibility and virtues of his mind.

"Like the greatest of modern painters, he delighted to trace from the actions of familiar life the lines of sentiment and passion; and from the populous haunts and momentary peacefulness of poverty and want, to form his inimitable groups of childhood and maternal tenderness; with those nobler compositions of Holy Writ, as beneficent in their motives as they were novel in their design, which open new sources of invention from the simplest texts, and inculcate the duties of our faith.

"In piety, the minds of Michael Angelo and Flaxman were congenial. I dare not assert their equality in Art; yet the group of Michael and the Fallen Angel is a near approach to the grandeur of the former; and sanctified as his memory is by time and glory, it gained no trivial homage in the admiration of the English sculptor, whose Shield of Achilles his genius only could surpass.

"But I trespass too long on the various business of this evening. To be wholly silent on an event so afflicting to us all was quite impossible. I know the great and comprehensive talents that are around me—I know the strength remaining to the Academy, but knowing likewise the candour that accompanies it, I feel that I may safely appeal to this assembly for their acknowledgment with mine, that the loss of Mr. Flaxman is not merely a loss of power but loss of dignity to the Institution. Deep and irreparable loss to Art! to his country and to Europe! Not to posterity, to whom his works, as they are to us, will be inestimable treasure, but who, knowing how short and limited the span that Providence has allotted to the efforts of the longest life and the finest intellect, and learning that his genius (though his career was peaceful) had inadequate reward, will feel it to be their happier destiny to admire and not to mourn him—to be thankful that he had existed, and not like us to be depressed that he is gone—to revere and follow him as their master, and not, as is our misfortune, to lament him as their friend!

" He died in his own small circle of affection, enduring pain, but full of meekness, gratitude, and faith, recalling to the mind, in the pious confidence of his death, past characters of goodness, with the well remembered homage of the friend.

"And ne'er was to the bowers of bliss conveyed
A purer spirit, or more welcome shade."

To this high and authentic praise nothing need be added, except the remark in The Intellectual Repository for the New Church of the time:—

" The world's admiration can confer no lasting benefit ; and Mr. Flaxman had the happiness of feeling his proper home was heaven."

Very soon after the earth had received his remains, there arose a desire to have preserved in some permanent form what could be collected of his, in his studio and elsewhere, and have a Flaxman Gallery. University College, Gower-street, was decided to be the appropriate place, and the authorities willingly gave their assent.

Miss Denman was delighted at the respect thus shown, and presented 140 models, casts, &c.; and a collection of his drawings was afterwards obtained.

Samuel Rogers, the poet and banker, called attention to the project by a circular, asking for contributions to defray the expenses incurred in carrying it out. These were contributed, and the permanent home for this interesting collection was secured.

In 1867, Mr. Henry Crabb Robinson, the last remaining personal friend of Flaxman, died, aged 90 years, and bequeathed £2,000 to the Council of University College, so that the Flaxman Gallery might always be kept in good order, and be open on certain days of the week to the public.

His fame increases with time, and, as is justly remarked by Mr. Teniswood, " The term Flaxmanic is now synonymous with the highest conceptions of imaginative sublimity, ideal beauty, purity of sentiment, and tender pathos."

Grateful to the Lord, who has already shown us such men, who have walked in the light of the Holy City for our examples, we close with Flaxman these Sketches of NEW CHURCH WORTHIES.

BY THE SAME AUTHOR.

The Divine Word Opened. Third Edition. Crown 8vo., cloth, 7/6.

From Egypt to Canaan; The Progress of Man from the Unregenerate to the Regenerate State. Crown 8vo., cloth, 6/-.

The Divine Wisdom of the Word of God, as seen in the Spiritual Sense of the Histories of Samuel, Saul, David, Solomon, and Daniel. Crown 8vo., cloth, 5/-.

Magnificent Scenes in the Book of Revelation. 8vo., cloth, 2/6.

Scripture Paradoxes; Their True Explanation. Crown 8vo., cloth, gilt edges. 2/6.

Twelve Discourses on the "Essays & Reviews." 12mo., cloth, 3/-.

Great Truths on Great Subjects. Six Lectures delivered at Brighton. 39th Thousand. Fcap. 8vo., cloth, gilt edges. 1/-.

Who are these New Church People? To which is added a Week of Prayers. 18mo., sewed, 2d.

On the Chaldean Account of the Deluge and the Ark, with some remarks on the Rainbow. 8vo., 1d.

The Unity of God. Fcap. 8vo., sewed, 1d.

The Lord Jesus Delivering the Keys to Peter. 8vo., 1d.

The Second Coming of Christ. Christ is Coming, but How. Fcap. 8vo., 1d.

How Sins are Remitted and how they are Retained. 8vo., 1d.

Christian Instruction for Young People who are of age for Confirmation; or Dedication of Themselves to a Christian Life. 18mo., sewed, 6d.; cloth, 1/-.

Observations made during a Tour through Norway, Sweden, Finland, and Russia. 8vo., sewed, 8d.

Second Reading and Spelling Book. 6d.

Swedenborg Verified by the Progress of One Hundred Years. 2/6.

www.ingramcontent.com/pod-product-compliance
Lightning Source LLC
Chambersburg PA
CBHW032355230426
43672CB00007B/706